Convicting the Mormons

Convicting the Mormons
The Mountain Meadows Massacre in American Culture

Janiece Johnson

The University of North Carolina Press CHAPEL HILL

© 2023 Janiece Johnson
All rights reserved
Set in Merope Basic by Westchester Publishing Services
Manufactured in the United States of America

Library of Congress Cataloging-in-Publication Data
Names: Johnson, Janiece L., author.
Title: Convicting the Mormons : the Mountain Meadow Massacre in American culture / Janiece Johnson.
Description: Chapel Hill : The University of North Carolina Press, [2023] | Includes bibliographical references and index.
Identifiers: LCCN 2022036530 | ISBN 9781469673523 (cloth ; alk. paper) | ISBN 9781469673530 (paperback ; alk. paper) | ISBN 9781469673547 (ebook)
Subjects: LCSH: Mountain Meadows Massacre, Utah, 1857. | Mormons—United States—Public opinion. | Mormons—History. | Mass media—United States—Influence.
Classification: LCC F826 .J74 2023 | DDC 979.2/020882893—dc23/eng/20220823
LC record available at https://lccn.loc.gov/2022036530

Cover illustration: "Mormonism in Utah—the Cave of Despair," editorial cartoon from *Frank Leslie's Illustrated Newspaper*, 4 February 1882. Courtesy of L. Tom Perry Special Collections, Harold B. Lee Library, Brigham Young University.

publication joined with a grant from
Figure Foundation

To the victims and their justice long delayed

Contents

List of Illustrations xi
Prologue xiii
Crime Meets Punishment

Introduction 1
A Mormon Massacre

CHAPTER ONE
Mormon Savagery 23
Murder an' Massacretion

CHAPTER TWO
Circumscribing Civilization 51
The White Hellhounds

CHAPTER THREE
Relinquished Manhood 73
Be Men

CHAPTER FOUR
Prosecuting Mormonism 97
The Tyrant of the Mormon Church and Theocratic Despotism

CHAPTER FIVE
One Punishment Is Not Enough 112
Lee's Second Trial, Execution, and Aftermath

Epilogue 136
Ex Uno Disce Omnes

Acknowledgments 151
Notes 153
Bibliography 183
Index 211

Illustrations

0.1	John D. Lee sitting on his coffin	xiv
0.2	Mountain Meadows	9
0.3	"The Massacre at Mountain Meadows, Utah Territory"	14
0.4	Patriarch-in-the-Box	16
0.5	"The Cave of Despair"	18
1.1	Joseph Smith "imagined" preaching in the wilderness	27
1.2	"Mormon Allies at the Mountain Meadows"	30
1.3	"132 Emigrants Killed by Mormons and Indians"	32
1.4	*American Progress*	35
1.5	Mormons painted as Indians	37
2.1	"Murdered by Supposed Friends"	55
2.2	"Can We Allow Foreign Reptiles to Crawl All Over Us"	67
3.1A–C	Murdering women and children	82–83
3.2	"Like a Tigress at Bay"	85
4.1	"Brigham Young's Wealth, Wisdom, Wives, Etc."	99
4.2	Trial portrait of John D. Lee	104
5.1	John D. Lee writing his confession	118
5.2A	John D. Lee at Fort Cameron, Utah, circa 1877	121
5.2B	John D. Lee in his coffin	121

5.3A&B "Justice at Last!" 122–23

5.4 *Mormonism Unveiled* 128

5.5 Brigham Young cabinet card 130

6.1 "The Flag of Truce at Mountain Meadows" 139

6.2 "The Real Objection to Smoot" 141

Prologue
Crime Meets Punishment

Leaving under the cover of darkness on an early spring night in 1877, a federal marshal brought John D. Lee over a hundred rough and ragged miles to a remote desert mountain valley in southern Territorial Utah. This was the plaintive spot where Lee had committed his crime twenty years earlier and now a U.S. Army detachment waited for him there. After a restless journey facing a double-barreled shotgun and a Methodist minister, Lee broke the "monotonous silence" and confessed that he killed "five emigrants possibly six."[1] He begged the marshal to just shoot him and end the insufferable suspense.[2]

Perhaps the federal prosecutors' plan was beginning to work. They had hoped that the chosen place could accomplish what they had been unsuccessful at doing: eliciting remorse and finally producing a "true" confession from Lee. It seemed that they would accept nothing less than a confession directly implicating Brigham Young, leader of the Latter-day Saints.

The site was carefully chosen so that Lee might relive the crime he committed there two decades before. On a now notorious 11 September in 1857, a local Latter-day Saint militia recruited Native Americans to help attack an emigrant company from Arkansas as it prepared to cross the desert—initially the Indians were to do the particularly "dirty work" of killing women and children.[3] The Latter-day Saint militia with their Indian confederates slaughtered 120 members of that company in the Mountain Meadows valley—the same valley where Lee now stood. After years of minimal action, federal prosecutors indicted John D. Lee in 1874 for his participation in what had become known as the Mountain Meadows Massacre. Lee's first trial ended with a hung jury in 1875. The following summer, a second trial convicted him and a federal judge sentenced him to death.

The morning after his arrival to the Meadows was bright and dry as John D. Lee quietly stumbled his way to punishment.[4] The word had gotten out. Though kept away from the immediate place of execution, a few hundred people gathered at a distance to watch his final moments. A court reporter stood ready to record his last words in shorthand.[5] The U.S. attorney,

FIGURE 0.1 Photographer James Fennemore captured this iconic image of John D. Lee sitting on the edge of his coffin at the place of his crime just before his death and sold it as a collectible cabinet card. The press circulated engravings of the image with detailed accounts of Lee's execution throughout the country. Fennemore, "Execution of John D. Lee cabinet card." Courtesy of Church History Library.

marshal, and a minister gathered with Lee in a final bid for clemency if he would implicate Brigham Young. He offered the names of a few others, but not the Latter-day Saint prophet. The reverend steadied him as Lee walked to the place appointed. There the wearied old man shed his overcoat, sat on the edge of his coffin, and gazed out at the valley (see figure 0.1).[6] As Lee waited to hear his final judgment, he asked the photographer who was present to capture the event to send his wives copies of his final photograph. Five recently deputized assistant marshals gathered in preparation for the expected execution, hidden from the onlookers' sight by two wagons draped in blankets.

Lee gave his final words from the edge of his coffin, indicting Young for offering him as a sacrifice to satiate the federal desire for punishment but not implicating Young in the crime. The Methodist minister offered a prayer before five bullets cracked toward Lee, shredding his chest and quickly killing him before lodging themselves in the grass beyond the coffin.[7] The photographer documented the scene as the court reporter climbed the telegraph pole and the execution account began to work its way around the world. The "Mormon Menace" and "Butcher of Mountain Meadows" was dead.[8] The state had extracted its punishment. Yet would it expiate the Mormon sin at Mountain Meadows? Would Lee's execution fulfill the American desire for punishment?

Convicting the Mormons

Introduction
A Mormon Massacre

John D. Lee remains the only individual ever convicted for his role in the 1857 murders at Mountain Meadows. Even that small measure of justice occurred two decades after the crime. The massacre's many other participants, most of whom were members of the Church of Jesus Christ of Latter-day Saints, went unpunished, and the 120 victims unavenged. Why this very American story continues to endure is a central question of this book.

It wasn't because Americans were unaware of the broad contours of what had happened. After the 11 September atrocity, it did not take long for news of the massacre to travel to the West Coast and then across America. The first rumors of an Indian massacre followed the California trail and reached southern California at the beginning of October, with details gleaned from Latter-day Saint freighters and two emigrants who had traveled for a time with the massacred train.[1] Within a week, the rumors began to take shape, soon suggesting that those allied with the Indians were Mormons. A month after the massacre, residents of Los Angeles "convened at the Pavilion, on the Plaza" in a "mass meeting," their objective "to investigate the facts in the recent massacre, on the Salt Lake road of more than one hundred Americans." Two days later, a citizen committee "unanimously adopted" a series of resolutions condemning the massacre and the "rapidly gathering cloud of troubles" the Mormons created. The Los Angeles residents' petition declared, "We firmly believe the atrocious act was perpetrated by the Mormons, and their allies the Indians." They petitioned "the President of the United States, to exert the authority vested in him by the Constitution; that prompt measures may be taken for the punishment of the authors of the recent appalling and wholesale butchery of innocent men, women and children." If the president did not act, the Los Angeles committee argued, "many emigrant trains, now on their way from the Western States to California, [were] liable to meet the same fate."[2]

Specifically, which "prompt measures" the United States might take against the Mormons remained open to question in the 1850s, as they would for decades to come. The Los Angeles residents focused their concerns on the alterity of the Mormon people as a whole—an Other—instead of the specific individuals at fault. The petitioners saw a clear link between a massacre in Utah and polygamists in California. Both were Mormon sins. They believed that the federal response to the massacre should target the entire Mormon community rather than the perpetrators of the violence specifically. The group ordered the petition published in local papers in both English and Spanish to reach all citizens.

Two weeks later, the news of the massacre reached San Francisco, a city already rife with conflict between pro- and anti-Mormon newspapers.[3] The *Alta California* republished the demands of the Los Angeles residents to which the editors added their own specific requests.[4] Beyond safeguarding American emigrants, the *Alta* editors demanded "immediate and determined action" so that "the Mormon traitors . . . [will] be rooted out of our territory, fully and finally." Building upon the already present antagonism toward the Mormons, the *Alta* editors argued the inevitability of war with the Mormons as soon as the government "received the most indubitable proofs" of their "treacherous, murderous conduct." The *Alta*'s report of Mountain Meadows would be soon transmitted to Washington offering those "most indubitable proofs."[5] These California efforts marked the beginnings of a saga of searching for action to punish the Mormons for the Mountain Meadows Massacre.

The central topic of this book is not simply the massacre itself, but rather what that massacre meant to America. As the California newspaper accounts show, the Mountain Meadows Massacre almost immediately became a weapon with which concerned citizens sought to battle the Mormon incursion on expanding American civilization. In the decades after the massacre, discussions of punishment occurred within a larger narrative of other Mormon transgressions against American civilization, including polygamy. This book will follow the search for punishment for the massacre through official legal channels and in the American popular press from the 1850s to the 1920s. Despite recent scholarly attention to the Mountain Meadows Massacre, the equally important tale of its aftermath remains. In this book, I examine the relationship between efforts to convict specific individual perpetrators and punitive endeavors aimed at a minority religion—endeavors that ultimately impeded the prosecution of the perpetrators and justice for the victims. In its quest to punish the Mormon people as a whole, the nation failed to prosecute most of the specific individuals who organized and carried out the Mountain Meadows Massacre, even though the prosecution of the case lasted for nearly forty years. In the same way that the citizens of Los Angeles united in their opposition to the massacre and to polygamy, the investigators, lawyers, judges, and politicians who pushed forward the prosecution and the editors, journalists, authors, and entertainers who publicized it consistently focused on the religious affiliation of the White perpetrators. The sensational narrative of the massacre taught American readers and audiences that such behavior was not singular but represented the greater whole of Mormon sin.

My work on the Mountain Meadows Massacre began as an attempt to fill a historical lacuna of understanding the two trials of John D. Lee, the only individual to be prosecuted and punished for his involvement. Unlike many nineteenth-century trials, his had extant court reporter notes, which enabled extensive analysis. The legal actions leading to John D. Lee's first trial have been briefly mentioned by several historians but never adequately interrogated. In evaluating the court records, it quickly became clear that despite prior historical analyses, John D. Lee was not the central focus of the narrative, and the project expanded. I became general editor of the two-volume *Mountain Meadows Massacre: Complete Legal Papers* which laid out the documentary foundation for the prosecution and legal actions for the massacre.[6] Similarly, though many historians had previously waded through much of the sensational press about the massacre as they tried to construct a complete history of what happened, most disregarded popular perception in their search to uncover the veracity of the event (or used elements of the popular narrative as accurate representations of it). What people believed to be true—no matter how outlandish—was significant.

For this book, four specific tropes emerged in the initial stages of documentary analysis of the official massacre investigation by federal appointees. The themes that pervade the court records align with the proliferating popular press accounts of the massacre. The official investigation and prosecution were intrinsically connected to the enduring popular attention to the massacre—a story that would continue to flourish long after the prosecution ended.

In individual chapters, this book examines those four tropes of Mormon sin highlighted by the Mountain Meadows narrative: savagery, repudiated civilization, relinquished manhood, and despotic theocracy. The themes all closely fit within a nineteenth- and early twentieth-century American construct of civilization—the prevailing discourse in a time of Manifest Destiny. Chapter 1 examines the perception of the Mormon relationship with American Indians, assesses claims to Mormon savagery and violence prior to and during the prosecution, and uncovers how those claims evolved in the wake of the massacre. Chapter 2 addresses the contested racial identity of the

Mormons, the role that identity played in the prosecution and the popular massacre narrative, and the larger Mormon question regarding the expansion of American civilization and its limits. Chapter 3 evaluates the centrality of manhood to the prevailing discourse on civilization, that discourse's specific role in the prosecution for the massacre, and the growth of a popular narrative both highlighting the failings of Mormon men and opening the possibility for Mormon redemption. Chapters 4 and 5 address the function of theocracy in the story of Mountain Meadows, including the potential narrative of redemption in the person of John D. Lee as he walked the path to execution. As the massacre narrative developed, stories about Brigham Young's involvement grew from rumor and innuendo to a generally accepted narrative of guilt, which authors used to critique Mormon theocracy. The epilogue will consider twentieth-century attention to the Mountain Meadows Massacre and the story's enduring appeal to the present day.

Atrocity at Mountain Meadows

Although this book is about the aftermath of the Mountain Meadows Massacre, it's important to establish at the outset what happened during the event itself. The 1857 massacre was a multiday siege that occurred within a broader context of significant and growing tensions between Latter-day Saints and the United States. By the mid-nineteenth century, Mormons had been the focus of sustained attention from Americans for almost thirty years. The official name of the church popularly known as the Mormon Church is The Church of Jesus Christ of Latter-day Saints. However, few nineteenth-century Americans would recognize the official name of the church—all they knew were Mormons. "Mormon" began as a pejorative term based in disdain for their new scripture, but one that the Latter-day Saints appropriated themselves by the 1840s. The label "Mormon" is a popular construction as much as much as other labels considered in this work. As such, here I endeavor to use the appellation "Mormon" when reflecting perceptions of those outside the faith and "Latter-day Saints" when considering the members of the church.

Though the Church of Jesus Christ of Latter-day Saints was a home-grown American religion, some Americans consistently contested its place within both the American religious landscape and the American polity. After decades of local clashes that pushed the church's members from upstate New York across the North American continent, the Saints felt secure in their mountain refuge. Though it was part of Mexican territory when they arrived in 1847, the land they called Deseret soon became a part of the United States with the Treaty of Guadalupe Hidalgo. In 1850, the U.S. federal government called the place Utah and granted it territorial status. Testing out the safety of their refuge, Latter-day Saints publicly announced their practice of polygamy in 1852, wagering that freedom of religion would guarantee the unencumbered practice of their peculiar marital system. Instead, polygamy quickly became a lightning rod for criticism from Protestant reformers, government leaders, and sensational novelists. A handful of antipolygamy volumes in the 1850s were only the beginning of what would become a cottage industry of anti-Mormon literature. Concerns over polygamy and theocracy transformed Mormonism from an item of local concern to one of the fashionable questions or problems of the day—"a veritable national pastime."[7] Articles on the "Mormon Question" or the "Mormon Problem" routinely filled newspaper column space, and politicians such as Stephen Douglas claimed that it would "become the duty of Congress to apply the knife and cut out this loathsome, disgusting ulcer" if and when any "authentic evidence" of Mormons' wrongdoing were to reach Washington.[8]

After significant clashes with the Latter-day Saints in Salt Lake City, the first federal judges appointed to territorial Utah returned to Washington with reports of Mormon tyranny and rebellion. U.S. president James Buchanan dispatched 1,500 federal troops to Utah in May 1857 in the first federal action against the Latter-day Saints. Determined to prove popular sovereignty did not absolve Mormon accountability, Buchanan acted against the advice of his cabinet.[9] More than a year passed before the federal troops on their Utah Expedition entered the Salt Lake Valley. Between the time when Latter-day Saints learned the U.S. Army was on its way and the troops' arrival, tensions reached a fever pitch. On the verge of calling martial law, territorial governor and president of the Latter-day Saint Church Brigham Young directed the Saints to stockpile grain and portable foodstuffs so they might be self-sufficient if they were called to desert their cities and retreat to the mountains. Some Latter-day Saints scolded or beat down those who defied such orders by trading with emigrants whether it was for money or kindness. Rumors about the coming army and advance spies began to spread to southern Utah, and some worried that another division of the army would soon be also marching on Utah from southern California.[10]

Thousands of emigrants passed through Utah that year, journeying by wagon through a tense territory that was on high alert. The emigrant train that would clash tragically with the Mormons was composed of two extended family groups, the Bakers and the Fanchers, mostly from the northwest corner of Arkansas. While many emigrants chose the less populated northern route, the Baker-Fancher party elected to take the southern trail to California—as did many others in 1857. Led by the experienced Alexander Fancher, who was making his third trip there, they were traveling along the same trail some Utah residents worried could soon likewise bring the federal army from California and they would have to battle from both the east and the west.

As the emigrants moved south through the territory, they solidified as a company, picking up a few individual travelers—including a "Dutchman" with a short fuse and plenty of bluster. The train had a few run-ins with the locals on their way south, twice camping in winter feed ranges in Provo and Salt Creek—just south of present-day Payson—which led to intense standoffs. The run-ins included the Dutchman boasting that he had helped push the Mormons out of Missouri in the 1830s, calling Latter-day Saint women "whores, &c.," and that he hoped to shoot Brigham Young while taking target practice. When John Pierce Hawley traveled with the train for a few days, the "captain of the company" blamed the Dutchman for "all of the trouble" they had because the Dutchman ignited tense moments when he "was sassy with officers in these places." Insulting Latter-day Saint homes, land, and religion did not help dissipate the tension. Though a frequent eighteenth- and nineteenth-century literary trope, some rumors also included women wanting to leave Utah and joining the train.[11] Both real actions and rumors worked together to create tension on the part of the Utahns as well as the emigrants. The farther south the emigrants traveled, the more their tension raised. Though opportunities to barter on their trip south had been difficult, any possibility would vanish when the trail turned to the west to cross the sparsely populated desert. The emigrants arrived in Cedar City eager to prepare for the desert crossing that lay ahead.[12]

Separated by 250 miles and at least three days' travel from Salt Lake City, it was a stretch to define Cedar City as a city in 1857. At that time the largest outpost in the territorial south, the close-knit Latter-day Saint settlement was still remote. Rumors wound their way to Cedar City without the neutralizing corrective of additional information. The town stood on edge as residents heard news of the U.S. Army's approach. The general store was out of supplies, though the emigrants were able to get some grain from a couple of individuals who ignored territorial directives. When the owner of the mill wanted to charge them a whole cow to mill their grain—an unreasonably steep price—the emigrants' frustration escaped in the form of abusive and inflammatory language. Later accounts alleged that some claimed involvement in the murder of Joseph Smith and other Mormons, threatened to kill more, and warned they would accompany the army from California to Cedar City. Those incendiary comments landed badly on sensitive local ears. This, coupled with rumors and behavior that later accounts said ranged from killing chickens to verbally assaulting women, led some Latter-day Saint men to determine that something must be done—their honor had been damaged. Once the emigrants left Cedar City and headed to the east toward the Mountain Meadows valley, a lush place to graze their cattle fifty miles to the west of Cedar City, these Cedar City men made a plan to "brush" the emigrants—rough them up and take some of their cattle in a show of power.[13]

There was no division of church and state in 1857 in southern Utah territory. Isaac Haight was mayor of Cedar City, a major in the Iron County militia formed only a few years prior, and a Latter-day Saint stake president presiding over the church in that town. (A stake is essentially a Latter-day Saint counterpart to a Catholic diocese.) Haight and other Latter-day Saint men, including local bishop Philip Klingensmith who served under Haight's direction, hatched the plan to brush the emigrant men, and from the beginning they hoped to recruit local Paiute Indians to attack the emigrants.[14] Looking for endorsement of this plan, Haight sent a messenger to his militia superior William Dame, the Iron County colonel and likewise a stake president over his own city, Parowan, twenty miles to the northeast. Haight's messenger waited as Dame discussed with his council how to respond. After discussion, Dame sent the message to Haight to ignore the emigrants' threats, saying "words are but wind." However, Haight had already decided there *must* be a response.[15]

As he waited for his messenger's return, Haight worked to recruit others to his vigilante cause. His principal confederate was John D. Lee. Ultimately, Lee's role would be far better known than Haight's, but Haight brought Lee into the plans. Lee's life suggested many reasons why Haight might have wanted to enlist his help. Born in Illinois in 1812, Lee lost his mother as a young child. Subject to abuse from an alcoholic father and an aunt, he left his aunt's home at sixteen. He worked in a variety of scrappy jobs before serving as a soldier in the Black Hawk War. After returning, he married Agatha Ann Woolsey, and they opened a successful store and farmed in Illinois. There they joined the Church of Jesus Christ of Latter-day Saints in 1838, and Lee showed his consistent dedication. They gathered with the Saints and were subjected to persecutions as the Saints were pushed to the west. In addition to introducing polygamy in Nauvoo, Illinois, Latter-day Saints likewise adopted sons to leaders constructing expansive kinship networks. Then

Apostle Brigham Young adopted Lee in addition to many other sons, and Lee took pride in this connection. A devoted Saint, Lee served several missions and married several women polygamously. Over time, several of his wives divorced him. He replicated the violence imposed on him in some of his own relationships. A couple years after arriving in Utah, Young asked Lee to settle in southern Utah. It appeared a perfect fit for his dedicated but caustic personality, and space from others and room to work would be good, but more run-ins with others would follow.[16]

Like Haight, Lee was also a major in the militia, and Brigham Young, as governor, had appointed him to a federal position as farmer to the Indians. Because of that existing relationship, Haight trusted that Lee could lead the Indians to attack the emigrant men. According to Lee, the two talked nearly all night long on Friday, 4 September, and Haight detailed a long list of supposed grievances against the emigrants. They had "insulted, outraged, and ravished many of the Mormon women," poisoned water, claimed they had the gun that killed Joseph Smith, and wanted "to kill Brigham Young and all of the Apostles." Haight convinced Lee that the emigrants would carry out their threats if nothing was done to stop them, and Lee responded with fervor. Their plan was to "make it an Indian massacre and not have any whites interfere with them." Of course, nothing would have occurred without White interference; they just hoped to hide their own violent machinations. Lee warned Haight that the Indians would likely also kill women and children, and yet they proceeded to plan. Finding someone to blame appeared to have been more important to them than who died. Although zealous in his participation, Lee asked Haight if they should consult the local council before moving forward. (This is, at least, how Lee later remembered the story. As with much of the massacre narrative, witnesses consistently clouded their own participation but readily testified to others' actions.) Haight convinced him that moving forward now was essential and said he would bring it before the council the next Sunday, 6 September.[17]

Manipulating the close relationship between Latter-day Saints and the Paiutes through local proselytizing and agriculture efforts, Lee recruited the usually peaceable Paiute Indians to "kill the Mericates" (Americans). On Saturday, he set out toward the Mountain Meadows with a group of Paiute men and several other White Latter-day Saint militia members. They tracked the movements of the emigrants as they wended their way to the Meadows (as depicted in figure 0.2) and set the tragic sequence in motion.[18]

Rachel Hamblin's home stood at the northern end of the Meadows. Her husband away, she watched as the emigrant train passed. They asked a ranch

FIGURE 0.2 "Mountain Meadows, from nature by S. H. Redmond." Lithograph, San Francisco: Pacific Art Company, 1877. Courtesy of the Library of Congress.

hand working on the corral for directions to water, and he pointed them to the spring at the southern end of the Meadows valley. Though both Rachel and the worker had heard the rumors rippling from Cedar City, the emigrants made their encampment near the spring without incident. Feeling comfortable, the train set up camp indiscriminately and settled down, positioning men only around their grazing cattle presumably to guard against wild predators. A peaceful Sunday passed at the Meadows, for Rachel only punctuated by an emigrant asking if he could purchase butter and cheese, of which she "had none."[19]

In contrast, the Latter-day Saint settlement at Fort Harmony, about twenty miles southwest of Cedar City and John D. Lee's home, was abuzz that Sunday. Lee sent a message to the Paiutes to gather while he prepared the men for "the extermination of the emigrant train." Lee threatened those who didn't agree, and Sunday morning rallied the rest of the community instead of holding church. Parroting the laundry list of grievances originally presented by Haight, Lee paralleled the Saints' earlier persecutions in Missouri and Illinois with current events. He then heightened the danger as he elevated the emigrants' threats, claiming they had threatened the Saints' leaders as well as "every other damn Mormon." He declared that Haight approved the extermination plan and stretched reality to include William Dame in that endorsement. When the Indians began to arrive at Fort Harmony, Lee styled himself a solider with a red sash and sword and marched them repeatedly around the inside of the Fort. Townsfolk witnessed between forty and seventy-five Indians from various areas in southern Utah that day, though that was not as many as Lee had wanted.

Back in Cedar City that Sunday afternoon, Haight met with local ecclesiastical leaders and again recited a litany of emigrant offenses as he sought their support for his plan. Cedar City bishop Philip Klingensmith later testified that a couple of individuals present at the meeting supported the killing, but Klingensmith excluded himself from that group. Laban Morrill, a member of the stake high council, remembered that some "more radical members" of the council "suggested harsh measures," but not necessarily "wholesale killing." Morrill stood up to Haight, asked what authority he had to react so severely against the emigrants, and proposed that they pause to receive counsel from the Latter-day Saint prophet Brigham Young. This suggestion cut off the momentum of Haight and his supporters, and the council agreed that they should ask Young. It would take another decade for telegraph lines to make it to southern Utah, so this could only be accomplished by a skilled rider with several days to spare. Morrill instructed Haight to send off a rider and headed home.[20]

Had Lee stuck to the original plan, there would have still been enough time to call it off, yet sometime that night Lee decided to attack. As Monday morning, 7 September, dawned, Lee and the Indians moved into position and launched their offensive. Although they killed a few emigrants, the besieged party quickly began to defend themselves and return fire, causing casualties among the Indians. Rachel Hamblin heard gunshots that lasted for half an hour.[21]

After the early attack, the emigrants quickly corralled their wagons, dug trenches, and moved earth as an additional measure of protection, creating a "wagon fort." Several emigrant men went out to gather livestock that had scattered in the chaos; two struck out following the trail back to Cedar City in their search. William Stewart and Joel White, two militiamen supporting Lee and watching the emigrant company from afar, set out after the two escapees, determined to run them down. Both emigrant men had joined with the Baker-Fancher company to cross the desert. One was eighteen-year-old William Aden, on a grand adventure to the west, and the other was the

"Dutchman," whose early boasts and threats had ignited the tension in Cedar City. Stewart asked to borrow Aden's tin cup for a drink and then mercilessly shot him in the head. A lightning-quick reaction enabled the Dutchman's escape back to the camp.[22]

The siege would continue for the next five days until the fateful Friday, yet at this point everything shifted. The truth was beginning to emerge. The emigrants now knew it was not just the Indians attacking them. Soon the leaders in Cedar City and Parowan would know that Haight and Lee had disobeyed the councils. A runner from the Meadows arrived in Cedar City around noon alerting Haight to how much had already occurred. Haight hadn't yet sent off the rider to Brigham Young and now debated what to tell him. As he sent the rider off Monday afternoon, he withheld any information about the Latter-day Saints' role in what had already occurred. He repeated his grievances against the emigrants—they were "verry mean"—and claimed they had gotten into another tussle, this time with the Indians. He laid the path to "make it an Indian massacre."[23]

Once the rider left, Haight focused on the escalating situation for which he was responsible. If the emigrants were allowed to go free, they would tell others that the Saints had attacked them. He thought the federal army from California would surely then march on Utah to bolster the army that was already marching from the east. Moreover, additional emigrants were due to arrive at the Meadows in a matter of days. Haight had to act. He sent a second rider to the Meadows with a message that Lee should back off—a tenuous proposition after Lee had riled up the Indians toward the emigrants. Haight gave Lee permission to entice the Indians with beef if needed to quell them but declared that the emigrants should be protected. Despite Haight's orders, things only continued to escalate.[24]

As word of what had already transpired began to wend its way to Cedar City and Parowan on Wednesday, Haight feigned ignorance to what was happening. Reflecting both an allegiance to the chain of command and an astute covering of his tracks, Haight headed north, himself this time, to Parowan and William Dame. Dame reconvened the church council, which again decided that the emigrants should not be attacked but helped. Once again, Haight worked to circumvent the council's decision. After the meeting, Haight proposed he and Dame continue the conversation alone. Only then did Haight begin to reveal just how far the destruction had progressed at the Meadows, yet he also lied, saying that most of the emigrants had died in the initial siege. Likely much of the conversation circled around how to cover up White Latter-day Saint involvement. On his own without the support of the council, Dame gave way to Haight's impulses. Though they would later argue over the specifics of their discussion, Haight left believing he had Dame's permission to call out the militia and exterminate the remaining emigrants.[25]

Haight returned to Cedar City, and on Thursday morning he called out the militia—all Latter-day Saints. Some later reported that he continued the ruse that the emigrants had already been killed and the militia was needed to "bury the dead." John Bradshaw, a private in the militia, responded to Haight's call to "muster up" and brought a spade with him. Haight asked him where his gun was and Bradshaw responded, "I didn't know we wanted a gun to bury the dead with." Haight called him "a fool" and sent him home because he "didn't understand things."[26] Some of those who assembled already knew what was going on at the Meadows. About 15 percent of the large Iron Military District militia responded to Haight's call.[27] A messenger from the Meadows arrived saying there had been three major attacks, the Paiutes had lost men, and some were ready to desert the effort. Haight's response did not waver: he told Lee to "finish his dirty job, as he had started it," already shifting responsibility away from himself.[28]

On Friday morning, 11 September, John D. Lee entered the emigrant wagon fort under a white flag of truce. He persuaded the emigrants that the Latter-day Saint militia held their best hope for survival. Though many of the emigrants were suspicious, their options had disappeared in the last several days along with their ammunition and water. Lee directed the wounded and the smallest children into a wagon, with the women and older children following close behind. They walked to the north on the trail through the Meadows valley until they passed over a ridge and out of sight. The militia leaders had tasked the Paiute men, hiding nearby, with killing the women and older children. Then Lee sent the men and bigger boys filing out alongside Latter-day Saint militia members, who outnumbered the emigrants two to one. Though he hesitated to give the final order, when militia major John Higbee gave the signal word, "Halt," chaos erupted and the slaughter began.

The killing would not be done in an instant. It was a messy, bloody affair. If the plan's purpose was to make the killing efficient, this was not that. All the Latter-day Saint militiamen had emigrant men and boys at close range, but in the moment, some refused to attack and fired their guns into the ground or the air. Some of the emigrant men escaped for a few more moments until other militiamen more intent on killing were able to chase them down. Farther up the trail, Indian interpreter Nephi Johnson "gave word to the Indians to fire." Guns were not their only weapons, so "women and children were knocked down with stones, clubs, and gun barrels, struck in the neck and butchered like hogs." There was nothing sterile or antiseptic about the massacre. The militiamen driving the wagons with the smallest children, the sick, and the wounded killed the adults. When the cold-blooded affair was over, seventeen small emigrant children were all who remained alive. One hundred and twenty people were dead. Despite plans and repeated attempts to "make it an Indian massacre," Johnson later testified that the militiamen killed most of the emigrants.[29]

That evening, the men gave an unprepared Rachel Hamblin charge of the seventeen children blanketed in blood and trauma, some injured themselves. The next day, Latter-day Saint women from Cedar City found homes for the children where they stayed until federal appointees returned them to relatives in Arkansas in 1859. The Latter-day Saint militia members later testified that they buried the dead, but neither their bodies nor their memory would stay buried. The bloody annihilation of the Baker-Fancher party would soon become known as the Mountain Meadows Massacre.[30]

FROM THE 1850S TO the first decades of the twentieth century, the Mountain Meadows Massacre became a defining feature of how many Americans perceived Latter-day Saints. It became a tale to enumerate Mormon transgressions—specific junctures where they contravened popular American sensibilities and the limits of many Americans' conception of civilization. Massacre reports met contemporary consternation over the "Mormon Problem" head-on. Just as it had in both Los Angeles and San Francisco, the story of a Mormon massacre built upon existing perceptions of the Mormons.

Though Latter-day Saint polygamy acted as a lightning rod for attention, the scrutiny that Americans placed on the Mountain Meadows Massacre in the second half of the nineteenth century and into the first decades of the twentieth—like the earliest stories in Los Angeles—demonstrated that polygamy was never the only Mormon offense. The explosion of popular sensationalist literature became the perfect medium for the story of Mountain Meadows. As the legal investigation and prosecution of the massacre proceeded, reports in the popular press ignited and spread across the United States, incorporating some factual elements of the massacre yet also becoming more elaborate and more sensational as time went on, fitting the contours of public expectation. Newspapers in major urban centers reported on the massacre, as did those in small towns across the country. As shown in figure 0.3, Mountain Meadows made the cover of *Harper's Weekly* in 1859, two weeks before Americans could read Horace Greeley's famous interview with

Figure 0.3 *Harper's Weekly* touted itself as *A Journal of Civilization*. It had published on "the question of the Mormons" since the serial's inception. The Mountain Meadows Massacre became front-page material for the first time in 1859. "The Massacre at Mountain Meadows, Utah Territory," *Harper's Weekly* 3, no. 137 (13 August 1859): 1–2. Courtesy of L. Tom Perry Special Collections, Harold B. Lee Library, Brigham Young University, Provo.

the Latter-day Saint prophet Brigham Young.[31] The massacre was a consistent presence lurking on the edges of the "Mormon Problem."

Very literally demonstrating the massacre's place in the "Mormon Problem," in the pointed political cartoon of figure 0.4, a creepy old patriarch-in-the-box pops up out of the domed Mormon Tabernacle (the most obvious Latter-day Saint building prior to the completion of the Salt Lake Temple in 1893).[32] Already with women falling from his neck, the emerging clown uses his four hands to trap even more women in his elongated polygamous grasp. Beyond polygamy, the folds of the patriarch-in-the-box figure's neck label the various threats of Mormonism: "fanaticism[,] deceit[,] falsehood," and "despotism." A Mountain Meadows signpost to the right ensures the reader will not forget the massacre—a sure Mormon sin. Dead bodies litter the ground around the sign and cross the image beyond the clown elevating the perception of Mormonism from a moral danger to a real physical threat. Meanwhile, around the edges of the cartoon various newspaper editors attempt to break down the "ignorance" and "superstition" protecting the creepy Mormon clown. Not only newspaper editors attacked the "Mormon Problem" or debated the "Mormon Question." Ministers, novelists, entertainers, authors of all kinds, cartoonists, federal officials, and interested individuals similarly spread the warning of the Meadows. Mountain Meadows correspondingly became a frequent rallying cry for disgruntled Utah federal judges when they wrote letters to Washington.[33]

Popular sources worked in tandem with official ones in the years to come, constructing a massacre discourse for Americans as details became available from government correspondence, reports, affidavits, and requests for action. I have examined both the popular media accounts and the official record in tracing this story, including extensive court records that spanned nearly forty years. These court records include the work of federal judges, grand juries, indictments, arrest warrants, subpoenas, the extensive trial transcripts for two court trials, appeals, and dismissals. The transcripts of John D. Lee's first trial, in particular, are a precious cache of source material with uncommonly exhaustive detail. Attempting to collect all the extant legal documents created a collection of almost 5,000 pages published in the *Mountain Meadows Massacre: Complete Legal Papers* and at mountainmeadowsmassacre.org.[34] This book is not intended to be a legal analysis of the prosecution for the Mountain Meadows Massacre—that should be the work of legal scholars. However, by thoroughly evaluating the legal record alongside the stories that were told about the massacre, I have come to better understand the cultural narrative that surged out of this single event, how

FIGURE 0.4 Newspaper editors attack the Mormon Patriarch-in-the-Box to break down ignorance, superstition, and polygamy while the Mountain Meadows sign surrounded by dead bodies signals certain Mormon sin. Charles W. Carter glass negative collection, circa 1860–1900. Courtesy of the Church History Library.

that narrative reflected the larger American social and political context of the late nineteenth century, how it helped Americans create and police the boundaries of civilization, and its continuing appeal in a wide variety of instances to exclude Mormons. The cover image, figure 0.5, likewise portrays a shadowy and violent perception of Mormonism and Mormon men in particular.

The discourse of civilization in America was pervasive throughout the last half of the nineteenth century and into the twentieth. Several scholars including David Axeen, George Stocking Jr., Nancy Cott, and Gail Bederman have examined concepts of civilization through the lenses of gender, war, anthropology, and race.[35] Savagery, Whiteness, manhood, and theocracy were all pressure points in this constructed rubric of civilization. Analyzing the official discourse alongside the popular creates an illuminating microhistory that highlights the profound concerns many Americans detected in Mormonism—that which "lurked" behind polygamy and might violently erupt. Scandalous stories of compulsion, sexual deviance, and violence worked to alienate many marginalized groups in the popular American mind. The Mountain Meadows narrative reinforces much of this analysis—exposés of Mormon violence worked to demonstrate Mormon Otherness to many Americans, but Mormons were not exceptional in this regard. Tales of Indians capturing Whites have a long history in North America.[36] Accounts of Black men raping White women expanded and grew without regard for evidence in the late nineteenth century.[37] Reports of young girls entrapped by Catholic priests to serve out their lives in convents similarly scattered across the country.[38] Published as sensational serials, these narratives and their depictions of Others became normalized for many Americans. In similar fashion, the scandalous plots that spun from the Mountain Meadows Massacre painted Mormons in shocking crimson hues that many Americans thought to be too steeped in blood for the American flag. The stories that swirled around the violence at the Meadows indicted all Mormons and taught Americans that they did not belong.

They Ain't Whites. . . . They're Mormons

Around the turn of the twentieth century, fiction expanded as a foray for the story of the Meadows. Fiction enabled multiple threads of discourse—ideas of savagery, White civilization, and manhood all to be woven into a narrative that centers the Mormons. In Jack London's 1915 reincarnation novel *The Star Rover* (*The Jacket* in the UK), prison officers torture Darryl Standing, an

FIGURE 0.5 Often political cartoons demonstrate the place of Mountain Meadows in depictions of the Mormon Problem. In "The Cave of Despair," the Utah skull's gaping mouth is ready to swallow women and children "sealed" into polygamous relationships. Mountain Meadow stands as the warning signpost along the way. Prolific British anti-Mormon pamphleteer William Jarman pulled the narrative across the Atlantic and appropriated the image for his own pamphlet, labeling it the "gate to Hell." "Mormonism in Utah—The Cave of Despair," *Frank Leslie's Illustrated Newspaper*, 2 February 1882. Courtesy L. Tom Perry Special Collections, Harold B. Lee Library, Brigham Young University, Provo. Jarman, *Hell upon Earth*.

imprisoned university professor, with a straitjacket that could be laced tight enough to induce severe angina. Standing learns that by putting himself into a trance he can escape the effects of the torture. While in his trances, he travels back through the stars to experience past lives. One of these past lives is that of the ten-year-old boy Jesse Fancher, fictional son of one of the leaders of the emigrant train murdered at Mountain Meadows—a boy quickly maturing to manhood.[39]

Within the narrative, the Mormons and the Indians stood in the way of the emigrants making it to California—"the dream land, the myth land." The adults who surround Jesse cannot see the truth about the Mormons; however, Jesse, the child, sees past the Mormon deception. Jesse is told to be quiet when he says he wants Laban, the epitome of Western manhood and pointedly the name of one of the major antagonists in the initial Book of Mormon narrative, to add Mormon scalps to the Indian scalps he keeps on his belt. Jesse wishes he could go "gunning" for the Mormons when he grows up. His parents only tell him to be quiet.[40]

A little girl complains to her mother, "They're white like us. . . . Why don't they come in to us?" In a straightforward expansion of an argument in John D. Lee's first trial, the little girl, like the adults in the narrative, did not understand why Whites were there allied with the Indians rather than helping them. The Americans expected Whites to be Americans who would help them in their desperate need. Though wary of "the swoop of [his] mother's hand," Jesse declares, "They ain't whites. . . . They're Mormons." His father says there must be good Mormons and bad Mormons, but Jesse reminds him, "We haven't found any good ones so far." For Jesse, Mormons fit in a single category.[41] The Whiteness of the Mormons only made them more dangerous because the emigrants had an expectation that they would come to their aid.

Notwithstanding their appearance of Whiteness, the Mormons plotted against the emigrants. The Mormons made the emigrants wait until they were so desperate, they would agree to give up under a flag of surrender. Only then did the adults begin to see the possibility of Mormon duplicity, and the mother asks, "But what if they intend treachery?" The Mormons have pushed them to the brink of destruction so that their options are either to starve to death or to accept the possibility of a treacherous Mormon offer.

Jesse's scalp-wearing hero, Laban, repents of his antagonism toward the Indians, declaring that "scalp wearin' is a vain and heathen thing" when he knows his life is short. He prepares himself to meet his Maker. Laban dreams of "Californy" where "everything grows large" only to meet his death by the

Mormon militia firing squad.[42] The Mormons murdered Laban, the embodiment of American manhood, and their annihilation extended from there. All became black to Standing's vision as the boy Jesse died following two little girls running from the White Mormons and their Indian allies.

The Star Rover is a classic Jack London story demonstrating his enduring obsession with White civilization and American manhood in both his fictional characters and his journalism.[43] London often set up his characters in opposition to women, to men of color, to foreign men. *The Star Rover* follows the same pattern: the manhood of the central character is established in opposition to other inferiors. Often manhood is established through battle or the ability to take a beating.[44] In *The Star Rover*'s Mountain Meadows chapter, Jack, the young boy, is transitioning to manhood. He interacts with his parents, who are too trusting, and Laban, the heroic and honestly faulted example of manhood ready to die in battle. Unencumbered by the diplomacy of his parents Jack can see the Mormons for who they are. He admires the valiant Laban as he plunges into battle and prepares for a manly death. But Jack is most explicitly juxtaposed against the "damned Mormons."[45] Young and perceptive Jack offered the promise of America.

In London's narrative, the Indian savages were initially seen as a stumbling block as civilization moved west to a California paradise representing a millennial hope. (Ironic, considering Standing is imprisoned in San Quentin Prison in California.) By the end of the chapter the adults, in the narrative and in London's audience, learn the truth that the boy, Jack, already knew—the Mormons were the real threat. They looked White, but they were a threat to civilization. For London, Whiteness alone was not enough. Manhood and independence additionally bolstered civilization. By the time London wrote, the Mormons had convinced America they were American enough to gain Utah statehood, but if Americans were to follow the Mormon lead, Mormons would strip their manhood and they would be denied millennial civilization. Americans had given Mormons multiple opportunities to reform themselves and be redeemed in the sight of American civilization, but Mormons did not accept the offer.

One of the fifty books a prolific London wrote in the last sixteen years of his life, *The Star Rover* was certainly not London's most influential book, though it still sold over 30,000 copies the first year. It was popular enough that in 1923 producers made it into a silent film. Its popularity continued to increase over time with a London biographer calling it a "cult classic."[46] Even after the official entrance of Utah and the Mormons into the Union,

London and other novelists would continue to see the fictional potential of the Meadows and further contribute to the larger narrative of Mormon transgression. Mormons breached the boundaries of civilization in numerous places.

As in London's novel, the discourse surrounding the massacre never converged on a single strain or theme. It was always multiple dialogic threads woven together not to punish the individual perpetrators of the massacre, but to create a much larger argument of the complexity of the Mormon Problem and its seriousness. No single Mormon sin was enough to eradicate the Mormons, but the convergence of Mormon sin, their multifarious transgressions of the boundaries of civilization, might require more substantive action.

In his influential 1859 treatise *On Liberty*, John Stuart Mill noted the existence of a *"civilizade"* against the Mormons.[47] Though Mill wrote after the massacre, it was not yet a consistent element of the popular narrative that expanded regarding the massacre's place in the Mormon Question. Mill specifically referred to the American legislative and popular press war on Mormon polygamy. Nevertheless, the Mormon Question could easily be recast as a *civilizade*. The way both the official and popular sources shaped the Mountain Meadows narrative demonstrated concerns about American civilization on many fronts, not just marriage. The fact of the Mountain Meadows Massacre strained Americans' evolving definition of civilization in the late nineteenth century, particularly regarding race, gender, theocracy, and violence. In consequence, boundary maintenance became more important than justice. This discourse would successfully punish Mormons for their infractions well into the twentieth century and again surge in the early twenty-first century. Its success would both limit the work of bringing massacre perpetrators to justice and ensure the continued allure of the story of the Meadows and the search for Mormon punishment.

Sometimes the goals were vague anti-Mormonism or meeting a popular clamor for violent and salacious tales, but generally the massacre narrative became a tool that was strategically deployed to punish Mormons for their sins against the American polity. Mormons could not unite with Indians if they were participants in American civilization; such a collaboration suggested something was amiss. Mormons looked White, but appearances could be deceiving. Perhaps they were not White at all, or they had betrayed their Whiteness. Gender likewise demonstrated the liminal place of Mormons. Rather than adhering to prescribed gender roles, Mormon women were acting as men and Mormon men were giving up their manhood by surrendering their allegiance to another man, one they called prophet. Evaluating the role of the massacre within the American perception of Mormons helps us to better understand the construction of civilization's carefully circumscribed limits and the battle for American citizenship in the latter half of the nineteenth century. Moreover, it enables a more complete understanding of why the Mountain Meadows Massacre became an effective stumbling block to full enfranchisement and acceptance of Latter-day Saints as Americans in a violent nineteenth century, as it ultimately blocked a complete prosecution and justice for the victims.

CHAPTER ONE

Mormon Savagery
Murder an' Massacretion

Just weeks after the massacre, the *San Joaquin Republican* reported under the headline "Mormons in the Capacity of Savages" that "the well known fanatical enmity of the Mormons" caused many to suspect Mormon involvement in instances deemed Indian depredations. By the end of the article, the editors maintained, "We are fully convinced that the Mormon people, and they alone, are responsible for *all* the murders and robberies that have been committed upon the immigrants. . . . We are safe in the dogmatical assertion that the Mormons, and not the Indians, have robbed and killed the people who have been robbed and killed on their way to California." Rather than a single massacre, Mormons were now responsible for *all* violence on the trail west.[1]

Reports of Mormons committing "wanton and atrocious 'Indian' depredations" on California and Oregon trails continued to proliferate in western papers.[2] Personal and public accounts told of Mormons "in the guise of Indians . . . painted and costumed" for the attack.[3] Rather than merely the rhetoric of western antagonisms, the escalated trope became widely disseminated and repeated over time. Once the Mountain Meadows Massacre offered definitive evidence of Mormon savagery, Mormon "desperados" consistently shed their civilized dress, clothed in savage attire, instigated Indians, and then used them as tools.

Already a significant concern of many Americans, savagery became a salient element as the story of the Meadows expanded. This chapter will evaluate ideas about savagery and civilization, the role of Mountain Meadows in a popular understanding of Mormon savagery in the nineteenth and early twentieth centuries, assessing the perceived dangers of Mormon and Indian unity, the tradition of Mormons and other Americans "playing Indian," and Mormons' contested relationship to civilization before examining how John D. Lee's trial employed the narrative of Mormon savagery in divergent ways. Moreover, it will address the ways in which this discourse changed over time.

Consistently, official and popular sources considered Mormons more accountable for their actions than their Indian cohorts who they assumed did not know any better. Mormons were capable and yet chose to repudiate civilization and revert toward savagery. They grew more egregious and more dangerous for the deception. For the prosecution as for many Americans, the Mountain Meadows Massacre evidenced the depth of Mormon savagery and provided a rationale for excluding Latter-day Saints from American citizenship. During John D. Lee's first trial for the Mountain Meadows Massacre, the prosecution utilized the discourse of savagery in its attempt to indict Mormonism in general and Brigham Young in particular, rather than a direct attempt to convict massacre leader Lee, the professed subject of the trial.

Savagery and Civilization

Circumscribing citizenship and civilization was nothing new. Defining "American citizenship" as an ideological position rather than a geographical term came to be a central project in the new republic. On his own initiative and with the support of George Washington, lexicographer Noah Webster began the project of defining a proper American citizen in opposition to British subjects to a king. A Federalist, Webster fixated on creating a new language for defining both what and who could classify as Americans for the new nation. In his *Grammatical Institute* reader and later through his showpiece, the 1828 *Webster's Dictionary*, he worked to unify the country and create true Americans through his process of categorization.[4]

Webster and many of his contemporaries saw humanity involved in a great millennial contest progressing toward civilization. The discourse of White civilization pervaded nineteenth-century America, though it had extended from Europe. In his dictionary, Webster defined civilization and savagery on a binary in opposition to one another:

> CIVILIZATION, *n.* The act of civilizing, or the state of being civilized; the state of being refined in manners, from the grossness of savage life, and improved in arts and learning.
> SAVAGE, *n.* A human being in his native state of rudeness, one who is untaught, uncivilized, or without cultivation of mind or manners. . . .
> SAVAGISM, *n.* The state of rude uncivilized men, the state of men in their native wildness and rudeness.

Despite Webster's succinct definition, the classification of groups as savage has always been slippery. As with most labels, "savagery" is historically constructed and used in a wide variety of situations to denote difference and Otherness.

In the nineteenth century, Americans frequently associated the term "savage" with native peoples and people of African descent; often, the terms were treated as synonyms. Though classifications of color often provided the basis for labels of savagery, that was never the only starting point. The category has been applied across a wide spectrum of groups based on religion, ethnicity, race, and geography. During the Protestant Reformation, opposing reformers labeled radical reformers, such as Thomas Müntzer, savages.[5] In the process of staking out Protestantism, those who were thought to contravene acceptable boundaries of change were scorned as savage. The label "savage" was never a precise descriptor, yet it effectively signaled dissimilarity and opposition.

In the nascent American republic, charges of savagery went hand in hand with contested American citizenship. With the swell of Irish immigration beginning in the 1840s, Americans imported English prejudices and differentiated the Celtic ancestry of the Irish from the truly White Anglo-Saxons. For the greater part of the nineteenth century, the Irish were also derided as savage and "their behavior [compared] with that of the 'Indian savages.'"[6] Throughout the 1860s and 1870s, the "savage" rioting Irish in New York were thought to stand in opposition to the "civilized" Anglo-Saxon Americans. Through sensationalized tales of violence, Americans understood the behavior of the Irish to demonstrate their lack of civilization—and, implicitly, their lack of Whiteness.[7] Any perception of a collective violation of acceptable boundaries could bring the label "savage." Whatever the source, savagery stood as a stumbling block to the forward progress of civilization and needed to be overcome to enable America to reach its millennial destiny.

Early nineteenth-century Americans saw "the Indian, in his savage nature [standing] as a challenge to order and reason and civilization."[8] This polarized narrative of savagery and civilization was a powerful trope, yet one always muddled by counternarratives. Americans defined themselves in opposition to the natives, but paradoxically looked to the Indian for an aboriginal return to their roots. By the 1830s, Americans "finished" the "removal" of native peoples in the east, but Indians were a volatile presence on the western frontier throughout the nineteenth century. Paradoxically, White appropriation of aboriginal genesis became a growing positive source for American self-definition while native peoples still retained their "savage" otherness.[9]

"Playing Indian" has been a consistent American pastime.[10] In the late eighteenth century, Whites painted as "Indians" in the Boston Tea Party were able to use their "fury" to move toward civilization through the Revolution. A century later, Buffalo Bill disguised himself as an Indian to rescue his sister from savages in his Wild West Show.[11] In the early twentieth century, former president Theodore Roosevelt took up the accoutrements of a "savage" to kill on the plains of Africa to establish his manhood, and Ernest Thompson Seton's Woodcraft Indians program taught young American boys to play Indian, inducing their evolution to become men.[12] Playing an Indian—whether actual, fictional, or ideological—could be a way to grasp the aboriginal strength of the noble American savage. Performances that encouraged revolution, manifesting manhood, or developing manliness pushed civilization forward, all while demarcating its limits.

Mormonism arose within this complex fusion of discourses about civilization, savagery, and the place of native peoples, its presence pushing the boundaries of what was considered acceptable for White citizens of the new nation. The Latter-day Saints were never a completely cohesive ethnic group, which made categorization difficult, but the perception of a collective violation of acceptable boundaries also brought upon them the label "savage."

"Mormon Indian-uity"

The narrative of Mormon savagery did not develop with the outrages at Mountain Meadows; it began with the earliest origins of Mormonism. A perceived Mormon alliance with the Indians became a significant element of the rhetoric of Mormon savagery. Published in 1830, the Book of Mormon narrative linked the Latter-day Saints to Native Americans in a peculiar theological understanding of native peoples. The Saints understood the Lamanites (the major antagonists, then protagonists, in the Book of Mormon narrative) as modern-day Native Americans and an explicitly stated audience of the text. Though initially cursed, they would be blessed in the latter days. The Book of Mormon taught "the red man . . . of his elevated origin."[13] Moreover, Latter-day Saint missionaries' first abortive mission attempted to proselytize native peoples just months after Joseph Smith published the Book of Mormon and organized the church. Terryl Givens points to the Saints' relations with Indians as one of the early and consistent sources of conflict with America, while Paul Reeve most thoroughly outlines the predicament in his monograph *Religion of a Different Color*.[14] Americans perceived Mormons as attempting to join forces with Indians and "playing Indian"—

FIGURE 1.1 Latter-day Saints elevated the theological position of the Native Americans. Here Joseph Smith is imagined preaching to native peoples, "squatters," and "a respectable company of negroes" in Missouri. Such broad inclusion did not fit in the narrative of White civilization. Mayhew, *Mormons or Latter-day Saints*, 60. Courtesy of L. Tom Perry Special Collections, Harold B. Lee Library, Brigham Young University, Provo.

disguising themselves as Indians or taking on Indian characteristics. For most Americans, Mormons could never engage in acceptable Indian play.

In 1833, vigilante action initiated the first collective Latter-day Saint expulsion in Jackson County, Missouri. As depicted in figure 1.1, Jackson County citizen Samuel Lucas noted that "their threatened association with the neighboring tribes of Indians" constituted a part of the rationale for the Mormons' forced expulsion.[15] Reeve argues that charges of a "Mormon-Indian conspiracy" appeared in every escalating conflict between the Saints and their neighbors.[16] In 1836, the anonymous "Habitator Montium" reported in the *New*

Mormon Savagery 27

York *Spectator* that the effect of the "Holy Ghost" on Mormons induced a variety of "fanatical" and sensationalized markers of "playing Indian," including "exhibiting various feats of Indian warfare, such as knocking down, scalping, ripping open, and tearing out the bowels." The "Holy Ghost" also ignited "fits of speaking Indian dialects."[17] Sensationalized depictions of native peoples coalesced with those of the Latter-day Saints.

In the 1840s after the Saints left Nauvoo, Illinois, to begin their western trek, there were rampant "rumors of Mormon machinations" to band together with the Indians and annihilate White Americans on the frontier.[18] Warren Foote detailed his contemporary encounter with a Nebraska woman and her perceptions of this dangerous alliance between Mormons and the Indians. When Foote tried to sell something to her, she commented on the "great many Indians up there where you are camped." Though Foote answered that he hadn't seen any, she believed rumors that the Mormons were "building forts" and "marrying with the Indians, . . . combining together and are coming down here to kill us all off." In his journal Foote commented, "If they are not killed until the 'Mormons' kill them they will live a long time."[19] Warren Foote expected that "long time" to last forever; a decade later the perception became a reality.

In 1852, the *American Whig* published a monthly serial account of Mormonism under the name "R. W. Mac," demonstrating the "most dangerous and disorganizing social doctrines" of Mormonism for the *Whig*'s readership. Mormon and Indian alliances were sure evidence of the danger. The serial recited tales of the chaos in Nauvoo after Joseph Smith's murder in 1844. The Mormons "blustered in the streets, and shouted with the energy and savage fury of their red brethren, whose example they professed to emulate."[20] The Mormons possessed a "blind and revengeful fury characteristic of the North American savage." This savage wrath "humiliate[ed] . . . the refined feelings of a civilized gentleman."[21] The serial expanded the rhetoric of alliance once the Saints left civilization and headed westward. The *Whig* detailed a laundry list of Indian tribes including "all the wild tribes of the deep valleys and lofty crags of the Rocky Mountains"—all Mormon confederates. Mormonism taught the natives "to hear the voice of the Prophet, submit to his teachings, and to give their untamed barbarian energies, and employ the tactics of their destructive warfare to the establishment of the Mormon supremacy."[22] Though the actual author was unclear, the message was unmistakable: civilization was a safe place of order; if Mormons were left unbridled, chaos would reign and civilization would be rejected.

Such rumors painted the Mormon and Indian relationship in broad strokes: complete alliance and complete unity. The reality was much more fraught. The Latter-day Saints colonized native people's land when they arrived in Utah Territory in 1847 and generally saw the Indians as less evolved peoples despite their theological potential. Early on, the Latter-day Saints focused on bringing agriculture and Christianity to the native peoples whose traditional resources had been decimated by their arrival. However, they had little success in those efforts, and depredations led to such violent standoffs. Brigham Young, territorial governor and superintendent of Indian Affairs, authorized a "limited extermination" in the early 1850s. In his battles with the federal government during the Utah War, Young hoped to secure strong alliances with the native peoples, though such alliances were always tenuous. Tribal leaders preferred to let the Americans and the Latter-day Saints fight it out while they waited to see who would win. At that critical point, Young decided to no longer stand between American emigrants and Native Americans, not wanting to risk Latter-day Saint lives for Americans if the federal government continued to send troops to quell Utah's perceived rebellion.[23] Later, Young transitioned once again, deciding that it was more effective to feed Indians than shoot them. Initial paternalistic efforts transitioned to the more American act of extermination and removal—the creation of treaties and reservations in the 1860s.[24] None of the Mormons' policy reversals were included in popular rumors about Mormon and Indian unity; the reality was always too complex to fit the clearly polarized discourse. As illustrated in figure 1.2, the infamous 11 September 1857 Mountain Meadows Massacre gave credence to the well-established fears, rumors, and innuendo of decades.

Popular narratives about Mormon-Indian unity emphasized that it did not just include shared military action but also encompassed familial and religious ties. To many Americans' distaste, marriage or baptism reportedly reinforced those alliances. Though Mormons were baptizing and marrying some natives in the mid- to late nineteenth century, the popular perception grew out of step with the reality. The *Chicago Daily Inter-Ocean* reported that Mormons baptized armies of Indians.[25] Newspaper reports embellished singular events with speculation to establish an unqualified Mormon and Indian alliance. In a *Scribner's Monthly* article, editor John Beadle alerted Americans of Mormons sent to Northern Idaho, where they were "specially instructed to marry Indian women as extensively as possible, and to form close alliances with the savages."[26] Rather than being seen as the Saints' own

MORMON ALLIES AT THE MOUNTAIN MEADOWS.

FIGURE 1.2 Though the reality of the Saints' relationship with native peoples was considerably more complex, Americans imagined complete and consistent alliance between Mormons and Indians. Triplett, *History and Romance and Philosophy*, 197. Courtesy of L. Tom Perry Special Collections, Harold B. Lee Library, Brigham Young University, Provo.

efforts to civilize the natives, the fact of these marriages and baptisms further cemented the perception of Mormons and Indians united together in savagery. An anti-Mormon pioneer folk song "advised a Mormon to go back to Utah because he married a squaw." Rhyming certainly factored into the choice, but the song implied that neither the Mormon nor the Indian was "the right sort of person."[27]

Make It an Indian Massacre

After the massacre, the earliest official reports were of an Indian massacre. To conceal Latter-day Saint involvement, massacre participant John D. Lee blamed the depredation on the Indians—just as he and Isaac Haight had planned. Immediately after the massacre, John D. Lee began to tell a story of an Indian massacre with the Mormon militia coming out as an act of mercy to end the suffering of the emigrants. Many Latter-day Saints, who assumed it impossible that they could be involved in such an event, correspondingly continued the narrative of an Indian massacre. In his federal position as farmer to the Indians, Lee was to aid the Paiute Indians with farming, working alongside the Saints' efforts to both Christianize and agriculturalize bands of Indians in Utah. A few weeks after the massacre, Lee officially reported the bloodshed to Young. He claimed that the emigrants "poisoned Beef & gave it to the Indians & several of them died. They poisond the springs of water several of the saints died the Indians became inraged at their Conduct & they surrounded them on a prairie." He continued his account absent any Latter-day Saint involvement: "The Indians fought them 5 days untill they killed all their men. . . . They then rushed into their Carrell & Cut the throats of their women & Children except some 8 or 10 Children which they brought & sold to the whites."[28] Young had recently staved off a possible Indian war in northern Utah when Latter-day Saints stepped between emigrants and Indians, so he initially saw the massacre as another failure of bellicose federal Indian policies.[29]

The day after Lee gave an account to Young, federal Indian agent George Armstrong also sent an official report to Young. In his letter, Armstrong reported a retributive Indian massacre at Mountain Meadows. He similarly told a tale of the misdeeds of White emigrants provoking the Indians.[30] Federal appointees soon replaced Young, and he no longer had any official jurisdiction over the case. In the ensuing weeks, the story began to change. Another Indian agent, Garland Hurt, also reported the massacre; he acknowledged Indian participation, yet he placed primary responsibility on the Latter-day Saints in his official report to the new federal Indian agent, Jacob Forney.[31] By November, reports of the massacre would reach across the country.[32] Though the initial official reports were of an Indian massacre, a more complete description began to emerge. News of Latter-day Saint involvement came in the subsequent weeks.[33]

Contemporary accounts never questioned the Indian presence at the massacre, though the number of Paiutes present varied greatly—from fifty to hundreds.[34] Despite the limits of the earliest news reports, as illustrated in figure 1.3, some commentators very quickly suggested the alliance of Latter-day Saints and Paiute warriors at the massacre. Many San Francisco papers assumed Mormon culpability before it could be verified. The center of significant anti-Mormon sentiment, San Francisco was already awash in a

MOUNTAIN MEADOW MASSACRE—132 EMIGRANTS KILLED BY MORMONS AND INDIANS.

FIGURE 1.3 Mormons and Indians in league together suggested something amiss. "Mountain Meadows Massacre—132 Emigrants Killed by Mormons and Indians," in Beadle, *Life in Utah*, 182. Courtesy of L. Tom Perry Special Collections, Harold B. Lee Library, Brigham Young University, Provo.

newspaper war between pro- and anti-Mormon newspapers.[35] In an early report of the massacre, the *Daily Alta California* asked, "Who can be so blind as not to see that the hands of Mormons are stained with this blood?"[36] The *San Francisco Herald* immediately identified the massacre as a precursor to the expected battle between "ten thousand fighting [Mormon] men . . . in close alliance with at least fifty thousand hostile Indians."[37] The crafted, long-standing narrative of a Mormon and Indian alliance had led Americans to expect violence.

As the news reports spread in the weeks and months after the massacre, some individuals called for government intervention. The massacre directly affected former Arkansas state senator William C. Mitchell, who lost two sons and many other family members who were members of the emigrant train. Anxious for action against the Mormons, he used his political connections. He wrote to his U.S. congressional representative, noting, "I see from the California paper . . . that there have been a great many meetings asking the President to chastise the guilty." Mitchell doubted the efficiency of the army, "to whip the Mormons and Indians, for rest assured that all the wild tribes will fight for Brigham Young." Like many Americans, Mitchell had heard rumors of a Mormon and Indian alliance for years. Some saw Buchanan calling out U.S. troops to quell the Mormon Rebellion in Utah as folly, yet as Mitchell grieved the loss of family it was not enough. He felt he "must have satisfaction for the inhuman manner in which they have slain my children."[38]

Questions from the press of what would be done about the Mormon massacre continued in numerous articles across the country in the following years to no discernible result. The following February, an Arkansas press echoed Mitchell's vengeful language: "What will the Government do with these Mormons and Indians? Will it not send out enough men to hang all the scoundrels and thieves at once, and give them the same play they gave our women and children?"[39] In 1859, a number of Arkansans publicly continued the plea for action. The massacre was not considered a singular instance of Mormon and native unity, but an example of a continued alliance, demonstrating the real danger of Mormonism. The Arkansas resolution called on the government to "immediately adopt decisive measures for subduing the spirit of insubordination and treason" among the Mormons.[40] Mitchell and his fellow Arkansans did not have an opportunity for revenge, but Mitchell's efforts were central to recover the seventeen surviving children.[41] Almost two years after writing to Washington with requests for government help to retrieve them, Mitchell was on his way to Fort Leavenworth, Kansas Territory, "with a couple of two-horse wagons and a nurse" to accompany the children on the final leg of their journey back to Arkansas, where they were reunited with their relatives in 1859.[42]

The federal government returned the surviving children but left the larger calls for military action against the Mormons and the Indians unheeded. As such, the polarized discourse expanded from western papers across the country without impediment. A Massachusetts paper reported in May 1858 that "a large body of [well-armed] Indians of various hostile tribes" were reportedly gathering in Washington on the Red River under the direction of "the Great Chief of the West"—Brigham Young. The "Mormon Indian-uity" apparently plotted to "exterminate the white settlers on the frontiers."[43] The 1863 Bear River Massacre, when 250 Shoshone were murdered by a White U.S. militia, also produced reports of Mormon and Indian alliances. However, the massacre was a militia response to attacks on Latter-day Saint settlers by the Shoshone, who were starving as a result of White settlement.[44] The rhetoric led the American public to await the next Mormon massacre.

This narrative was similarly reflected in official reports. The secretary of war's 1859 annual report stated, "Mormons are never molested by the Indians."[45] If Mormons controlled the lesser-evolved Indians, then Mormons never had to worry about hostile Indians themselves. On 19 March 1860, the Senate resolved to gather all information regarding the massacre. The president published the response in Senate Executive Document 42 on 4 May 1860. The 139-page document detailed multiple affidavits and correspondence regarding the Mountain Meadows Massacre. Yet it also included dozens of accounts of additional reported Indian "depredations" on any trail to California between 1855 and 1860. While the report laid out important knowledge of the massacre, its larger work reinforced the popular perception of a consistent alliance between Mormons and Indians.[46]

That alliance was a clear sign to many Americans that Mormons had left "civilization" behind them. In 1859, federally appointed Utah territorial judge Delana Eckels explained his understanding of civilization to U.S. Attorney General Lewis Cass and its role in the Mormon Problem as he detailed how any man, "when removed beyond the *currents of civilization*, fast recedes towards barbarism." Utah was without "the civilizing effects of commerce, christianity and government," so it was logical that civilization would "languish."[47] As shown in figure 1.4, the popular painting *American Progress* by John Nast famously depicted ideas of Manifest Destiny bringing light to a dark continent.[48] As she floats above it, Columbia—the White female personification of America dressed in white—brings civilization and knowledge, via the telegraph line, to the frontier. Indians are found in the dark edges fleeing from the light as the White settlers move west. Feminizing notions of civilization hid the darker and violent aspects of civilizing the frontier and reminded American men of their responsibilities to protect civilization. Though Latter-day Saints could have been understood to be in the wagons moving west with the light of civilization (they saw themselves that way), within the Mountain Meadows discourse Mormons fled from the light to hide in the darkness. Rather than bringing light and civilization to the dark frontier, Mormons had elected to leave the light of Christian civilization and enter the savage darkness.[49] Popular sources reinforced Judge Eckels's view as they detailed the Mormon menace to the American public. In the *Atlantic Monthly*, Fitz-Hugh Ludlow maintained that in contrast to ironically peaceful islands that shielded the atrocities of foreign savages, the "bleak and rugged face" of the Utah landscape appropriately and "poetically . . . indicate[d] the abode

FIGURE 1.4 As the personification of Manifest Destiny, Columbia brings light and civilization to the dark frontier. Did Mormons bring light with other pioneers or choose to escape civilization to the darkness? George A. Crofutt print of John Nash, *American Progress*, 1873. Courtesy of the Library of Congress.

of savages and ogres."[50] This choice to leave civilization behind necessarily had consequences.

White Indians

The perception of the alliance between Mormons and American Indians had several facets. Mormons playing Indian—dressing the part, wielding their tools, and performing violent acts—endured as one significant aspect of the perception. U.S. Army soldiers stationed at Fort Bridger, Wyoming, purportedly wrote a ballad as they waited through the winter to enter Utah. The song propagated the story of Mountain Meadows and Mormon sin. One verse began,

> On a crisp October Morning
> At the Mountain Meadows green

> By the light of bright campfires
> Lee's Mormon bullets screamed.
> At a word from Lee, the pistols blazed,
> The women and children came.
> They shot them down in Indian style.
> O Utah, where's your shame![51]

Despite being wrong about the month the massacre occurred, the song advances the idea that Lee's actions were not just those of a violent individual with a gun; Mormonism produced Lee. He shot "Mormon bullets," suggesting a pattern of Mormon behavior and a history of similar violent actions. Lee killed the emigrants "in Indian style"—perhaps the weapon was not considered Indian, but the savagery employed was thought to be. All Mormons, or at least all the Mormons in Utah, should have been ashamed, yet they were not. The emotive ballad decried a breach of civilized boundaries for which all Mormons had to be held accountable.

Before the Mountain Meadows Massacre, other Whites who were similarly accused of transgressing the boundaries of acceptable civilized behavior were labeled "white Indians." Newspaper reports throughout the nineteenth century noted their existence. Americans saw these "white Indians" as an object of curiosity and bewilderment; American observers believed them to be choosing savageness rather than attempting to recover a lost aboriginal past as they played Indian. The arguments denied both the agency and the intellectual capacity of native peoples. Whites were "the worst persons in Indian raids" because they "add[ed] the skill of one race to the savageness of the other.... One white Indian [was] worse than ten red ones."[52] In the 1850s, there were numerous reports of "white Indians" attacking emigrants on the northern trail to California and Oregon.[53] These White men were said to "urg[e] Indians to commit depredations on emigration."[54] Brigham Young warned the people in Salt Lake City that "numerous and well organized bands of *white* highwaymen, painted and disguised as Indians, infest several points on the road, who drive off stock by wholesale, and recent murders are rumored from that quarter."[55] A flurry of reports came in documenting Whites attacking emigrant trains in conjunction with the Indians.[56]

However, the nature of the reports of White Indians changed significantly after the Mountain Meadows Massacre. At that point, White persons choosing to involve themselves with natives in the Mountain Meadows Massacre demonstrated that they were worse than the savages. The *Chicago Daily Tribune* told of "atrocities too horrible to be related, and which seemed to shock

The Mountain Meadow Massacre.

FIGURE 1.5 Rather than a depiction of an Indian massacre, in this version of the massacre all the Mormons were painted as Indians—there were no native peoples present. Freece, *Letters of an Apostate Mormon to His Son*, 27. Courtesy of L. Tom Perry Special Collections, Harold B. Lee Library, Brigham Young University, Provo.

the savages themselves."[57] After his personal investigation of the massacre that same year, army lieutenant James Lynch claimed to have uncovered "attending circumstances far exceeding anything in cruelty that we have ever heard of or read of being perpetrated even by savages."[58] As depicted in figure 1.5, for some there were only Mormons at the massacre. Both public and personal commentators began to see the event through the same lens of hypersavagery.

Indicting Savagery

As the Latter-day Saints and federal appointees vied for control of Utah and most of the country focused on the Civil War, little judicial progress was made against the perpetrators of the massacre until the early 1870s. In 1871, upon prompting by a disaffected former Latter-day Saint, massacre participant

Mormon Savagery 37

and former Cedar City bishop Philip Klingensmith filed an official statement about the massacre. Though then U.S. district attorney George C. Bates expressed a desire to move the prosecution for the massacre forward, nothing happened in the months that followed. At some point word got out, and the following summer Klingensmith's affidavit was stolen from Bates's office. Within weeks, it appeared in both the *New York Herald* and the *New York Times*, published on the same day. Other papers across the country quickly followed suit. The next year, Latter-day Saint defector Thomas H. Stenhouse published the affidavit in his book, *The Rocky Mountain Saints*. Klingensmith reignited the smoldering ember of the massacre.[59]

One of the federal appointees' consistent claims about the Latter-day Saints was that they would not convict their own, no matter the crime. Some thought any attempt at prosecuting polygamy or the perpetrators of the massacre would be useless. However, Klingensmith's affidavit, in addition to the 1874 Poland Act which placed Utah's judiciary securely under federal control, changed things; ultimately the state moved forward with prosecuting both polygamy and Mountain Meadows.[60] Indictments were brought by a grand jury in 1874. Nine people were indicted separately for murder of a number of Johns Does—fictitious members of the emigrant company. Those indicted included Isaac C. Haight and John D. Lee, without whom the massacre would not have happened; William Dame, the militia commander; Philip Klingensmith, who supported Haight at the Cedar City council meeting and actively participated on the massacre field; and John M. Higbee, who on the field gave the order for the killing to begin. The indicted also included some individual Latter-day Saint militia members: William Stewart, who began the killing with the murder of nineteen-year-old William Aden; participants Ellott Willden and George Adair Jr.; and a politically motivated inclusion of a southern Utah judge who was not involved with the massacre other than caring for one of the victims' children.[61] Haight, Lee, Higbee, and Stewart went on the run almost immediately. Marshals arrested Lee and William Dame first—Lee as he hid in a chicken coop and Dame as he waited for the marshals in his home.

The press took liberties with the colorful element of the chicken coop and "drew a vibrant picture of Lee emerging from the straw while his wife Rachel aimed a double-barreled shotgun" at the marshal and his deputies. The marshal's own account was not as theatrical—Lee came out and invited the officers to breakfast. Lee offered an initial confession in hopes of a plea deal, but prosecutors rejected his confession, crafted a second indictment that included the charge of conspiracy, and brought him to trial.[62]

Legal actions never operated independently of the surrounding culture. The relationship between official legal actions for the massacre and the sensational tales told about it demonstrate a consistent interdependence. Many authors saw sensationalism as a tool to engender passion and highlight the Mormons' rejection of civilization. In a genre similar to Indian captivity narratives, in a post-massacre Mormon captivity serial tale, "Saved from the Mormons," the Indian savages were preferable to the Mormon savages who sold their young into polygamic slavery.[63] Savagery was one of several highly sensationalized themes to bring about larger goals. Thomas B. and Fanny Stenhouse were perhaps the most successful authors in a series of verbose nineteenth-century former Mormons. After the initial success of her husband's book, Fanny Stenhouse called herself an "open enemy" of the Mormon hierarchy and wrote a *"Tell It All"* exposé of Mormon polygamy in 1874, including a chapter on the Mountain Meadows Massacre.[64] In the first edition, the title page touted an introduction by Mrs. Harriet Beecher Stowe. However, in every edition after the first, Stowe had to share space on the title page with promises of additional massacre details.

When John D. Lee was first tried before the bar the following year, and Lee's defense attorney Wells Spicer made his opening statement, the defense attorney castigated members of the prosecution for relying on Mrs. Stenhouse's account of the Meadows in their retelling (this would not be the only time they depended on antipolygamy tomes for their argument). For Stenhouse, this was hopeful. In a later edition, she gushed, "The author rejoices that it has been her good fortune to contribute so much toward the final consummation of even-handed justice in the punishment of the guilty."[65] Mrs. Stenhouse saw her work as an effort to correct the social ill of Mormonism—polygamy. For many like Mrs. Stenhouse, both opportunity and religious duty required that they contribute to the general downfall of Mormonism. Mrs. Stenhouse's volume would go through no fewer than three dozen editions (the latest in 2003) with multiple publishers and at least one Spanish edition.[66] Moreover, Mrs. Stenhouse would continue offering anti-Mormon lectures for the rest of her life. The profitability of the project did not discount the evangelical zeal with which she pursued it.[67]

Fanny Stenhouse dedicated herself to showing the larger American public, particularly antipolygamy advocates, the treachery from which she had escaped. As she wove her narrative, she emphasized the deceptive nature of the Mormons. The Arkansas emigrants took for granted that the "savage Indians . . . were their only enemies." They might have thought the Mormons were odd, yet the reality seemed impossible—"Coldly, strangely as they had been treated at the Mormon settlements, they never for a moment supposed that white men could be in league against them or could meditate their destruction." The travelers could not guess that some of the men they saw as Indians "were only painted devils, mocks of humanity, wretches who under the mask of a red-skin's color were eager to perpetrate the foulest of offences—scoundrels a thousand times demanded in the opinion of men and by the decree of God." Though Mormons might have looked like other Americans and appeared civilized, they were imposters. Though important, the savage identity of the Mormons was only a part of the greater Mormon Problem—only one element of many that placed the Mormons in opposition to nineteenth-century American ideals. In detailing the deception of Mormon savagery, Stenhouse ensured that others would not similarly fall into the Mormon trap.[68] Even with consistent expansions on the Mountain Meadows narrative in subsequent editions (and her titular claim to tell it all), Stenhouse avowed, "This is the story—most imperfectly told." As many after her would repeat, she "dare[d] not sketch its foulest details," preferring to leave the complete story to the sensationalized imaginings of the reading American public.

Savagery in the Court

With John D. Lee's trial, the public didn't need to wait for the next exposé in book form, the newspapers would step in to continue the sordid tale of civilization lost. On 23 July 1875, U.S. Attorney William Carey opened the much-anticipated case against John D. Lee, the "butcher" of the Mountain Meadows, to a packed makeshift courtroom above the local saloon in Beaver, Utah, and to the larger United States via the newspapermen in attendance.[69] Initially a dusty Latter-day Saint settlement, the southwest Utah town of Beaver sustained a significant influx of miners in the late 1850s and a military presence as the U.S. Army built Fort Cameron in 1873. The recently relocated federal court tried Lee for murder in concert of action with nine others as participants in the massacre. This "most important criminal case" garnered widespread attention in the press across America, and among competing Utah papers.[70] The court gave the press choice seats near Marshal George Maxwell, son of the Methodist minister in town.[71] The press provided significant trial coverage that traveled across the country and even across the sea to Europe, shaping the public perception of the Mountain Meadows Massacre and the Mormons.

Fully engrossed at the beginning of the trial, reporters provided ample copy of the proceedings, publishing trial transcripts (though only through the first three witnesses), additional massacre reports, and salacious additions to the story of the Meadows. Numerous papers published former LDS bishop and massacre participant Philip Klingensmith's testimony.[72] Many reporters also briefly summarized the testimonies of other witnesses, while a few reported on all of the witnesses. The prosecution cast a wide net for such witnesses, sometimes focusing on the sensational. A "former" wife of John D. Lee found herself included on the witness list, though she was never summoned. Mrs. Theresa Phelps was married to Lee "five or six years after the massacre."[73] Phelps was one of many who were subpoenaed but apparently not reputable enough to be called to testify. Several papers printed assertions from these "witnesses."[74] Others reported a variety of spurious stories.[75] Defense attorney William W. Bishop detailed, "The reporters for Associated Press and several specials are here, all busily engaged hunting items and manufacturing news when there is a scarcity of items."[76] Since the rise of the penny press in the 1830s, what qualified as news grew broadly, and it became the provenance of all, not just the upper class. By the 1870s, the number of newspapers had more than doubled, and their reading public had grown exponentially.[77] The press ensured that a public with burgeoning enthusiasm for crime reports and legal trials across the country could gorge on "the horrible romance of the Mountain Meadows Massacre . . . reawakened by the trial of John D. Lee."[78]

The trial opened with William Carey as the prosecuting U.S. attorney and newly appointed Robert Baskin as his assistant with two more attorneys, C. Myron Hawley and Pressley Denny, as associate counsel. Lee initially claimed Wells Spicer as his attorney, later adding Enos D. Hoge and William W. Bishop. They worked together with Dame's attorneys, George Bates and Jabez Sutherland.[79] The prosecution opened and closed with this strategy: the Mormons did not belong in civilization and were imposter Americans. The prosecuting U.S. attorney William Carey asked, "You cannot believe that civilized men, white men, men who were born amongst many of our own tribes and kindred, American Citizens, could volunteer to go forward" and commit such a "sickening crime."[80] Despite their appearance as White Americans, these Mormons had rejected civilization. The Indians stood a "little better than the Mormons." Later Carey's co-counsel, Robert Baskin, would argue the Mormons were incapable of killing children, yet here Carey argued that the Indians, rather than the Mormons, at least "had superstition enough—enough Christianity in their bosoms to preserve the children." The Arkansas emigrants should have been able to assume that other Americans would be civilized enough to protect them and that

Mormon Savagery 41

Lee "had been reared under the benign influences of the holy religion of Jesus Christ, and therefore under its benign influence *he could not possess*, as the savage possessed the treachery and disregard for human life." Surely White Christian America had evolved past the ability to possess such "treachery." Alas, the emigrants "were mistaken."[81]

This discourse of civilization and savagery lays a critical framework within which the attorneys constructed arguments at John D. Lee's first trial. Not a single witness used the term "savage" in relation to native peoples or Latter-day Saints. Yet the attorneys' arguments consistently focused on savagery. Interestingly, the prosecutors argued this narrative of Mormon savagery before a mostly Latter-day Saint jury. Baskin asserted he feared faithful Saints on the jury would not find John D. Lee guilty regardless of the evidence.[82] Nevertheless, he pleaded with the jurors to remain true to their judicial oaths, reminding them they would "answer in the great day of judgment . . . before the final judge."[83] His decision to appeal to the jurors' religiosity seemed a gamble. For much of the nineteenth century, most American Christians did not view the Latter-day Saint gospel as religious at all, but a counterfeit.[84] For Baskin, the possibility of true Christian belief seemed the Mormons' only hope for change. They could throw off the shackles of Mormonism and return to civilization if they so desired. Despite the possibility of offending a majority of the mostly Latter-day Saint jury with an argument of Mormon savagery, Baskin proceeded, divulging that his focus lay beyond his immediate audience. The narrative bolstered Baskin's larger goal of further indicting the Mormons as a whole before an extensive American audience with "incontrovertible" evidence.

John D. Lee's first trial demonstrated the complexity of contemporary views of indigenous peoples to build a perception of Mormon savagery. By the 1870s, popular images of Indians had grown "increasingly ambivalent" as some felt compassion for the plight of native peoples, though negative constructions of assumed simple Indian savagery remained.[85] The prosecution and the defense offered competing visions of savagery, with the defense initially calling on this earlier narrative of Indian savagery—albeit fractured—and the prosecution demonstrating an ambivalence toward Indian savagery, replacing their barbarity with that of the truly savage Mormons. John D. Lee, the Mormons, Mormon leaders, members of the slain emigrant party, and Native Americans were all argued to be savage at different points in John D. Lee's first trial.

Setting up his strategy in his opening argument against John D. Lee, prosecuting U.S. attorney Carey indicated that the alliance of Mormons and

Indians signaled impropriety afoot. For Carey, the frontier location was right—it was a liminal space outside the grasp of civilization, where malfeasance could occur. John D. Lee could boast of his crime in southern Utah because the "eyes of civilization" did not reach there, but when he traveled to Salt Lake City the boasting had to stop. Carey insisted that "it was getting a little too near the place where it would be proclaimed to the world that a white man . . . was engaged in that massacre."[86] Movement from a small rural area to a city was not necessarily important, yet more than Latter-day Saints resided in Salt Lake City. The Gentile (non–Latter-day Saint) population of Salt Lake made it the doorway to the civilized world. And that civilized world could not let such a crime stand.

Second District territorial judge Jacob Boreman had instructed the jury that the Mountain Meadows Massacre stood as "a crime of appalling magnitude, planned and carried out with a demon-like ferocity, unparalleled in modern days, or among civilized people."[87] Prosecuting attorney Baskin echoed Boreman's categorization; he deemed it "a crime against humanity, a degree of crime deeper in its dye than history records." Mormons "disgrace[d] . . . civilization." Nothing "since [had] darkened the annals of the nineteenth century."[88] As we will consider more fully in chapter 2, the judge and the prosecution did not innovate, but continued the earlier rhetoric of an "unparalleled" crime. Lee, and all Mormons by implication, held the "treachery and disregard for human life" of a non-Christian savage. As a Mormon, Lee allied himself with Indians and behaved "worse than the savages." In his closing argument, Assistant U.S. Attorney Baskin argued that in contrast to Christianity, Lee's "religion was to kill." Mormonism "betray[ed] and then . . . kill[ed] young women and children." This duplicity was evident in Lee's choice to arm himself "with a flag of truce" to allow the emigrants to feel safe before brutally betraying that trust. People across the earth understood a flag of truce as a symbol of "security" for every "savage and every civilized nation."[89] Both the civilized and the barbarian conformed to the conventions the white flag demonstrated, but not the Mormon.

Replete with a late nineteenth-century ambivalence toward the Indian, Baskin argued, "The Indians might have been civilised, but the white man over them was not." There was "no greater savage . . . in that band" than John D. Lee, the leader. Baskin pointed out, "While he (Lee) wears the skin of a white man he bears a heart blacker and more degraded—more contemptible than an Indian."[90] The Mormon rejection of civilization, then, made the Mormons worse than the Indians Baskin thought innately savage. Baskin argued that the emigrants never would have trusted the white flag of surrender from Indians, but since the flag had "a white man's guarantee upon its face," they believed they could "succeed." Lee desecrated the white flag, "relying upon that with a lying tongue worse than [an] indian's tongue in his mouth."[91] Returning to a native pejorative, Baskin drew out Carey's earlier implication, suggesting that Lee was not the exception to a group of upstanding and moral Christians—the Mormons as a whole "were lower than the Indians."[92] Mormonism reversed the effect of civilization, reducing its adherents to "mere barbarians."[93] It "converted Christians into fiends. It . . . made them wild; [and] made them dumb beasts."[94]

The cohesive and consistent message of the prosecution stood in stark contrast to the panoply of theories the defense presented, yet the defense likewise fixated on savagery, offering a narrative that could be found somewhat palatable to the Latter-day Saint members of the jury. Curiously, the defense began in the same place as the prosecution. Defense attorney Wells Spicer also opened his case arguing that the level of savagery exhibited at Mountain Meadows was exceptional—never "excelled in horribleness, in fiendishness."[95] The defense also wove a narrative of savagery versus civilization, deploying many of the same elements as the prosecution. Wells Spicer detailed the great drama and "horrid treachery, in all its ghastliness" and in similar fashion questioned how anyone might believe that "civilized men, white men, men who were born amongst many of our own tribes and kindred, American citizens, could volunteer to go forward and tear the infant from its mother's breast and stab them both to death; could murder in cold blood and without warning."[96] He too developed a foundational argument that civilized Whites simply could not perpetrate such savagery, an argument that relied on the jury judging Lee to be civilized.

At this point, the defense narrative diverged from the prosecution and argued that civilized White American citizens could not do such a thing; it must have been the Indians. The defense continued John D. Lee's earliest claims that Mountain Meadows was "nothing more nor less than an Indian massacre." Spicer went to great lengths to describe the Mormons living in fear of attacks in the Utah Territory and building "walled cities" to protect themselves from the "savage" native peoples.[97] He conceded the presence of White men at the massacre but claimed their numbers were limited to twenty or thirty—"a handful, at the mercy of the savages. . . . Most of them had wives and families at home unprotected."[98]

This initial defense narrative shifted after a recess (and a lively discussion among the defense attorneys) to raise the possibility of White Indians.[99] Spicer claimed that if investigators examined "all the massacre[s] that have ever happened or been perpetrated by savage Indians" in the history of America, they would "always find that white men were there." These could choose to "fall to the lowest depths of crime and hellish deeds" encouraging the uncivilized, "the untutored Savage, the Barbarian, or the cannibal," those who could not choose civility.[100] He continued by saying the White men there had "hearts as black and corrupt as ever worn by an Indian"—the same language as prosecution attorney Baskin would later use to describe John D. Lee.[101]

To support this line of defense, they argued the best points of comparison were the Deerfield and Wyoming Massacres. In 1704, French and Pocumtuc forces attacked an English settlement in Deerfield, Massachusetts, and in July 1778, British loyalists allied themselves with the Iroquois people to attack American settlers in Pennsylvania's Wyoming Valley. In both instances, White military detachments allied themselves with native peoples to attack other Whites.

Despite the defense team infighting, members of the defense converged in their closing arguments on this last strain of Spicer's opening argument: there were savage White men at the massacre, but not John D. Lee. They ultimately focused on two prosecution witnesses and massacre participants: early confessor Philip Klingensmith and Joel White. Involvement both in an initial council and on the massacre field made Klingensmith appealing. Both he and Joel White possibly recruited additional Native Americans to participate. Moreover, White chased down two emigrants that escaped, he was there when William Stewart first killed William Aden, and he and White were known as some of the most bloodthirsty on the field.[102] As the defense argued, they were the White savages on the massacre field.[103] Neither the prosecution nor the defense originated the narratives of savagery utilized in Lee's first trial; the attorneys harnessed the ubiquitous discourse of civilization and an already present rhetoric of Mormon savagery to their own ends.

Shock[ing] the Savages

In his closing argument of John D. Lee's first trial, prosecutor Carey argued that Mormons were more savage than the perpetrators of other comparable massacres because they had employed natives to do their dirty work.[104] Carey assumed Mormons could manipulate the Indians because of their superior intellectual capacity, thus negating Native Americans' agency. For Carey, this action at the Meadows made the Mormons both more accountable and more savage than the Indians. Carey was building on a notion begun in the popular reports after the massacre, that Mormons were now hypersavage.

Even after Indian "containment" and virtual extinction, many White Americans generally accepted outrageous tales of nefarious acts of Indians on the frontier and assumed that savage Indians almost constantly and predictably committed "depredations." Over time, the Mormon role in depredations similarly became a given. Moreover, the earlier narrative of Whites playing Indian began to transform into a perception of Mormon hypersavagery after the massacre and was further cemented by Lee's first trial. In 1875, just after John D. Lee's first trial ended with a hung jury, the anti-Mormon *Corrine Reporter* built on popular fears and claimed that a thousand Indians were conferring with a Mormon bishop and plotting to "clean out" the Gentile mining town of Corrine, Utah, "a la mountain meadows."[105]

The *Virginia Enterprise* in Virginia City, Nevada Territory, was a volatile anti-Mormon press. In the weeks following John D. Lee's second trial and in the wake of the contemporary Battle of Little Bighorn, the paper demonstrated a growing compassion for the native peoples fighting to protect their families—though not considered their equals. Its editors asked why more serious Mormon savagery was treated with mercy when they were led by a "*souless* [sic] *dictator* who, upon superstition, fraud and murder, has built an alien empire in the midst of our Republic?" Sitting Bull was "a very bad Indian," but Brigham Young, "that old Sitting Bull who holds his seat by Salt Lake, and in blasphemy calls himself 'the Lord's anointed,' is worse than any savage of the plains."[106] Young's sin was both political and religious. Young didn't just act as a "soulless dictator," but coupled it with the blasphemy of calling himself a prophet, and the *Enterprise* found that even more egregious. Chapters 4 and 5 will more thoroughly consider the role of Brigham Young in the massacre discourse, but for our purposes here it's sufficient to note that none of these thematic threads function independently; all are woven together to demonstrate Mormonism as a counterfeit religion. Savagery, alienness, and a despotic theocracy all pointed to a place for Mormons on the dark edges of Christian civilization.

Not all anti-Mormon authors approved of the reliance on the sensational to ensure action against the Mormons. As a strident objector to polygamy, Salt Lake City Episcopal reverend Ballard S. Dunn ardently believed that Mormons had contravened the marital boundaries of civilization, and he worked to battle against that Mormon sin. The principled Dunn was no less zealous in his anti-Mormonism than other authors, yet he differed in strategy. He grew frustrated as he saw the narrative around Mountain Meadows spin out of control, describing Utah as a shadowy place of ubiquitous violence. Though Lee was clearly a "fiend" and the massacre a horror that would stay with the Mormons, he maintained that "wild, sensational, and for the most part baseless rumors, intended to affect not only the Mormon leaders, but the whole population, have been telegraphed throughout the country, with the view of arousing public sentiment, in the hope that it will take shape in the form of summary proceedings of the Mormons." Recognizing the rumors and insinuations of vigilantism as such put Dunn in the minority. For Dunn, the growth of the Mountain Meadows narrative distracted from the real problem, which was polygamy.[107] He trusted that the real Mormon sin of polygamy was injurious enough to civilized society to require a constitutional amendment prohibiting its practice.[108] The wild and sensational focus on rumors would not ultimately be effective against the Mormons because they were "wicked and false." The end did not justify the means, and for Dunn, false means would injure the ultimate goal. He argued that Mormons were not "pre-eminently a criminal people." In fact, Dunn believed the Mormons were "less stained with blood than any community of equal size south of Missouri, and west of the Mississippi River." A recent study of the comparative level of violence nuances Dunn's claim, though, like Dunn, Scott Thomas negates the popular idea of Utah as an overwhelmingly violent territory. Thomas notes Utah had comparable levels of vigilante justice in comparison with other western states.[109] This stands in direct opposition to the greater popular Mountain Meadows discourse in the nineteenth century. The violence at Mountain Meadows made the Latter-day Saints more like their American counterparts.

The discourse continued to pervade American culture over time in a variety of different means. However, the sensational accounts would continue. Frank Triplett's books offered the aura of historical authenticity through eyewitness accounts and affidavits while leaning heavily upon fictional expansions.[110] As he crafted his massacre narrative, he employed elements from the trial testimony and then built on it. In an 1884 account, he described how a Mormon, with the oath of his counterfeit religion, played Indian by stealing the accoutrement of the "more merciful savage" and "sank it into [an emigrant girls'] skull." Though Triplett argued that "sanction by the whole Mormon people" made all Mormons accountable, he focused on the accountability of John D. Lee particularly. He pulled an element mentioned in Klingensmith's testimony and expanded on it in his narrative: a merciful Indian chief captured two fifteen-year-old girls "wish[ing] to save their lives, but Lee ordered him to shoot one of them, while he himself dashed the other one to the ground and cut her throat, the blood pouring in a torrent over him and dyeing his clothes with the horrid hue of murder." In multiple graphic examples within Triplett's account, the savages were more merciful than the Mormon Lee.[111]

Performing the Massacre

News of the Lee trial and accounts of the massacre became so ubiquitous in the last quarter of the nineteenth century that people could also now watch accounts of the massacre as entertainment. This met the public's yearning for the salacious as it prescribed acceptable behavior through performance. Civilization's boundaries could be established in a variety of ways; performative genres, such as anti-Mormon melodramas and Wild West Shows, employed emotive or sensational narratives to specific ends. Indians were a staple of Wild West Shows, though their parts were usually portrayed by White actors. Buffalo Bill Cody cast a large number of Indians to perform his story of the West. In 1878, Cody salvaged a flailing market for his Wild West shows with his play *May Cody, or Lost and Won*, though in this show Cody dressed as an Indian to rescue his sister not from Indians but from the savage Mormons. Advertisements prominently featured the Mountain Meadows Massacre and Brigham Young. The show opened with a two-week run in New York City and then successfully crisscrossed the United States for another twenty-nine months, exciting audiences. This included one night in Denver, Colorado, where malfunctioning fireworks landed on the corpse actors causing them to resurrect: "An immoderate amount of profanity bubbled from resurrected lips."[112]

A wide variety of other performers also worked Mountain Meadows into their western stage shows, but Cody's reaped the most success.[113] In *Performing American Identity in Anti-Mormon Melodrama*, Megan Sanborn Jones argues that wholly economic analyses of western melodrama ignore the political and social critiques the melodramas provide.[114] Cody playing Indian reinforced the perception of an alliance between Mormons and Indians while highlighting the Mormons' negative appropriation of Indian characteristics. Cody's appropriation of Indian attire and actions brought about civilization as he saved his sister from the Mormons. The Mormons attacked civilization as they played Indian.

Pawnee Bill (Major Gordon W. Lillie) led another Wild West Show that repeatedly used the Mountain Meadows narrative around the turn of the twentieth century. Lillie took on the persona of an Indian, and his company successfully traversed the country reenacting the massacre.[115] It was suitable for some Whites to play Indian in a positive return to their aboriginal roots, as did Pawnee Bill. While violence on the stage would never be comparable to actual violence, playing Indian worked for some. Following a pattern well established by the turn of the century, Pawnee Bill's early twentieth-century biographer, J. H. De Wolff, used the biography as an opportunity to write a chapter on the massacre. He wrote that Lillie focused on Mountain Meadows because of its "crimson blot upon the bright pages of American history." De Wolff also asserted the exceptionality of the massacre, claiming, "Nothing in the pages of war surpass[ed the massacre] in savagery, cruelty, and sanguinary character." His analysis concluded with a declaration of Mormon hypersavagery: "These 'Latter-Day Saints' were worse than mountain tigers and more bloodthirsty than the hideous redskins of the warpath."[116]

Violence might be a necessary casualty of the forward movement of civilization, but only some kinds of violence were acceptable. Within the Mountain Meadows narrative, Whites killing other Whites demonstrated a severe transgression. The glaring comparisons to the violence of the Civil War were absent in the Mountain Meadows discourse; the Latter-day Saints' violence was not sanctioned by the state.[117] As New England's *Bay State Monthly* opined, the Mormons' actions at Mountain Meadows "surpasse[d] in atrocity any act of the savage tribes by whom they are surrounded." The sin of Mountain Meadows "stained indelibly the Mormon church."[118]

The Eyes of Civilization

The U.S. attorneys incorporated elements of this popular discourse surrounding Mountain Meadows as they framed their arguments in John D. Lee's first trial. Such a tactic demonstrated a greater concern for their nationwide audience via the newspapermen in attendance rather than their Latter-day Saint–majority jury. Prosecutors declared Lee's trial would finally bring the savagery of the Mormon Church to "the eyes of the whole civilized world," so they worked to do their part, building on already prevalent perceptions of Mormons.[119] The prosecution did not create an original narrative in constructing the "savagery" element of its argument against the Saints. Rather, employing the popular discourse already in place, the prosecution expanded the rhetoric of a Mormon and Indian alliance and the specter of Mormons playing Indian, transforming these tropes into a perception of Mormon hypersavagery. The prosecution's narrative of Mormon savagery rallied public sentiment against the Mormons as it reified the Mormons' lack of fitness for citizenship.

In his closing argument, Assistant U.S. Attorney Robert Baskin argued that John D. Lee's trial was to Mormonism what Dred Scott was to the institution of slavery. The 1857 Dred Scott Supreme Court decision, *Dred Scott v. Sandford*, considered whether enslaved persons could earn their freedom when moved to a free state. Writing for the majority, Chief Justice Roger Taney argued that the lack of civilization in enslaved peoples of African descent negated Scott's right to sue in a federal court. The case invalidated the Missouri Compromise and congressional efforts to curb slavery. Baskin asserted that "the whole system of negro slavery was involved . . . in the person of Dred Scott." In the same manner, John D. Lee's trial put the Mormon Church on trial, Baskin argued, and "there [was] no use to disguise the fact."[120] Baskin maintained the Mountain Meadows Massacre was a "most wonderful commentary" on the institution of Mormonism which confirmed the suspicions of the "civilized world."[121] In the middle of the trial, the stridently anti-Mormon *San Francisco Post* recommended extreme measures: "We should deal with those Mormon savages as we would the Indians, their allies and tools in the work of butchery. No Mormon should be left in the United States."[122] Within the rhetoric of acceptable violence to expand civilization, such action could be condoned. Throughout this book runs the threat of vigilantism in tension with pleas for a state-sponsored action against the Saints. A mix of vigilantism and state-sponsored violence had pushed the Latter-day Saints across the country. Would it continue?

The prosecution's goals were not as extreme, however. The Dred Scott decision had argued that a territory should remain a territory until it was demonstrated that the territory was "a civilized community, capable of self-government."[123] That was central to the prosecution's aims. The evidence of savagery and the absence of civilization in Utah could be a significant step to deny any possibility of statehood, and by extension full Latter-day Saint citizenship, as it had been for native peoples.[124] Though Lee's first trial would end in a hung jury and no one would yet be punished for the Mountain Meadows Massacre, the prosecution effectively utilized a powerful discourse that worked to further separate Mormonism from civilization in the eyes of many Americans. However, savagery was only one of the ways in which Americans racialized Mormons in the Mountain Meadows discourse.

CHAPTER TWO

Circumscribing Civilization
The White Hellhounds

Even before the new superintendent of Indian Affairs in Utah Territory, Jacob Forney, arrived in the territory in June 1858, he had a charge to investigate the Mountain Meadows Massacre that he would later describe as "without a parallel in human history for atrocity."[1] His investigation into the massacre would eclipse all other concerns during his short tenure. Although he initially sent others to report to him, in the spring of 1859 he continued the investigation himself in southern Utah. That August, he sent his full description of the "massacre of such unparalleled magnitude on American soil" to the U.S. commissioner of Indian Affairs, Alfred Greenwood. It was, Forney wrote, "inhuman." His annual report similarly pled that "a massacre of such unparalleled magnitude, on American soil, must sooner or later demand thorough investigation."[2] As a federal Indian agent, this was not the kind of violence Forney expected to encounter on assignment. He expected Indian violence as civilization expanded, but the Mountain Meadows Massacre had been planned and carried out by a people Forney did not anticipate.

For Forney, "white hell-hounds" inflicted this atrocity that stood alone in a violent nineteenth century: "Bad men for a bad purpose magnified a natural circumstance for the perpetuation of a crime, that has no parallel in American history for atrocity."[3] His label of White hellhounds was not unlike the label of White Indians previously discussed, though Forney saw no comparison. By the end of his brief investigation, Forney felt confident he knew what happened. "These Indians received their instructions from white men. . . . This massacre was concocted by white men and consummated by whites and Indians."[4] His basic assessment was correct. That spring, he had passed on his evidence to the appropriate federal judge and believed it would be enough to soon convict the "white hell-hounds, who had disgraced humanity."[5]

Though his descriptive repetition in multiple sources could highlight Superintendent Forney's limited vocabulary to describe the massacre, he was not alone.[6] There is surprisingly significant consistency in the chosen superlatives people used to classify the massacre no matter the source.

Descriptions detailed the massacre as exceptional: "unparalleled," the "most atrocious," the "most perfidious act of cruelty," or an act "never excelled in horribleness," among an extensive variety of Mountain Meadows sources, both official and popular.[7] Authors most often employed this superlative categorization in an act of moral hyperbole to establish a need for punishment. Writing to his superior officer in 1859, Brevet Major James Henry Carleton queried, "The question [of] how this crime that for hellish atrocity has no parallel in our history, can be adequately punished, often comes up, and [one] seeks in vain for an answer."[8] Utah Second District judge Jacob Boreman declared it "one of the most cruel butcheries ever known to civilized society" in his charge to the grand jury in September 1874 as he urged them to bring charges against participants of the massacre.[9] However, beyond moral hyperbole, the consistent need over time to categorize the Mountain Meadows Massacre as something without an adequate comparison in civilization usefully highlights which facets of the massacre were perceived as the most egregious and how Americans fit the massacre and its perpetrators into a larger narrative.

From his first official report, for Superintendent Forney the "hell-hounds" were the White individuals who participated in the massacre. Forney did not include the whole of the Latter-day Saint people or their leaders, but such restraint was uncommon among federal officials.[10] Many more antagonistic federal officials quickly made the jump from the individual participants of the massacre to action against Mormonism as a whole.[11] Forney complained that there was a "greater anxiety to connect B[righam] Young and other Church Dignitaries with every criminal offense, than diligently endeavor to punish the actual perpetrators of the crime."[12] This tension runs through the prosecution for the massacre. Was it more important to punish the "hell-hounds" who brought about this evil or the system that produced them?

As introduced with the discussion of Mormon savagery in chapter 1, the place of Latter-day Saints within America was already contested. As Paul Reeve argues, the religion's critics "began a prolonged process by which they replaced Mormon individuality with traits they assumed applied to all members of the group."[13] This move rendered outsiders unable to see how the Saints might be more similar to than distinct from other Americans. In the aftermath of the massacre, the focus almost instantaneously shifted to the Mormon people as a whole, rather than punishing the individuals at fault.

Within the narrative crafted around the Mountain Meadows Massacre, this language of the greatest atrocity served a specific rhetorical function. It evoked emotion as it reinforced the possibility that Mormons were not capable of civilization or Americanization. Moreover, as Forney pinpointed with his descriptor of *"white* hell-hounds," the contested race of Mormons became a central element to this discourse. While many cultures have similar myths, in Greek mythology the hellhound, Cerberus, watched over the gate to hell for Hades. Lexicographer Samuel Johnson defined a hellhound personified as an "agent of hell."[14] Johnson's definition reflects agency—a hellhound personified is not inherently of hell, but a creature that chose the liminal space of a boundary between heaven and hell. The hellhound elected to exist on the boundary—just as the Mormons chose to leave White Protestant America and civilization.

This chapter will consider the combination of exceptionalist tropes describing the massacre with the racialization of the Latter-day Saint people. Both the legal prosecution of the massacre and the larger Mountain Meadows narrative focused on the non-Whiteness of the Mormons as a way of contesting their citizenship as they highlighted their sameness and their inherent duplicity. Debates over the liminal standing of Mormons shaped the prosecution for the massacre and reinforced American ideals of expansion, empire, and exclusion with claims of Mormon foreignness and rejection of civilization. Notwithstanding the American origin of the Latter-day Saint church, in the latter half of the nineteenth century the categorization of its members reflected popular fears.[15] For some, Mormons were not Americans valiantly conquering the West; they were an alterity, an Other. The Othering of Mormons would become central to any response to the massacre and consistently overshadow any strides toward justice. Ironically, this racialization simultaneously opened the way for Latter-day Saint redemption. Since they were originally White, they could choose to return to civilization.

The Politics of Comparison

The label "massacre" itself evokes passion no matter the number of individuals murdered. A litany of Americans, both those in official positions and those writing in the popular press, saw Mountain Meadows as not only a massacre but a massacre without parallel in civilization.[16] Yet as a violent nineteenth century progressed, hundreds of what are labeled as massacres today littered the nineteenth-century American frontier; they became almost expected.

One major massacre occurred prior to Mountain Meadows, the Sacramento River Massacre. John C. Fremont and his U.S. Army expedition slaughtered hundreds of peaceful Wintu people, as many as a thousand, on the banks of the Sacramento River in the spring of 1846. It was initially labeled a battle, as were many similar events because of military involvement, shielding such bare aggressions under the rubric of war. This massacre began a genocidal wave that would virtually wipe out Californian native peoples before the century was out.[17] As the bloody century progressed, several other contemporary massacres likewise left hundreds of dead in their wake: the 1863 Utah Bear River Massacre (250), the 1864 Sand Creek Massacre (140), the 1870 Marias River Massacre (173), the 1871 Camp Grant or Aravaipa Massacre (at least 100), and the 1890 Wounded Knee Massacre (325). (All numbers of the dead are estimates.) All these massacres involved White military detachments or militias murdering Indians, though all of them were originally categorized as battles. During the Dakota War of 1862, also known as the Sioux Uprising, different bands of Dakota people in Minnesota killed hundreds of Whites.[18]

Of these barbarities, the Sand Creek and Wounded Knee massacres were perhaps the only ones to receive contemporary nationwide attention comparable to that of Mountain Meadows.[19] Some considered the U.S. Army killing Indians to be a part of the forward march of civilization across the continent. Likewise, many Americans of the time anticipated Indians killing Whites—perhaps as unavoidable collateral damage from the expansion of civilization. In the nineteenth century, many Americans expected Indian-on-White violence and White-on-Indian violence. A refusal to see similarity among the numbers dead implicitly denied the personhood of native peoples.

A significant point of commonality in these examples is that White military leaders or militias initiated most nineteenth-century massacres, including at Mountain Meadows. The Latter-day Saint militia acted like other American militias. Yet the popular narrative that spun around the Mountain Meadows Massacre, including the investigation and the prosecution, ignored any military component. Though a few images depicting the massacre including figure 2.1, exhibit what looks like a militia line formation, a naval magazine is a singular example of a nineteenth-century account of the massacre that focused on the local militia. Even in that case, the magazine prefaced its analysis of the militia by focusing on the egregious effect of Mormonism on society.[20] Notwithstanding militia involvement, the narrative produced about Mountain Meadows did not see any resemblance to examples of analogous violence.

The lack of attention to the Sacramento River Massacre, the only major massacre to predate Mountain Meadows, could explain the initial exception-

THE MOUNTAIN MEADOWS MASSACRE.—MURDERED BY SUPPOSED FRIENDS.

FIGURE 2.1 Depictions of the massacre revealed much about which elements of the Mountain Meadows story an author considered most important. Though absent in the text, this image was one of the few images that demonstrated the Mormons as a militia in a military formation. The flag could be a striped American flag, an element only mentioned in Prosecutor Carey's opening argument in Lee's first trial. Young, *Wife No. 19*, 249. Courtesy of L. Tom Perry Special Collections, Harold B. Lee Library, Brigham Young University, Provo.

alist descriptions of Mountain Meadows. However, even as other massacres piled up as civilization progressed across the continent, Mountain Meadows continued to be described as the most egregious or outrageous monstrosity ever to blight the land. Notwithstanding the numerical similarities between Mountain Meadows and other contemporary massacres, the Americans writing about the massacre saw no comparison. The tale of Mormons in league with Indians to kill Whites superseded any potential narrative of military atrocity. Without White Mormon instigation and participation, the massacre might return to the multifarious atrocities of the nineteenth century—it would be one further example of reciprocal White or Indian violence.

Moreover, some of the elements of the Mountain Meadows narrative that could have been used to highlight exceptionality were ignored. In a principal point of difference, Mountain Meadows deviated from the assumed racial makeup of nineteenth-century massacres, in that Indians were neither the victims nor the principal aggressors. Perhaps more importantly, at Mountain Meadows White Mormons killed White Americans. Whites killing Whites in nineteenth-century America was not exceptional, yet using the label "massacre" to describe such violence was rare. Many assumed that Whites did not collude with Indians to kill other Whites in civilization, despite glaring evidence to the contrary.[21] Those atrocities labeled "massacres" did not include the sum of all nineteenth-century violence. However, nor did authors see a comparison in violence that was generally White-on-White violence—the brutality of contemporary Bleeding Kansas or even America's very bloody Civil War.

The violence in turbulent Kansas (and in neighboring Missouri) in the 1850s provided another contemporary point of comparison absent from American conversations about Mountain Meadows. The violence there continued over a six-year period preceding the start of the Civil War, even if sensational press accounts exaggerated the actual number of deaths in Kansas.[22] In 1856, the White abolitionist John Brown and his familial militia murdered five proslavery Kansans in what would be quickly labeled the Pottawatomie Massacre.[23] Prior to John Brown's activities, proslavery advocates had already racialized White abolitionists with the label "Black Republicans"— considered an epithet. After John Brown's involvement with the Pottawatomie Massacre and then the siege at Harpers Ferry, proslavery advocates expanded the use of the term "Black Republicans" to include all Republicans, including moderates like Lincoln, to paint them all with the same racialized violent stripe as Brown. While not numerically similar, the contested Whiteness of participants in the Pottawatomie Massacre and then the popular expansion of guilt to all Republicans through the chosen epithet stands as a significant parallel.[24]

The arc from Brown's involvement in the Pottawatomie Massacre to the tinderbox of Harpers Ferry and the proceeding brutality of the Civil War cannot be exaggerated. The war years saw a significant drop in the number of Mountain Meadows publications, but the decades of war that followed offered many opportunities for comparison consistently and unsurprisingly ignored—war is rarely seen as comparable to anything else. This conspicuous absence further cemented the perceived Otherness of Mormons. Not simply understood as one of the many political conflicts of the tumultuous 1850s and '60s, the Mountain Meadows Massacre was seen as a different kind of violence.

A Singular Prosecution

Moreover, in contrast to most atrocities across the American West, Mountain Meadows was exceptional in that it was investigated and prosecuted, and that the state punished someone. Prosecution efforts stretched for nearly forty years after the massacre.[25] No convictions of White men came from any of the other numerically similar nineteenth-century American massacres. (All prosecutions in Kansas were also dropped, though Brown was later executed for leading the raid on Harpers Ferry.) Against local sentiment and amid threats of vigilantism, President Abraham Lincoln pardoned all but thirty-nine Indian participants in the U.S.-Dakota War.[26] After multiple investigations into the Sand Creek Massacre and the resignation of Colonel John Milton Chivington, the military denounced Chivington and his troops but never acted to further punish those involved.[27] After the Camp Grant Massacre, an Arizona grand jury indicted more than 100 U.S. Army raiders, and President Ulysses S. Grant threatened to put the territory under martial law if prosecution did not occur. The prosecution then defiantly used the trial to enumerate Apache depredations, and the jury acquitted all those indicted after nineteen minutes of deliberation.[28]

A lack of legal action was thus the prevailing trend for most nineteenth-century massacres, though White soldiers who were prosecuted fared significantly better than Indian combatants or Black enslaved insurrectionists. For example, General Nelson Miles held an inquiry after which the Wounded Knee raiders were brought to trial. Of those, 323 were convicted and 309 were sentenced to death—every single known Indian participant in the fighting. Slave insurrections or even rumors of slave insurrections were consistently and swiftly prosecuted.[29] John D. Lee's Whiteness coupled with a conviction became a point of distinction, although this was never a part of either the official or the popular narrative.

Additionally, most twentieth-century Mountain Meadows Massacre histories emphasize the lack of prosecution, arguing that only one individual, John D. Lee, ever came to trial and that Lee, the scapegoat, was the only one who ever paid the price for the massacre with his life.[30] However, out of a litany of numerically similar contemporary massacres, Lee was perhaps the only White man ever convicted, found guilty, and executed for similar massacre involvement in the nineteenth century. For any White person to be brought to trial, found guilty, and then executed was a complete departure from other similar American massacres. However, for most commentators,

Mountain Meadows stood as a singular atrocity in the abundance of nineteenth-century American violence.

A Question of Race

After finishing his term as a U.S. Army teamster during the Utah occupation, James Lynch headed south to the Arizona Territory looking for a new adventure. On his way he met up with Indian Agent Jacob Forney, who was traveling to southern Utah to retrieve the surviving children from the Mountain Meadows Massacre. Rather than continuing south, Lynch and his companions helped Forney. After collecting the children, Lynch returned to Salt Lake City and there provided a statement of his experience. Two months later, he wrote a second, more extreme account elevating his claims against the Mormons.[31] Lynch's role in retrieving the massacre survivors "marked some sort of turning point in his life, and thereafter he lost no chance to tell the story and plead their case."[32] His statements would be a source for many future massacre accounts.[33]

For Lynch, convicting the perpetrators of the massacre became a matter of American integrity. In his second statement, he urgently pled with Americans, "No longer let us boast of our citizenship, freedom, or civilization." It was the time for action, as Mormon atrocity required a response. White involvement proved a great surprise when "attending circumstances far exceed[ed] anything in cruelty that we have ever heard of or read of being perpetrated by savages." Hypersavagery from these people that seemed White required a response. The hyperbole emphasized that Mountain Meadows was not simply an Indian massacre even though there was Indian involvement. Mormon involvement prompted the necessity of swift punishment. In a flourish of millennial hope, Lynch saw the possibility of the "dawn" of "a new state of things" where retribution and vengeance would come to the Mormons. Though Lynch's statements were in the form of affidavits, their increasingly serious tone reflected his desires that his account would be disseminated and used to rid the world of "Mormon Avarice, fanaticism & cruelty."[34]

Like many authors here evaluated, Lynch's religious affiliation is unknown. However, his response to the surviving children and their trauma provided his continuing motivation. For others, angst concerning the Mormons could stem from theological boundary maintenance against a fake religion, or it could be a political concern warning the American polity against subversive un-Americans. In many cases, exact motivations are obscure and potentially complicated. Whether they considered Mormons fanatics of a fake religion or religious zealots ultimately didn't matter; it was a distinction without a difference. Perhaps for some it was simpler. Captain Samuel Montgomery, an Arkansan serving in the Utah Expedition, forwarded Lynch's second affidavit to fellow Arkansas native and U.S. Indian superintendent Alfred Greenwood. Lynch's affidavit encouraged him; he hoped its contents and Greenwood's symbiotic "interest and sympathy" for the murdered Arkansas citizens might make a difference, since, he declared, "we are all Sick of the mormons."[35]

Americans like Jacob Forney and James Lynch saw Mormons as White but could not reconcile Mormons' actions with their perceived Whiteness.[36] Massacre accounts repeatedly note astonishment that Whites could be involved in such an event. Americans expected savagery from some groups, but Americans had to explain how Mormons, a people who looked White and seemed capable of civilization, had regressed toward savagery rather than progressing forward with civilization. Notwithstanding appearances, race could be at the root of the atrocity. Perhaps they were not White. Questions of Whiteness and civilization were specific to determining where the Mormons fit in the American polity, if they fit at all.

U.S. Army surgeon Roberts Bartholow also visited Utah as he traveled with the Utah Expedition. On his journey, he examined Utah not unlike an explorer detailing fascinating foreign populations. Alongside his descriptions of Utah's fauna—grizzly bears and prairie dogs—he noted the presence of unique *homo sapiens* as the most important discovery. Bartholow noted that these humans were "most curious in every relation," and he eagerly declared the creation of a new Mormon race. Polygamy had given birth to this new race clear in the physiognomy of the Mormons. He contended that "Oriental" polygamists were prepared for polygamy "as a recognized domestic institution for ages"; time had molded Asian polygamists to the practice, Bartholow argued, so they did not find it degrading. In contrast, he asserted that Mormon women saw "their wide departure from the normal standard of Christian civilization."[37] For Whites, conversion to Mormonism had the same effect as interracial marriage, then called miscegenation: it lowered them from their elevated status. Their very faces revealed this degradation: "The yellow, sunken, cadaverous visage; the greenish-colored eyes; the thick, protuberant lips; the low forehead."[38] According to Bartholow's rationale, the purity of their blood and therefore their race were devalued. Whites could not participate in such uncivilized behaviors without becoming degraded. He continued to argue that if left alone, the Mormon race would die out because polygamy was contrary to the Mormons' original race, and this racial dissonance would lead to Mormon destruction.[39] Bartholow joined many prophesying the death knell of Mormonism.[40]

Though Bartholow's views were widely published, there was no consensus that Mormons constituted a new race. Some Americans debated the possibility in official settings, and the ideas continued to live in popular discourse, particularly that Mormons had degenerated.[41] Mountain Meadows writers and politicians informally worked through a similar understanding of Mormon racial dissonance as they investigated Mountain Meadows and evaluated what should be done with the Mormons. However, in contrast to debates grounded in the marked visage of Mormons, Mountain Meadows discourse rotated around Mormons' duplicitous appearance of sameness. They looked White and they looked Christian. This made the deception even more dangerous. Most did not go as far as Bartholow in explicitly declaring the existence of a new Mormon race and urging action to exterminate the Mormons. However, their debates centered around what to do with the Mormons and where they fit—what was their racial classification? The group's practice of polygamy persuaded some of their retreat from civilization, but for many the Mountain Meadows Massacre provided concrete evidence of Mormon racial dissonance.[42]

Most historians now persuasively argue that race is a fluid social construction rather than a static biological determinant.[43] As historian Colin Kidd eloquently contends, race is "a realm not of objective science, but of a cultural subjectivity and creativity."[44] Individuals construct race, and those constructions evolve over time. In response to earlier scholarship that conflated race and skin color, in the last few decades a litany of monographs has begun to untangle these constructions. Historians of race define Whiteness as color or colors, rather than merely the absence of color. They also consider multisensory constructions of color while examining the complexity of racial definitions and their central role in American history at the end of the nineteenth and beginning of the twentieth centuries.[45]

Philip Deloria argues that "Americans—particularly White Americans—have been . . . fixated on defining themselves as a nation" and race has "been a characteristic American obsession." Though a consistent fixation, the historically constructed categories of race shift and evolve over time. As Americans constructed categories of difference between racial groups to order their experience, the categories they employed were often contradictory and even paradoxical.[46] In 1751, Benjamin Franklin argued that numerous Europeans, including Germans and Swedes, were not White but "swarthy."

Since the Naturalization Act of 1790, "free white persons" had been eligible for American citizenship, although the definitions of Whiteness changed over time. At the time of the act's inception, Congress debated the Whiteness of Jews and Catholics, who were traditionally members of fixed ethnic groups. Over time this discussion of "free white persons" would expand to other immigrant groups. It would take nearly a century for the Irish and the Italians to be considered White.[47]

The one-drop rule originated in the antebellum period. In contrast to earlier multiple multi-racial categories, under the one-drop rule the presence of any amount of African blood determined Blackness, since appearances could deceive. Though not codified until the 1920s, the Civil War "accelerated" the concept, until it became the generally accepted manner to divide Whites and Blacks.[48] Expanding definitions of Blackness gave Whites from a wide variety of national and geographical backgrounds solidarity as they defined themselves against anyone labeled Black in a strict Black-or-White binary. In the period of flux before codification of the one-drop rule, legal inconsistencies were constant. In 1857 Louisiana, for example, Alexina Morrison, a slave with "blue eyes and flaxen hair," sued her master James White for kidnapping and enslaving her—though her mother was also enslaved. In three consecutive trials, Morrison's attorneys convinced courts that she looked and behaved like a White woman as she interacted with other Whites. The courts refused to rely on the testimony of her enslaver's attorney's "experts" who categorized Morrison as Black, because she acted White.[49] A decade later, in 1866 Michigan, William Dean's right to vote had been challenged because he was an American Indian. Michigan's state constitution limited voting rights to "white male citizens of inhabitants, and certain *civilized* male inhabitants of Indian descent."[50] Dean's representation argued that his lack of membership or participation in a specific tribe demonstrated his civilization. In contrast, after a physical examination the state determined that more important than any Native American tribal connection or estrangement, Dean was a part African—no more than one-sixteenth, but still African—even though he looked White. Despite his apparent "civility" and his personal claim on his Native Americanness, the state argued he should not be allowed to vote. In this instance, the court ruled that heritage trumped appearance, but the Supreme Court judge writing the majority opinion proposed legally extending Whiteness so that anyone under one quarter Black could be considered White.[51] Race was never objectively determined. After the Civil War, performance and appearance continued as key elements in determining citizenship.

The popular attention to the Mormon Question in the nineteenth century made Latter-day Saints prime candidates for categorization and racialization. This strain of thought labeled Mormons with an alterity that existed outside Whiteness. In his monograph *A Peculiar People*, Spencer Fluhman identified the "vexed whiteness" of the Latter-day Saints, while Paul Reeve's *Religion of a Different Color* further unpacked the racialization of the Saints and their wrestle to become White at the expense of their Black and indigenous coreligionists.[52] As Reeve persuasively demonstrates, the American racialization of the Latter-day Saint people began in the 1830s. At times, descriptions of Mormons appeared strikingly similar to those of Blacks and other racialized groups. In fact, some pictorial representations portrayed Mormons as visually similar to a variety of minorities likewise Otherized in the nineteenth century. As it worked in other arenas, the racial classification of the Mormon massacre became a way to signal Mormon difference; the massacre at Mountain Meadows was not the same as other similar events.

In contrast to Bartholow and those who saw extensive physiognomic differences between Mormons and other Americans, in most instances the massacre discourse focused on the White appearance of the Mormons. The problem was that they looked like other White Americans. They looked like they should be civilized. If Mormons were civilized and White, how could they kill other civilized White people? This would lead some to the possibility that Mormons were Whites who had rejected their Whiteness. They chose to devolve from Whiteness to leave civilization and embrace savagery.

Mormon Foreignness

Related to the vexed Whiteness of the Latter-day Saints, one of the epithets more frequently applied to Mormonism in the second half of the nineteenth century underscored their foreignness.[53] Complex casuistry lay at the root of the accusations. Using considerable exaggeration, some federal officials would claim Utah's population consisted of "nearly all" foreigners, a claim that did not consider any evidentiary support or actual analysis of ancestry.[54] Though a significant influx of Scandinavian immigration began in the 1850s, mid-nineteenth-century Latter-day Saints were in fact a more cohesive Anglo-Saxon group than at any later date. In 1870, at the zenith of nineteenth-century Utah immigration, a third of Utah's residents were foreign-born—with more than half of that number English immigrants.

For James Carleton, the U.S. Army captain who made his own investigation of the massacre, the Mormon immigrants were "Welsh, English,

Norwegians, Swedes, some Germans, and a few French."[55] Carleton was mostly correct (there were also a significant number of Scottish and Swiss immigrants), yet most of these immigrants were understood to be White by the second half of the nineteenth century.[56] Carleton maintained that if they were White, then class was to blame for their actions. They were "evidently of the lowest and most ignorant grade of the people in the several countries from whence they have come." Of course, other immigrant and racial groups equally offended Carleton. He took similar issue with the "peopling of the interior of our continent by our pig-tailed [Chinese] friends from the Celestial Empire!"[57] Mormon Otherness would be clearly established, but into which racial category did they fit?

As the Utah Territory federal judges and prosecutors worked to move forward the investigation for the massacre and corresponded with officials in Washington, they consistently attributed the number of foreigners in Utah as partial rationale for the Mormon Problem and in turn the massacre. For Judge Delana Eckels, the Mormons were "ignorant classes" of foreigners "whose want of intellectual culture, made them easy prey to [the] Mormon delusion."[58] Todd Kerstetter astutely noted the potential class critique likewise present in similar proclamations.[59] The consistent allegations that Mountain Meadows happened because of Mormon lust for wealth amplified this criticism.[60] Prosecutor William Carey described the emigrant train as "the best equipped and richest train that had ever crossed the Rocky Mountains," implying that Mormon greed triggered the massacre.[61] He built on information from Carleton's troublesome report.[62] Though the wagon train Carleton described was likely not the Baker-Fancher party whose members were massacred at Mountain Meadows, this single report would be repeated again and again.[63] Foreignness, ignorance, and thievery were understood to go hand in glove.

In broad hyperbolic strokes, Judges Cradlebaugh and Boreman—the two federal judges to prosecute Mountain Meadows—likewise pronounced most Utah inhabitants foreign. In multiple jury charges, they argued that the supremely high influx of immigrants caused them to explain legal processes more cautiously, since those foreign-born jurors knew "*almost nothing* of American ideas and principles."[64] As he addressed the grand jury that would soon indict John D. Lee and other massacre participants, Boreman posited "American law" should elevate society rather than dragging it down. He laboriously discussed his philosophy of law: "I make these and other remarks that would not be necessary in the States—but are necessary here because some two-thirds of the people of this Territory are of foreign birth or are the children of such, and have never been outside of the Territory." Boreman then precisely echoed Cradlebaugh as he continued, "Consequently [they] know almost nothing of American ideas and principles."[65] Stunningly, both Cradlebaugh and Boreman reinforced Mormon foreignness and Otherness in contrast to proper Americans, when addressing grand juries made up of a majority of Latter-day Saints.

Alien Mormons and Jury Selection

The racialization of the Mormons became manifest in action as they chose jurors for John D. Lee's first trial. Judge Boreman and the U.S. attorneys belabored the issue of citizenship as they interviewed jurors. The newly passed Poland Act placed Utah's judiciary securely under federal control with the goal of accelerating the prosecutions of both polygamy and Mountain Meadows. One of the elements of the Poland Act shortened the residency requirement for jurors to six months in the territory, a stipulation that incorporated more miners and other long-term, but nonpermanent, residents of Utah, often not Latter-day Saints, into the jury pool. At the same time, however, the Poland Act also opened the possibility of including more "foreign" Saints. To that end, the Poland Act added a stipulation that jurors must be able to read and write English. The judge and prosecution took issue with the citizenship of multiple jurors during jury selection. In the course of *voir dire*, two jurors were excluded for illiteracy. Latter-day Saints with immigrant parents were often rejected because the court challenged the naturalization of their parents. To demonstrate his citizenship, one potential juror argued that he had voted multiple times and lived in the United States since he was nine years old, but he was rejected as a juror. The court responded, "We do not think it is sufficient evidence he is naturalized. A great many vote without their papers." In another instance, the court rejected a Latter-day Saint juror when it judged as hearsay his memory of the naturalization of his father. As the jury selection wrapped up, the prosecution objected to yet another Latter-day Saint juror on the grounds that he had not been naturalized. This time the potential juror had lived in Utah for fourteen years and recalled the name of the judge who naturalized him. This juror became part of the jury only because the prosecution lacked further challenges.[66]

Despite the lack of direct connection to foreign roots or power among the Saints, logic did not need to be central to the discourse of civilization: paradoxes were viable within the larger narrative. Here the massacre provides an intriguing intersection of difference. Regardless of the reality that many Latter-day Saints were of Anglo-Saxon stock and most Americans considered Anglo-Saxons White, a claim of Mormon foreignness was one more way to demonstrate the incompatibility of Mormonism with American citizenship. Paradoxically, the focus on the foreignness of the Mormons would transition during John D. Lee's trial to center on original Mormon Whiteness and the Mormon rejection of that Whiteness.

Whiteness and the American Empire

In his emotionally charged opening argument for John D. Lee's first trial, William Carey painted a vivid picture of a violent, days-long siege led by "whites and their Indian allies" against a beleaguered group of "noble" emigrants. Miraculously, "a company [came] marching down under the stars and stripes" — apparently a company of Americans marching to their rescue. This flag "promise[d] protection" not for just anyone, but to those who had a "right to call for its protection." The American emigrants had that right. For Carey, they "hailed [the flag] with joy because [the flag meant] relief." It meant "life and liberty and rescue from the terrible savages" who surrounded them.[67]

Carey continued with the story of John D. Lee, the man who started out from the salvific company with a white flag — the "white flag of peace which is respected everywhere" — in both "civilized and savage nations."[68] Yet for Carey, Lee was not civilized nor was he American; he was a Mormon and a traitor. He looked White and he looked American, but he would not provide the "promise[d] protection."[69] John D. Lee divulged his true self as he negotiated away the emigrants' arms and led men, women, and children to a cruel and horrific death. To emphasize the treachery, Carey continued, "Neither were they enemies, they were not men of a foreign nation who were at war with this people. They were men of their own race — of their own lineage."[70] Within Carey's structure, fratricide should not happen in a civilized society, yet the Mormons had done just that — they killed their own when they killed American citizens. The vexed Whiteness of Mormons became central to Carey's initial argument to establish the group's duplicity.

Lee may have given the impression of being an American with his stars and stripes and his White skin, but for William Carey, Lee's Mormonness stood in direct conflict with widely held views of Americanness and civilization. Carey initially cued his audience with the story of "whites and their Indian allies." Whites and Indians in league together signaled something amiss. Then came two flags—the American "stars and stripes" and the universal white flag. Flags were a critical sign in the prosecution's strategy. The flags told Carey's intended story. For Carey, the image of a deceptive traitor leading innocent "noble" Americans to their deaths illustrated how he wanted the court and the watching country to classify Lee.

Throughout the variety of contemporary accounts of the massacre before and during Lee's trials, only Carey's account introduced an American flag. The actual presence is not important; what matters is Carey's use of the American Stars and Stripes to spotlight the way that Carey wanted his larger audience to see both Lee and Mormons in general. An American born in Illinois to parents from Virginia and Tennessee, Lee was not foreign-born. Yet Carey's argument constructed the Mormon Lee as one who had left Americanness and civilization. Lee looked American, and his Whiteness was seen as critical as he presented the American beacon of safety—the flag. For Carey, Lee's countenance concealed his counterfeit identity. The traitor maliciously presented the flag and then turned to savagely murder American emigrants. Despite his appearance and ethnic heritage, Lee was merely masquerading as an American; he chose to become a Mormon. Focusing on the deception of the White Mormons in the "guise of friends," Carey implied that Mormons were more dangerous than those who demonstrated their place outside civilization with obvious signs of malicious intent, including the color of their skin. In Carey's narrative, the Americans of the Baker-Fancher party knew not to trust the Indians, but they didn't think White Mormons could be "planning the destruction of the whole company." They assumed that "a man that talks as he does, a man that comes with that white flag of peace . . . certainly can promise us and fulfil all his promises. He can't mean any hurt."[71] Far from merely religious outsiders, Carey depicted Mormons as antithetical to Americanness and civilization. They were a people who had repudiated their Whiteness. Rather than protecting their American compatriots, "these white troops fire[d] and every white man [fell]."[72]

In the tale Carey wove, Salt Lake City appeared like an oasis in the desert to the emigrants. The "beautiful city gave them a promise of welcome, of protection."[73] However, appearances deceived. As they traveled through the city and began their trek south, they were treated "worse than they had been treated by the Indians"—the citizens of Utah didn't have the "common humanity" to feed the weary emigrants.[74] Labeling Salt Lake City, the city of the Mormons, as an oasis tacitly focused on the duplicity of the Mormons. Carey established that Mormonism's danger was as much in its similarity as

FIGURE 2.2 During the nineteenth century, Americans often suspected "foreign" Catholics and Mormons of similarly attacking the United States. Nast, "Religious Liberty Is Guaranteed." Courtesy of the Library of Congress.

it was in its difference, a critical point that distinguished this discourse from much that surrounded the Mormon problem. Mormon Whiteness did not guarantee civilization; in fact, the potential Whiteness of Mormons with their inherent deceit was even more dangerous than easily identifiable foes.

Returning to the politics of comparison, the prosecution employed the vocabulary of "the greatest atrocity" to highlight the extent of Mormon treachery. To find applicable examples of horror within "the great crimes of history," the U.S. attorneys in Lee's first trial straightaway moved beyond American examples of massacre and violence.[75] In his opening statement, U.S. Attorney Carey compared Mountain Meadows to the sixteenth-century massacre of St. Bartholomew's Day when Roman Catholics slaughtered thousands of Huguenots. Carey argued that the massacre occurred because of "the delusive doctrine that all the residents of France must be Catholic or Protestant."[76] The implication that Mormons were acting just like Catholics was rhetorically powerful. Both their race and their religious commitments revealed they were not the right kind.[77] Often Latter-day Saints and Catholics were similarly categorized as un-American and foreign powers rife with conspiracy. As shown in figure 2.2, the two were seen in tandem attacking the foundation of American liberty.[78] Moreover, Carey implied that the Mormons would eventually slaughter those who would not convert. The only example he could find that included "an order to kill women and children" was the biblical genocide of the city of Ai, but the people of Ai were Canaanite enemies. The emigrants were not "enemies" or "men of a foreign nation . . . at war with these people. They were men of their own race, perhaps many of their own blood."[79] There was no excuse or rationale for fratricide.

Circumscribing Civilization 67

An Un-American Sin

As the trial progressed, the prosecution argued that the malicious treachery of John D. Lee was not really the problem at issue. Rather, it was a cipher for the larger danger of Mormonism. Prosecuting U.S. attorney Robert Baskin later argued, "When the facts were known by a civilized world—when they heard of the matter[,] they spoke of it as a most wonderful commentary, upon this system [Mormonism] which has led to this most infamous and unchristianlike slaughter."[80]

This thread of the discourse continued after Lee's trials. After a short term as an assistant U.S. attorney, Baskin returned to private practice as he continued to warn Americans of the dangers of Mormonism, and like Carey he, too, turned to European history. At that point, he considered the massacre "more atrocious than either the massacre of Glencoe or St. Bartholomew."[81] At Glencoe, a clan of Scottish Highlanders worked to block the unification of Scotland and England by refusing allegiance to the king in the late eighteenth century. Though part of a complex narrative, in the essentials the Jacobite McDonald clan offered shelter to Campbell fighters who then later exterminated the McDonalds. Some participants were tried with a charge of "murder under trust." Scottish law considered "murder under trust" more contemptible than straightforward murder. The example again highlighted the weight of Mormon duplicity.[82]

The trial arguments would later be paralleled and expanded in the popular discourse of the massacre. Prolific massacre chronicler J. H. Beadle asserted that though Glencoe had elements worthy of comparison, it "pale[d] in comparison" to Mountain Meadows. The Mormon massacre was "scarcely equalled by aught in the old world." "The history of our English race" did not provide an apt comparison.[83] James Carleton had previously argued the impossibility of reforming Mormons. He wanted to give Mormons a year to leave the United States and then, "if after that they pollute our soil by their presence make literally *Children of the Mist* of them."[84] Carleton's allusion was also Scottish. He pointed to the actions taken against the clan McGregor beginning in fifteenth-century Scotland in an effort to encourage specific action to expel the Mormons. In 1646, Charles II labeled the clan McGregor "a traitorous band contrived in the north" against "God and country," and they were stripped of citizenship and exiled becoming children of the mist.[85] The children of the mist entered the American consciousness via Sir Walter Scott and other novelists' works published in the first half of the nineteenth century.[86] Like the Scots whom the English termed barbaric, the Mormons were comparatively considered unworthy of citizenship. For Carleton, their citizenship should be stripped and they should be exiled.

Repeatedly, the only examples possibly offering similar comparison were found beyond American civilization. In his opening argument, Prosecutor Carey scoured French and Scottish history for initial comparisons, then transitioned to clearly non-White comparisons beyond the reach of White civilization. Carey suggested the "Black Hole of Calcutta" was a more apt comparison. In that alleged 1746 event, "146 prisoners were enclosed in a room 23 foot square and before morning all but 23 of them were dead."[87] John Howell's late eighteenth-century first-person survivor account of the incident was so widely published that in the nineteenth century much of the western world understood the reference by simply mentioning "the Black Hole." Howell's tale claimed a similar number of dead in the Black Hole to the massacre at Mountain Meadows, and most readers understood it as an uncivilized colonial population committing an atrocity on British citizens. Moreover, the false assurance the Indian captain provided in Howell's account sounded quite similar to Lee's promise to the emigrants that they would be safe: "He assured me on the word of a soldier, that no harm should come to me."[88] British colonialists used Howell's Black Hole narrative politically to justify the subjugation of the Indian continent.[89] Orientalizing Mormonism did not innovate; Carey merely added to an already prevalent tradition.[90] The prosecution further focused Mountain Meadows discourse on the racial composition of Mormons and the prevalent question in the early investigation: Were the Mormons White? The official and the popular discourse merged to ask if Mormons could join civilization. Then, in turn, what would America do with those who were considered Others?

Furthermore, using "the symbol of the fall of Calcutta and the beginning of [the British] empire," Carey turned to the question of civilization and the responsibilities of empire building. The expansionist rhetoric most traditionally associated with the United States in the early twentieth century already stood in place by the mid-nineteenth. As the United States spread west, the question of empire developed as an inherent element of Manifest Destiny. By the last quarter of the century, most Americans accepted that the United States would spread from sea to shining sea, but many questions remained unanswered: Was the Pacific the limit of American expansion? Would this "empire of liberty" fill the whole of the Americas? How would Americans treat those they met in their attempt to enlarge the nation? What about the other empires now within America's expanding borders?[91]

The Mormon Question was also a question of empire.[92] These points of comparison central to massacre discourse would demonstrate that the

Mormon Problem expanded beyond polygamy. At issue was the progress of American civilization: Would Americans be able to manage the Mormon colony? Or was the massacre a prediction of future instability and greater insurrection? The Mountain Meadows narrative made the British model of empire more applicable to the U.S. context and advanced the imperative of federal action to quell the Mormons.

As some Americans questioned the position of Mormons within civilization, they wondered if Mormons had the capacity to rise to civilization despite their apparent rejection of it. These sources consistently focused on the inability of Whites, the English race, or Anglo-Saxon (or Anglo-Norman) blood to participate in such an atrocity, unlike their Indian or Black counterparts. Could the Mormon rejection of civilization through atrocity exclude them from Whiteness regardless of any Anglo-Saxon heritage?[93] The duplicity made it worse. For the U.S. attorneys, this regression ultimately made Mormons worse than any Asian counterparts. Returning to the Black Hole comparison, as Prosecutor Carey continued his argument, he noted the likelihood that "the fiend who placed them [in the Black Hole] was not aware that [the] foul air would kill them before morning." In a fascinating and almost compassionate retooling of this highly politicized account, for Carey, the Indian captain, though still "a fiend," was merely guilty of a mistake. He did not realize more than a hundred soldiers would be dead the next morning. In contrast, the White Mormon perpetrators certainly saw the end of their actions on the massacre field. Therefore, the Mormons were more accountable than Indians warring with British imperialists.

Similarly, in later years prolific popular author Frank Triplett drew on Carey's argument and expanded it, maintaining that "even to the fanatical emissaries of the Old Man of the Mountain, that chief of assassins and murderers, such wholesale butchery was unknown, and that so hideous a saturnalia of murder could occur within the borders of any country ruled by the Anglo-Norman race, almost surpasses belief."[94] The comparison of the Muslim Crusades leader Rashid ad-Din Sinan, known to westerners as the Old Man of the Mountain, correspondingly situated Mormonism outside American civilization. For Triplett, the massacre made Mormons not exactly like the "Hindoos," but they were worse than the uncivilized Hindoos.[95]

The Black Hole of Calcutta and Rashid ad-Din Sinan's order of Assassins were both highly politicized and exaggerated narratives that various authors employed to meet specific ends over centuries.[96] In 1905, J. H. Little published the first critique of Howell's Black Hole of Calcutta narrative—as

Little called it, "a case study in the perpetuation of error."[97] Although Howell's narrative had questionable facts, it served an ongoing rhetorical purpose. Many would likewise attempt to shape the Mountain Meadows narrative to address their own concerns about the Mormons in civilization through popular and official sources. Americans were to spread civilization and help America reach its millennial destiny. How would they deal with this minority Other within their borders? Would they subjugate the Mormons like the British did with indigenous persons within their empire? For some, the racial dissonance exemplified at the Mountain Meadows put civilization at risk. Americans needed to either tune out the dissonance or eradicate it through decisive action.

Restoring Whiteness

During the trial, the rhetoric of Whiteness provided a locus for discussing the massacre. At the end of Lee's first trial, Baskin rhetorically asked why the Mormons on the massacre field did not "assert their Anglo-Saxon blood" and refuse to participate in the slaughter. He declared, "They disgraced the Anglo-Saxon stock to which they belonged and is a stigma upon it."[98] Baskin further argued they gave up their Whiteness when they became Mormons; in fact, they "became criminals."[99]

However, Whiteness in the mid-nineteenth century was still an unstable social category, and signs of that instability are evident in another line of reasoning also used in the trial: that the Mormons' original Whiteness still affected their behavior. Some remnants of Whiteness remained. This is an early example of the "one drop rule" that governed the post–Civil War era. Within this understanding of race, a drop of Black blood would classify someone as Black. Conversely, without any Black blood (or any African heritage), someone could still be White. In spite of being culturally constructed with ambiguous borders, race was powerful.[100] For example, Baskin saw killing as an inherent characteristic of the American Indian race, but he argued that White Mormons had to nerve "themselves up to the task of slaying women and children"—it took effort to go against the innate demands of one's race.[101] Unable to prevail against the essential virtue of their race, the White Mormons imposed this task on the Indians.[102] In Baskin's view, their Whiteness made killing women and children untenable. Though their choice to enter Mormonism may have caused the Mormons to repudiate their race, their racial repudiation could only go so far. Their White blood could potentially rescue them. Unlike their native allies who lacked the capacity to choose, their White blood offered the Mormons agency. The discourse opened the way for Mormons to amend their transgressions and return to civilization. At different times and in different ways, other federal officials would similarly construe the initial Mountain Meadows legal proceedings as a potential avenue for Mormon redemption.[103]

CHAPTER THREE

Relinquished Manhood
Be Men

When Judge Jacob Boreman instructed a mostly Latter-day Saint grand jury considering Mountain Meadows indictments, he had many requirements. One was that they "be men."[1] Categorizing who was a man might seem a clear-cut act—to most in the nineteenth century, maleness seemed self-evident. However, there was never a consistent standard of manhood. What was manly or who possessed manhood was never consistent; its boundaries shifted dependent on place and time and the subject in question.[2] The majority determines what qualities constitute manhood and honorable behavior at a specific time and within a specific context. Yet like racial standards, manhood and its boundaries are historically constructed and dynamic. In the latter half of the nineteenth century, the discourse of civilization intricately connected race and manhood—both were White.[3] Just as Whiteness or Blackness could be slippery to define, so could manhood. Manhood became nearly unachievable for Blacks, native peoples, Hispanic, or Chinese emigrants. Mormons might look White, but they remained in a vexed position as to their racial identity as well as their manliness.

Though manhood was a central concern within the American discourse of civilization and Manifest Destiny at midcentury, there was no single standard of manhood. Two common and competing standards emerged. The first, which emphasized aggression and dominance, was exemplified by "the gray-eyed man of destiny," the controversial American colonizer and insurrectionist William Walker. In the 1850s, Walker was the pre-eminent exemplar of what historian Amy Greenberg has dubbed "martial manhood"—fearless, strong, arrogant, and independent. In 1855, Walker gained his fame as he and his band of filibusters overthrew the Nicaraguan government, and he became president of Nicaragua for a time. Just a few months before the Mountain Meadows Massacre, he surrendered to the commander of the U.S. Navy after another failed filibuster attempt at spreading the American empire into Central America. Notwithstanding his ultimate defeat and surrender, he became something of a folk hero to many Americans. Those like Walker defined manhood by excessive drink, dominance, strength, aggression, and violence.[4] Violence could be manly and honorable in the right circumstances. Moreover, martial manhood was not the only manly ideal.

At the opposite end of the spectrum from martial manhood stood restrained manhood, the second of the two poles of masculinity in the mid-nineteenth century. Whereas martial manhood was focused on the public sphere, restrained manhood excelled in the sphere of the personal relationships and work. The ideal of restrained manhood focused on family, Protestantism, business, work, and success. Moral men exemplified uprightness, bravery, and reliability. Individual men could exhibit qualities and characteristics of different categories. In the South, a culture of honor pervaded their concept of restrained manhood. In the liminal space of the West, multiple cultures of manhood were evident throughout the nineteenth century. American men understood manliness in different ways often dependent on place and time and whose manhood was in question.[5] The Latter-day Saints had their own ideals of manliness which rotated around priesthood and polygamy in the early Utah period. Though there were areas of overlap between restrained manhood and Latter-day Saint ideals, those outside the faith generally only saw transgressions of those boundaries.[6]

Both the restrained and the martial ideals of manhood, however, shared one common assumption: it was men's job to protect women and children, who were considered to be vulnerable and in need of male guardianship. In this goal of protecting women, Americans believed the Mormons had failed miserably. One of the major concerns antipolygamy advocates espoused was with the position of women. They viewed Mormon women as being in slavery—the same language used to describe Chinese women.[7] The 1858 Republican platform targeted two kinds of slavery: chattel slavery and polygamy. Protestant reformers consistently argued that through polygamy Mormon men degraded women and womanhood, and they failed to protect women and children. For many Americans, a few broad strokes adequately illustrated Mormon men by centering on the Mormon failure to meet the hegemonic ideals of male independence and female dependence. In the eyes of the American public, the Mormons' failure to uphold those gender ideals was evident in the case of Latter-day Saint apostle Parley Pratt, whose polygamous marriage to a California mother who was still legally married to another man was decried as a moral outrage. Pratt's murder in 1857 was widely viewed as an appropriate punishment for his act of enticing this woman to marry him, because the gender norms of the day required men to protect women from evils such as Mormon polygamy. Rather than protect her, Pratt had lured her away from home and family, which violated gender norms. In subsequent years, Pratt's murder became entwined in the public consciousness with the Mountain Meadows Massacre, as American readers and writers proved themselves quick to believe that the massacre had happened because the Mormons were seeking revenge for Pratt's death. While there was little evidence to support that interpretation, it gained traction because it fit the gendered expectations of Americans in the nineteenth century, who saw Mountain Meadows as the ultimate betrayal of men's duty to protect women and children.

For most Americans, polygamy created a dubious narrative of hypermanliness that both repelled and attracted men. Though violence could be considered manly for others in other situations, prosecutors at Lee's first trial argued that Mountain Meadows proffered compelling evidence that Mormon men were unfit as American citizens because they had relinquished their manhood. This chapter will evaluate the role of manhood in the popular massacre narrative and the legal prosecution for the massacre. Manhood could be circumscribed in multifarious ways, but within the Mountain Meadows discourse, the themes of dishonorable violence, failure to protect women and children, a Mormon lack of "individual independence," and Mormon cowardice demonstrated serious failings within an American rubric of manhood in the latter half of the nineteenth century. Mormon men were consistently described in opposition to honorable or brave American men as either lacking manhood or hypermanly but never meeting the gendered standard of civilization. These failings defined a repudiation of Mormon manhood; the legal action for the massacre would highlight these failings and offer the possibility of redeeming them.

Parley Pratt and Dishonorable Manhood

In May 1857, more than a thousand miles away from territorial Utah, a southerner, Hector McLean, killed Parley P. Pratt, a Latter-day Saint apostle, in Arkansas Territory. Four months later, a Latter-day Saint militia massacred 120 Arkansas emigrants in southern Utah at Mountain Meadows. Though the official investigation and prosecution did not see a link between Pratt's death and the massacre at Mountain Meadows,[8] the use of the story highlights an important facet of Mormon sin: Mormons had failed as American men. Pratt's death played a critical role in the story of failed Mormon manhood that was expanded and perpetuated over time by the popular massacre narrative.[9]

Eleanor McLean first met the Latter-day Saints in 1854, when she lived in San Francisco with her husband Hector. Though Hector gave his consent for her baptism, Eleanor's conversion exacerbated an already strained and abusive marital relationship. Hector threatened Eleanor with commitment to a mental institution shortly after her baptism (she was not the only one to risk commitment because of her Latter-day Saint conversion).[10] By this time Pratt had moved to San Francisco to preside over the Pacific Mission. He baptized the McLeans' children and became acquainted with Eleanor as she helped care for his ailing wife, Mary Brotherton. Hector secretly sent their children away to her parents in New Orleans to get them away from the Latter-day Saints; Eleanor saw it all as an effort to punish her. McLean left Eleanor, and she moved to Utah. There she married Pratt as a plural wife, though he likely knew that she was not legally divorced from McLean.[11]

The following year, Eleanor successfully reclaimed her children in New Orleans and began to head for Utah when Hector began his pursuit. Pratt came from the east where he had been on a mission and planned to meet up with Eleanor to accompany her and the children back to Utah. Yet after their reunion, they were arrested while in Arkansas on a spurious charge of stealing the children's clothing. When brought before the bar, the judge found the arrest was without cause, and Pratt was released after he spent a night in jail—according to Eleanor, for his protection. The judge warned Pratt to be careful, but McLean chased him down, stabbed him twice, and then shot him to death. Though local officials held an inquest, no one claimed to have seen McLean kill Pratt, and the jury ruled that an unknown assailant had committed the murder. The case did not go to trial. Though local reports noted McLean's alcoholism and abuse, newspapers across the country reprinted local reports that saw McLean as the victim of Pratt.[12]

With Pratt as a well-known loquacious public defender of polygamy "with his pen and from the platform," the Pratt and McLean saga provided considerable fodder to demonstrate the consequence of Mormons flaunting the American boundaries of marriage before the murder.[13] This exemplified "The Sad Story of Mormonism."[14] A military magazine noted, "The Mormons have a different way of putting the matter: they say he converted Mrs. McClean to the Mormon Church; but in all civilized communities, the crime was one of seduction." After Pratt's murder, the tone of newspaper articles became more virulent. Arkansas's Fort Smith *Herald* implied the counterfeit nature of Mormonism: "One Mormon Less! Nine More Widows!! Alas for the Mormon Prophet!!! If thou hast power to raise the dead, Parley, raise thyself!!!!"[15] In his own published version of the murder, McLean boldly declared,

"I killed him. I am not able to say how you will view the act but I look upon it as the best act of my life. And the people of West Arkansas agree with me."[16] It seemed that more than just Arkansas agreed with McLean. Many Americans would consider him completely justified in his murder of the "hoary headed seducer": McLean had done the honorable thing. In the nineteenth-century culture of honor, as historian Angus McLaren argues, "a murderer had few better defenses than to claim that his victim was . . . the seducer of his wife."[17]

When a company made mostly of Arkansas emigrants was slaughtered in a Utah Mountain Meadow valley four months later, a newspaper report in southern California of the massacre suggested a connection to Pratt's death among other reasons for the massacre, and a report in Sacramento reprinted the same possibility.[18] But as soon as the news of the massacre reached San Francisco, local newspapers focused on the view that it was an act of retribution for the murder of the "Sainted Parley."[19] Pratt had lived in San Francisco as head of the Pacific Latter-day Saint mission during a contentious war between Mormon and anti-Mormon newspapers. There Pratt's murder became a hot topic in the papers for months.[20] The idea of the massacre as retribution for Pratt's death expanded outward from San Francisco. The *New York Times* soon reported, "There is too much reason to believe that the unfortunate emigrant company were massacred by Mormon direction, in revenge for the killing of Elder Parley Pratt."[21] For some, it was only one in a broad array of theories attempting to explain the massacre. For others, it became the central rationale.[22]

In positioning Pratt's murder against the Mountain Meadows Massacre, Mormon antagonists found a useful aggregate narrative. It was only a segment of a larger narrative of dishonorable Mormon violence and lost manhood that swelled after the massacre with a sustained focus on the protection (or lack thereof) of women and children. Despite all the ink spilled over a connection of Pratt's death to the massacre, the construction does not hold historical water. This was one death in a string of murders of prominent Latter-day Saints in the two decades before Pratt's death. The Saints had no history of vengeance, even after the murder of their prophet, Joseph Smith, in 1844. Though the Saints reacted with grief and sometimes anger, there was no call for "earthly vengeance." Arguing to the contrary requires a series of conspiracy-laden jumps in evidence.[23] Rather than rationale behind the massacre, the ways in which Americans talked about Pratt's death cast more light on how Americans understood Mormon transgressions against civilization.

The narrative about Pratt's murder as motivation for Mountain Meadows only grew over time, multiplying in popular accounts. By the 1870s, it had become a consistent trope in the narrative of the massacre found in sensationalized newspaper reports and books—all presented as factual accounts.[24] Exposé writers such as Fanny Stenhouse argued that "a most unsaintly reason"—Pratt's murder—had caused the Mormon animus toward the Arkansans.[25] The details shifted wildly between accounts: sometimes Pratt and McLean were in the mountains, sometimes in the plains; sometimes McLean had a derringer, and sometimes he had a Colt. Hector McLean was called by different names, but the central narrative was the same: "a furious husband in Arkansas had killed Elder Pratt of the Mormon church who has stolen his wife, taken her to Utah and Mormonized her."[26] In defense of his wife and his children, McLean killed Pratt. The popular narrative denied Eleanor agency as it vaunted Hector's chosen violence. The *Arkansas Intelligencer* detailed "the unfortunate condition in which Mormon villainy and fanaticism" placed McLean. In the prevailing popular narrative, he had no other honorable choice. Most communities and even legal experts would condone "a husband with a wayward mate" moving to extralegal violence, even though the solution was "unpleasant."[27]

Though it was unlikely the reader needed a reminder of Mormon polygamists, McLean's example first warned the American audience just how completely Mormons disregarded the American convention of marriage. Pratt, the "amorous Apostle," had "run away with another man's wife."[28] Pratt's transgression was seduction by a religious imposter, and such action required a response. Dripping with southern ideals of honor, McLean defended family and his American manhood. McLean's failings as a drunkard, his alcoholism, threats, and violence against his wife did not have a place within the simplified story that continued to gain traction across the country. McLean's murder of Pratt served a consistent rhetorical function within the Mountain Meadows discourse: the dishonorable violence of the Mormons in the massacre was even further emphasized when juxtaposed against McLean's honorable violence caused by Mormon action.

For others, the refusal of Arkansas authorities to punish the perpetrator before the law solidified the connection of Pratt's death to the massacre: the absence of justice in the courts had prompted the Mormons to seek revenge. Judge John Cradlebaugh used the Pratt murder and the inaction of the Arkansas courts to his own end. In 1863, he capitalized on the murder as he repeated one of his frequent claims that Brigham Young went about "destroying and nullifying the Federal Courts in Utah."[29] He claimed that the inaction of the Arkansas courts in charging Pratt's killer caused the massacre and used the story to label Young a hypocrite. Even if the readers did not think the connection was strong, Fanny Stenhouse provided additional rationale. She claimed the intractable Mormons "argued that McLean was the enemy of every Mormon, and every Mormon was the enemy of McLean;—McLean was protected in Arkansas therefore every man from Arkansas was an enemy of the Mormons;—an enemy ought to be cut off—therefore it was the duty of every Mormon to 'cut off'—if he could—every Arkansas man."[30] Once the connection between Pratt's murder and the massacre was accepted, the narrative emphasized the Mormons' lack of manhood and their dishonorable violence.

Some descriptions of Eleanor McLean Pratt exemplified why American men needed to protect women. The *Pioche Daily Record* described her as she testified in the Pratt trial, "a woman of fine personal appearance. Her high, fair forehead, oval features, queenly deportment, and dignified behavior in giving her testimony were overpowering."[31] Eleanor was queenly and dignified, yet the Mormon delusion deceived her and made her desert her family.[32] Protecting his family, McLean had done just as any other American man would do. Just as her true husband McLean shielded her against the "hoary headed seducer," so too it was the responsibility of American men to defend American women and children.

The Failure of Mormon Manhood

The popular narrative about Pratt and McLean had a long and discernible history, as Americans in the nineteenth century attempted to work out their cultural anxieties through gender norms that shifted over time depending on race, class, and ethnicity. American men along the spectrum saw the protection of women and children as central to their responsibilities as men. Restrained men defended their families in their homes; martial men used similar justification to protect—or personally "annex"—women in Latin America and the Philippines (often from the "effeminate" men of their race).[33]

For a minority group, the manly standard moved unpredictably like quicksilver. Minorities were consistently understood to fail the code of manhood, whether the standard was martial, restrained, or some other manly ideal. Their caricatures were drawn with broad black and white strokes that left little room for fine brushwork. For example, in 1870s California, rumors of excessive numbers of Chinese prostitutes demonstrated a lack of Chinese manhood; it was a failure to protect female virtue. Chinese women were "female slaves," their condition blamed on the lack of Chinese manhood. Clearly, if Chinese men were in California rather than China, they didn't want to establish a home—another sign of an absence of manhood.[34] In the early twentieth century, fighting was manly for White boxer Jim Jeffries, the pinnacle of manliness, yet for his Black opponent and ultimate victor in the world heavyweight match, Jack Johnson, his boxing was emblematic of his savagery.[35] Toby Ditz maintains that gender norms can be created not merely because of crisis but also as a method to exert power over Others. Nineteenth-century manly ideals may have come because of the changing structures of society, but they were also an effective way that Americans could limit the power of minority groups.[36]

Like other minorities, Mormons were portrayed as existing outside the boundaries of manhood and Americanness. Fanny Stenhouse saw the Mormons as the ultimate hypocrites, for they were "sensitive themselves to the highest degree concerning their wives and daughters, [however,] they considered McLean a sinner for doing just exactly what any Saint would have certainly done."[37] Though Mormon men would claim to uphold the honor of their wives and daughters, they utterly failed one of their most significant responsibilities as men when they failed to protect women and children during the Mountain Meadows Massacre.

All the women and all but seventeen of the children were killed in the massacre. The flurry of narratives produced in the decades that followed focused on women and children almost exclusively; they often played central roles in the popular narrative. In one account, "Not one escaped, and even among the children, two of them, having said something that indicated knowledge of the affair, were afterwards strangled to death."[38] Although he was not present at the massacre, Samuel Jukes, a southern Utah judge, was likely indicted as a participant because of rumors that he took care of two children afterward and one of those children disappeared.[39] Stories of children not returned to their families in Arkansas proliferated. Another account was an attempt to again highlight polygamy. In that massacre story, "none but the female children of tender years were allowed to live."[40] Even though it was published after the Mormon disavowal of polygamy, in Langdon's *Authentic History*, Mormons only saved children who might grow to become polygamous wives.

In the massacre plan, Mormon militia members were to kill the men and intended that the Native Americans kill the women and the children, leaving what they considered the most egregious work to the Paiutes. In one account, these responsibilities were switched—"Indians killed the men, while the Mormons butchered the women and children in the most brutal manner imaginable"—crafting a perception of an even further heightened brutality on the part of the Mormons.[41]

Massacre imagery reinforced these gendered concerns. As shown in figures 3.1a–c, similar images depicted two girls during the massacre as well as the murder of women and children—a frequent focus in many Mountain Meadows stories. The story of the two girls depicted in multiple images originated in J. H. Carleton's report, which said they had "run some ways off before they were killed."[42] An Indian boy told Carleton of two girls that the Indian boy and his friend had attempted to help, but two other Indians pushed the boys away and shot the girls.[43] As the narrative of the massacre mushroomed, the two girls became a consistent component of the story. The elements were different, but the function of the two girls in the narrative was essentially the same. Usually, it was not Indians killing the two girls, but savage Mormons. Aligning with the original account, sometimes they were running away or trying to hide from those attacking them. Often the two girls were clothed in white dresses and sent to the spring to get water before the initial attack.[44] Sometimes the girls were shot at they tried to fetch water to save their families from dying of thirst—not surprisingly, the boys made it amid gunfire.[45] Often the images depicted them as little girls, though after Lee's first trial sometimes they were teenagers.[46] In a number of late fictional narratives, they were two boys dressed in white dresses, trying to fool those who surrounded them—even young boys were to protect women.[47] In Lee's first trial, a witness testified that he saw an Indian chief chase down two girls who hid in a thicket, though he did not know what happened to the girls.[48] In Lee's second trial, a different witness expanded on the story of the two girls and testified that Lee told him he and the Indian chief had each killed one of them.[49] This would become the basis of additional elaboration.

As these accounts expanded, often the victims were raped before they were murdered. These tales gratified certain Americans' "sexual fantasy of polygamy."[50] English explorer Sir Richard Burton found Mormons more truly Victorian than the Victorians despite their polygamy, yet Americans would not appropriate such analyses into their discourse.[51] Americans simultaneously abhorred polygamy and fantasized about it through sensationalized novels and melodramatic plays. These narratives followed the presumptive structure that polygamy led directly to rape and murder. The almost omnipresent chapter on the massacre in polygamy exposés and anti-Mormon melodrama built on this assumption and developed it. One account told of Lee united with an Indian chief in combat against the emigrants. They raped the two

The poor emigrants were dying of thirst; two little children were sent to the spring; their bodies were riddled with bullets.
Die armen Emigranten waren am Verdursten. Sie schickten zwei kleine Kinder zur Quelle. Dieselben wurden von Kugeln durchbohrt.

THE MASSACRE AT THE MOUNTAIN MEADOWS.

MURDERING THE WOMEN AND CHILDREN.

FIGURE 3.1A-C The story of two girls became a consistent element in the Mountain Meadows narrative with a number of images prominently focusing on the girls. Others focus exclusively on Mormons murdering women and children. *Das Leben und Bekenntniss*; Triplett, *History, Romance and Philosophy of Great American Crimes and Criminals*, 206; Young, *Wife No. 19*, 247. Courtesy of L. Tom Perry Special Collections, Harold B. Lee Library, Brigham Young University, Provo.

girls—in this story aged fourteen and fifteen—and then brutally cut their throats. The graphic narrative detailed the barbarism and humiliation the savages visited upon the young girls, whose "pure bosoms could not quiver 'neath the plunge of the cold steel blade, nor their white throats crimson before the keen knife's edge until they had suffered the torments of a thousand deaths at the hands of their brutal captors."[52] The lurid imagery was powerful. Rape was considered worse than murder and destroying the purity of women a greater affront to civilization.

Another instance purporting to be a firsthand account of the Mormons outdoing "the Indians in their lust" detailed multiple rapes of five girls by a group of Mormons before they "shot them through the head."[53] William Stewart, one of the nine men indicted for the massacre, was specifically singled out for raping young girls before murdering them.[54] Latter-day Saint stake president Isaac Haight—indicted massacre planner—was similarly included in the graphic tales of sexual violation and viciousness, despite the fact that Haight was not present at the massacre.[55] The primary focus of these

Relinquished Manhood 83

tales was not about providing evidence for the accusation, but expanding the larger discourse of Mormon transgressions with feigned markers of factual accounts including naming perpetrators. Many Americans accepted the tales uncritically because they fit into a familiar narrative of Mormon lust and violence.

These explicit tales go hand in hand with the myth of the Black rapist. The myth of the Black rapist gained traction rather suddenly in the 1880s South and grew unbridled even as the actual number of rapes decreased. Whites justified their lynching of Black men by claiming they were "uncivilized, unmanly rapists, unable to control their sexual desires."[56] Similarly, the genre of Indian captivity narratives repeated many of the same beliefs. The accusation that an aggressor "dashed out" infants' brains was a common trope in stories of Indian massacres and other depredations, such accusations helping to inflame readers against perpetrators.[57] In the growing massacre narrative, Stewart, Haight, and George Adair—another indicted participant—were all likewise depicted in different stories as bashing the heads of babies or young children on rocks or with clubs.[58] The accusations effectively harnessed emotion and anger toward the perpetrators of the massacre and Mormons in general, contributing to the already present narrative of Mormon savagery and further highlighting the Mormon failure to "be men."

Trying Manhood before the Bar

Federally appointed Utah Territory Second District judge Jacob S. Boreman held a great many opinions of the Mormons. A biographer called the Methodist a "theological crusader" against the Latter-day Saints.[59] He saw manifold failings in territorial Utah, but one of the ways that Mormons had failed was as American men. Mormon men might be placed on either end of a spectrum of manhood. They could be cowardly, lacking manliness, or they could be hypermanly, guilty of an overabundance of manhood. Either possibility transgressed Boreman's gender ideals. But transgressive behavior was a family affair. For Boreman, polygamy was certainly evidence of Mormon "outrages." Women, under polygamy, were "more oppressed, more degraded, more unhappy, than anywhere else in the whole United States." The blight of plural marriage affected the whole family: "The moral sensibilities of the men are becoming blunted and brutalized, and their children are losing their finer feelings and having their natures ruined for nobler and higher aspirations."[60] As shown in figure 3.2, the massacre likewise made American women act as men and defend their families against Mormon aggression.

She placed her baby on its dead father's breast, seized a knife, and stood like a tigress at bay!
Sie legte ihr kleines Kind an die Brust seines todten Vaters, ergriff ein Messer und stand dort wie ein verwundete Tigerin.

FIGURE 3.2 In this engraving, the emigrant woman, "like a tigress at bay," is left to defend her child against the "merciless Mormon assassins." The images from this pamphlet (published in English and German) focus almost exclusively on gendered images of the massacre. Just as Mormon men made Mormon women lose their fine feminine feelings, they also forced emigrant women to act like men. *The Life and Confession of John D. Lee, the Mormon* and *Das Leben und Bekenntniss von John D. Lee, dem Mormonen*. Courtesy of L. Tom Perry Special Collections, Harold B. Lee Library, Brigham Young University, Provo.

When Boreman addressed the grand jury empaneled in September 1874, he placed an onerous task on its Latter-day Saint members. He maintained that "the stain of . . . innocent blood" rested on the people of the Territory for the Mountain Meadows Massacre and it was the duty of the grand jury to expiate that sin through legal action against the perpetrators. It was now their responsibility. Were they to shirk, choosing not to bring down indictments for the massacre, it would give Congress no other option but to make "the laws in Utah still more rigid" than they already were. The only way the Saints could demonstrate that Utah was not a hostile and disloyal U.S. territory was to investigate and prosecute someone for "the black and bloody deed."[61]

The massacre at Mountain Meadows was unassailable proof of what further Mormon failure could destroy. For Boreman, the American legal system had the power to counter the Mormon outrages—what historian Patrick Mason labels "disciplinary democracy"—to enable the Latter-day Saints to

Relinquished Manhood 85

rejoin the body politic.[62] But for Boreman, the onus of responsibility was on the Latter-day Saints themselves—in this instance on those called to the grand jury. He declared, "If you quail before any outside influence; if you are too cowardly to be men and before God to do your duty, others will be found who will do their duty, without regard to what other men may say or do. That brand of infamy cannot be allowed to remain longer upon this Territory. Show to the world then that you have the manhood and are brave enough to investigate this and every other crime and bring to trial at the bar of justice every villain in the land."[63] For Boreman and many of his contemporaries, American men were meant to be autonomous, brave, and steadfast, shielding their families from danger of all kinds.[64] Ideals of the American West further entrenched such ideology. This ideal of autonomy was, and is, consistently juxtaposed between legal strictures necessary to the social compact and absolute freedom.[65] Latter-day Saints argued that federal involvement in Utah was limiting their autonomy, but clearly federal appointee Boreman saw the need to curb Mormon autonomy. He used their willingness to enter the legal process to determine their fitness for citizenship.

Establishing and maintaining the rule of law was an expectation for all territories vying for statehood, particularly considering the perception of a lawless West.[66] The rule of law enabled territories to harness the wilderness and promote civilization. Tension between vigilantism and the rule of law was consistent as territories became states. Utah first applied for statehood in 1849 and would request statehood eight more times before its inclusion in the United States in 1896—twice before the massacre.[67] Federal appointees came in 1857. Some appointees quickly ran away crying foul on the Mormons, claiming they chased them out of the territory; other, more pragmatic, appointees attempted to work with the Latter-day Saints.[68] From the 1860s to the 1880s, Utah came under increasingly strict congressional restraints aimed at Latter-day Saint theocracy and polygamy. Some historians position the West as a critical actor in the process of Reconstruction; Utah became the site of another Reconstruction as the federal government attempted to legally bend Latter-day Saints into submission and remake Utah's citizens.[69]

The Dred Scott Supreme Court case established the legal classification of civilization as a standard for statehood, setting a precedent in the same year as the massacre. If Utah were to become a state, it needed to demonstrate it was not only "a civilized community" but also "capable of self-government."[70] For Boreman, the onus of this responsibility was not his as a federal judge but belonged to the citizens of Utah Territory. Boreman submitted that by doing "their duty" bravely, before God and the American legal system, Mormon men had the opportunity to demonstrate their manhood, which was a requisite condition for civilization. By prosecuting the massacre and Boreman's list of other Mormon transgressions, Utahns could demonstrate their fitness for citizenship. Boreman continued, "Hoping and trusting that you will as freemen, show your individual independence and fearlessly and fully discharge the duties d[e]volving upon you."[71] The grand jury heeded his warning, indicting the nine individuals previously mentioned on 24 September 1874. Official indictments demonstrated substantive progress in the work to prosecute the massacre. Moreover, prosecuting the massacre could demonstrate Latter-day Saint preparedness for statehood and help them to avoid further congressional constraints. Using law to restore civilization to those who had transgressed the boundaries of civilization could signal Utah's preparedness to the rest of the country while simultaneously bolstering federal authority within Utah. If not, Judge Boreman would argue it was because of a lack of Whiteness—the Mormons were mostly foreigners anyway.[72]

Judge Boreman was not alone in his concerns about Mormon men. The first two witnesses for the prosecution in John D. Lee's first trial had both passed through Mountain Meadows in the weeks after the massacre. They could testify to the crime—*corpus delicti*—but not to the actions of any specific individual. Both testified to seeing bodies, almost exclusively those of women and children. With prosecutorial direction, they homed in on visceral descriptions of the wounded bodies of the massacred innocents.[73] As he returned from California, Robert Keyes testified, he saw two piles of bodies of "women and children [who] were thrown together promiscuously, crosswise and every other way."[74] The second witness, Ashael Bennett, corroborated, "I saw a pretty horrible sight to me, I saw the skeletons of women and children, small children, and long tresses of beautiful hair laid there, colored with dried on blood, pieces of calico."[75] Latter-day Saint militia members had claimed to have buried the victims; if they did bury their bodies, they did not remain that way for long.[76] The apparent lack of burial offended Christian sensibilities, but in remarking on the subject, Prosecutor William Carey's larger task was to evoke emotion and posit the possibility that jurors and the rest of the country would feel compelled to stand up to such cowardly and unmanly acts.

Keyes testified that all the bodies he saw were in a state of decomposition, dug up and torn apart by wolves, except for one female corpse. He claimed that when he crossed through the Meadows approximately two weeks after the massacre, he saw "one female that lay upon the south west side of the pile . . . that did not seem as though it had been mutilated at all. She looked almost as though she had gone to sleep." The wolves had left her alone. Apparently, he examined her perfectly composed body and when the prosecution queried if she was wounded, the witness replied that "there seemed to be a bullet hole on the left side . . . a little below the heart."[77] Another court reporter noted that the witness placed his hand on his heart to demonstrate the location of the bullet wound. A sensational novelist could not have done better: in shooting at her heart, the Mormons killed the example of female perfection. She lay unsullied as evidence of their unmanly acts.

Before witness testimony began, federal prosecutor Carey passionately laid out expectations from these first two witnesses in his opening argument. Though neither witness would testify to this, he detailed the offensive way the women were left "bereft of every shred of clothing. The savages had not even left enough to cover the naked remains of the women." Much in the same way as embellished tales of polygamy, Carey used the descriptions of the dead, vulnerable women to encourage an emotional response and simultaneously titillate his mixed courtroom audience, which included men as well as "many ladies."[78] This sensationalism heightened as he detailed the unexplainable presence of the one perfect woman: "Among them too for by some unaccountable reason that no man can tell, there lay one beautiful woman, as our witness will swear, on whose countenance was a placid smile of peace, as though she was lying asleep. No wolfe had marred her flesh, no vulture had pecked out her eyes, but she lay there a monument alone; all the rest had been mutilated but that woman alone. And that woman in her perfect state of preservation."[79]

In the trial testimony, her body was preserved as a monument to document the savage and unmanly actions of the Mormons. Even the ravenous animals did not disturb the monument. Those in the courtroom likely shared a common image in their minds on hearing this description—the *Sleeping Venus* in Giorgione's Renaissance masterpiece or Titian's better-known *Venus of Urbino* (*Reclining Venus*). Both paintings center on the mythological ideal of female perfection. Duplicated by hundreds of artists over centuries, by the nineteenth century the reclining female nude was a common visual trope. Reclining Venus is both sexualized and permissive, offering the voyeur permission to linger at the sight of the naked woman as had the witness. Carey exploited this trope to craft a graphic and persuasive call to his audience: the paragon of female perfection lay there in the Meadows as an astonishing witness against her assailants. The killing of other men might not elicit an emotional response, but the harm done to this ideal woman crafted a sensitive touchpoint. Carey built the anticipation of an appropriate emotional response by chronicling the witness's reaction to his experience at the Meadows. "The terrible sight was too much for him to bear and he hastened away from the field of death with that horrible sight, that horrible view, impressed upon his mind, and there it will remain until his eyes are closed in death."[80] Carey desired that his audience, near and far, would also maintain that "horrible sight" long enough to move them to action.

The lack of protection to women and children, the lack of Christian burial, and lack of respect for the female body all documented an absence of Mormon manhood. Real American men safeguarded women and children. Rather than acting as American men, Mormon men had relinquished their manhood and annihilated those who looked to them for shelter.

Assistant U.S. Attorney Robert Baskin, like Judge Boreman, accepted an American standard of Protestant Christianity that the Latter-day Saints did not meet. He argued, "The law of Christianity demanded—these should have lain down their lives rather than to have stained their hands in the blood of innocent women and children."[81] In his closing argument for John D. Lee's first trial, Baskin made the connection to manhood explicit. He stringently argued, "If there had been *men* at that field of blood with the true American stock in their veins they would have sacrificed their own lives rather than imbrue their hands with the blood of little children."[82] The Mormon participants in the massacre could not be true American men and still participate in the killing of innocents.[83]

Moreover, Baskin argued that it was not simply massacre participation that categorized them outside American manhood. For Baskin, any man who participated in Mormon temple rituals had already given up his manhood. He asserted, "They were members of an organization which the sequeal shows robbed them of their manhood. The moment they went through the Endowment House there they laid down their manhood, and they hadn't enough of the man left even to protest against that most hellish operation."[84] Baskin reasoned that in temple rites Mormon men gave up their manhood as they pledged allegiance to another man, one they called a prophet. They relinquished their own God-given right to individuality and their ability to qualify as proper American citizens. Baskin's mention of temple rites was both salacious and conspiratorial. As historian David Brion Davis argues, "secrecy cloaked . . . [with] unconditional loyalty to an autonomous body," here epitomized by the Latter-day Saint temple rite, was central to the claim of Mormon conspiracy against the United States.[85]

Without a single hegemonic ideal of American manhood during the nineteenth century, independence and individuality were characteristic of manliness across the spectrum and a point of tension between absolute freedom and protection from the state.[86] Both Boreman and Baskin subscribed to individuality as a necessary characteristic of manhood and, by extension, American citizenship. For Baskin, independence was given away when men participated in Mormon temple rites. He argued, "The Mormon community down there were nothing but dumb cattle"—and this to a mostly Latter-day Saint jury from southern Utah. Baskin was clearly more concerned with the wider audience in the court of public opinion than the people within the courtroom. The Mormon participants in the massacre, he continued, "had so given up their individuality[,] had so given up their manhood to this infamous system" that when they were "ordered they dared not ask a question. They did not ask a question from beginning to end with all the others, even upon [the massacre] field, when men talked together."[87] Their subservience stopped them from ever questioning their orders.

The Gentile presence was almost entirely absent from southern Utah in 1857, and for Baskin, this allowed unfettered Mormon dominance and acquiescence. The conversion of those Mormons on the field was so complete that no one dared rebel from the militia orders. Baskin's example further brought into relief the slipperiness of manhood: a soldier would be considered manly for taking orders and killing, yet for the Mormons it demonstrated an egregious absence of manhood.

In Baskin's closing argument, he presented Mountain Meadows as the most drastic symptom of a greater problem endemic to Mormonism. As Mormons "[gave] up their individuality to their leaders" and "laid down that manhood," Baskin argued they lost any sense of self or autonomy. They "allowed themselves to be made vassals [or] slaves."[88] Slavery ruled Utah—and Utah slavery was worse than southern slavery. For Baskin, women under polygamy were not the only ones in slavery; Mormon men who had once been autonomous beings had given away their individual power. It is supremely difficult to envision how any Latter-day Saint members of the jury could find this argument compelling, even if they thought Lee guilty. Baskin railed against the most sacred of Latter-day Saint rituals in their most holy place, calling the Mormon temple an "iniquitous institution" and possibly a "greese vat."[89] Baskin could have believed that his explicit condemnation would move the Saints to legal action against Lee to demonstrate that their temple rites were not incompatible with citizenship and American manhood. However, these inflammatory arguments lend credence to the idea that Baskin's primary goal was not to convict Lee at all, but to put Mormonism itself on trial.[90]

As they neared closing arguments in Lee's first trial, Baskin's ally and *Salt Lake Daily Tribune* reporter Frederic Lockley wrote to his wife, "It is not likely we shall get a verdict. There are two or three men on the jury whose obligations to the Church will prevent them finding a verdict according to the evidence, and the most we can hope for is a divided jury. Strange to say we are all hoping this will be the result, as the attention of the whole country is directed to this trial, and if the jury fail to convict it will under the insufficiency of the Poland Bill so manifest, that Congress cannot fail to give us additional legislation at the next session."[91] Baskin's actions at the trial reinforced this claim. Baskin deliberately calculated that he could use the platform of Lee's trial to bolster the popular fury against the Mormons and eventually bring further congressional strictures on Mormon citizenship. As Baskin prophesied and hoped for, the mostly Latter-day Saint jury did not find Lee guilty. It ended in a hung jury. Regardless of Baskin's hopes and Judge Boreman's threats, Congress did not act immediately. These official efforts would both frame and augment the popular discourse that already swirled around the massacre.

Repairing Dishonorable Manhood

Official legal means had failed to bring about justice or to heal the rupture to civilization caused by the Mormons. Though the prosecution never mentioned Pratt's murder in relation to the massacre, the aftermath of Lee's first trial saw a popular resurgence of attention to Pratt's murder by McLean. Megan Sanborn Jones establishes the "necessity of honorable violence" as a consistent element of anti-Mormon melodramas, which exploded in the 1870s.[92] McLean's murder of Pratt fit a narrative of justified vigilante violence within civilization. The popular press constructed McLean as an example of honorable violence portrayed in vivid hues. In one account, the American man McLean (though here called Smith), astride a "fine horse," chased after the clearly weak Mormon Pratt "on a little black mule."[93] McLean's horse and stature demonstrated his superiority. Pratt's mule could also be a satirical reference to reinforce Pratt's contested religiosity—an imposter riding a mule in the same manner that Jesus entered Jerusalem. As in the following version,

McLean's weapons were often an element of focus among dramatic (though conflicting) details:

> The mountains closed upon the defile[r], and the avenging husband closed upon the spiritual usurper of his marital rights. The five shooter of Colt rang on the morning air, one barrel after another, until the two pistols he carried were exhausted. The Apostle zigzagged down the narrow road, until a derringer's only and last ball cut his mule's cropper and entered his own back. Then the California[n]'s knife [hung] for a moment in the air and it sank deeply in Pratt's back. Thrice it was lifted, and sped before the Apostle tottered, and the Californian rode on avenged.[94]

McLean needed the tools of violence to avenge his family since the law had failed him. Vigilantism was an accepted option when necessary. The judge who first locked up Pratt and then allowed Pratt his freedom offered Pratt a knife and a pistol for his protection. According to the sheriff, Pratt refused the weapons, saying he relied on God to protect him. Though attacking an unarmed man without warning would be seen in most instances as an unmanly or cowardly attack, an assailant murdering an unarmed man from behind was never the chosen narrative here. (Pratt was shot from point blank range in his collarbone after being stabbed twice near his heart.)[95] After the legal system had failed to achieve justice, the narrative opened up the possibility of turning to vigilante action to ensure justice just as had McLean.

For many of the Mountain Meadows authors, the link from Pratt's murder in Arkansas to the Utah massacre of Arkansans was implicit. To insulate against the possibility that readers might miss the connection, many authors made the link explicit. Some argued that the emigrants were "from McLean's neighborhood"—though McLean did not live in Arkansas, nor was he a native Arkansan.[96] For the reporter C. F. McGlashan, "at least one man [in the emigrant train] was believed to have been interested in the killing of Apostle Parley P. Pratt." To ensure his reader did not miss his line of causality, he rhetorically asked, "Do you see the connection?"[97] Other accounts claimed explicit personal vendettas to clarify the connection. In a military magazine's description, Eleanor, "still full of hatred for all that came" from Arkansas, made her announcement of Parley's death amid the excitement in Utah as Mormons anticipated the arrival of the federal troops and singled out a specific emigrant company for vengeance, since "among this company were several who had helped kill the apostle." The tension of the time propelled her desires forward with the greatest possible force—"she could have chosen no fitter time or manner for wreaking vengeance on them." As a direct result of her announcement, the Arkansas emigrants were slaughtered.[98] Another newspaper account went so far as to place John D. Lee at Pratt's murder. From a feigned first-person vantage point, the writer described the aftermath— only referring to Eleanor (though she was called Smith in this account) and "a dark haired, stout young man, whom I remember as Lee. He seemed to adore the Apostle, and predicted vengeance for the act when he should report to Brigham Young."[99] Lee was at times described as stout, though he was not particularly young in 1857—he was forty-five. Nor was he physically anywhere near Arkansas at the time. Nevertheless, constructing an explicit connection used the Pratt/McLean saga to its fullest possibility. This story now efficiently implicated Brigham Young in the massacre, as we will consider in chapters 4 and 5, and gave John D. Lee a personal vendetta for his role in the attack.

Bravery and Cowardice

Just as Parley Pratt's death provided a gauge of honorable violence by which to measure the Mormons, within the popular story of the massacre itself the failings of Mormon men were likewise juxtaposed with the exemplary manhood seen in the brave Arkansan "defenders of their families."[100] The thread of Arkansan bravery continued to be woven with the story of John Calvin Sorrow, a seven-year-old massacre survivor. Calvin was one of two boys Indian Agent Jacob Forney brought to Washington, D.C., in 1859 in the hope that they were old enough to provide valuable testimony against the Mormons. When neither the federal judges nor the probate judges in Utah convened a court to hear the boys' testimony, Forney asked for permission to take them to the nation's capital.[101] Though the boys met with the attorney general and others, no record remains of the meeting, and the boys were soon returned to extended family in Arkansas. Judge John Cradlebaugh later related how John Calvin wanted to shoot John D. Lee himself because, he said, "I saw him shoot my mother."[102] In 1870, Latter-day Saint antagonist and Idaho senator Aaron Cragin asked members of the U.S. Senate, "Who in the Senate will say that this boy, now growing to manhood, would not be justified in the sight of God in carrying out that thought?" In Cragin's story, the boy was more of a man than the "cowardly, blood stained villains" who killed his family. Parroting the claims of many federal appointees that the Mormons were a law unto themselves, Cragin used the suggestion of vigilante action to propel Congress to further action against the Mormons. Extralegal action would at least stop the assassins, as "many of them have added new guilt to their souls by committing more murders since that terrible day." Presumably as an effective motivation to action against the Mormons, Senator Cragin offered Congress the option of proceeding with the rule of law and specific government action or allowing the victims of the Mormons to turn to extralegal means.[103]

The Mountain Meadows discourse could be molded to serve a variety of different ends. In her polygamy exposé, former wife of Brigham Young Ann Eliza Young fictionally expanded that narrative, arguing that some of the emigrant women and children were "killed by their husbands, father, or brothers" rather than being subjected to "the fiendish brutalities which [some] suffered before they were allowed to die." Owing to the onerous bravery of these emigrant men to kill their female relations, these women and children were "happy souls who thus escaped the most cruel torture."[104] Here again, violence could be an honorable and necessary element of manhood, particularly if it was employed to safeguard female virtue.

Author Frank Triplett maintained that "even John D. Lee . . . was forced to pay tribute" to the bravery of the Arkansans as "they moved under a perfect storm of bullets as coolly as if they were about ordinary household work."[105] The brave men and boys of the Arkansas emigrants stood in stark contrast to the Mormon "skulking cowards."[106] Treachery on the battlefield was nothing new, but for Triplett, Mormons deceiving the emigrants into giving up their arms and decoying them out of their stronghold in the wagon corral was considered the most egregious part of the battle. Triplett was certain that the Mormons would win in a fair fight because of "their overwhelming numbers." But rather than fighting a "manly battle," the Mormons used cowardly and unprincipled deception. He argued that Americans should not be surprised, for "this vile perfidy" was "constant . . . with the teachings of these infamous fanatics, and the nature of the miserable wretches that could be beguiled by the lustful promises of so infernal a religion."[107]

Similarly, Methodist reverend C. P. Lyford warned that the Mormons' "most heartless, cold-blooded deed" was demonstrative of the dangerous nature of the Mormon Problem. The examples of the absence of manhood were abundant. For example, Lee had "pretended to hold a council" with the Indians in his feigned bid to rescue the emigrants. As well, Lyford asked, what kind of man would stoop to hiding himself in a chicken coop when he was about to be apprehended by the authorities? Only a "dastardly coward" like John D. Lee would "hide in a chicken-coop when the officers came to arrest him!"[108] For Lyford, Lee was never the only target; his religion made him the monster that he was. Moreover, this would always be the outcome for people who trusted the Mormons: "The cowardly assassins . . . feigned friendship and sympathy, and induced these brave men to lay aside every weapon, and then shot them down like dogs! The venerable, gray-haired clergyman, the sturdy farmers, the stalwart young men and the beardless youth, all were cut down, one by one, and above their dead bodies waved the stars and stripes!"[109] While Lyford homed in on the "cowardly assassins" involved in the massacre, his didacticism was to warn of the danger for all. Mormons were pretend friends and pretend Americans, whose affectation of friendship could be deadly to more than just those who unfortunately found themselves at the Meadows.

Some wove elements into the narrative to demonstrate that Mormonism was on the wane and would naturally die out—as religious studies scholar David Walker coined, premature declarations of the "death knell of Mormonism."[110] After the publication of massacre details through trial testimony, in one intriguing trope of the massacre discourse a dichotomy was created between old Mormons and young Mormons. One story told of a young girl who clung to Lee's son for protection, only to be killed by Lee.[111] In reality, Lee had no son participating in the massacre, but the story offered a useful protestation of a generational shift: the assumption here was that Lee's son was not as brutal as his father. While previous depictions of Mormons had painted them as one monolithic group, some sources now began to see a possible hope of rebellion among the rising generation. Ann Eliza Young maintained that Mormons were not merely an indiscriminate mass, asserting, "To the honor of many of the men be it said,—the younger ones, especially,—they refused to join in this horrible work, and some of them made efforts to protect these helpless women from their fiend-like tormentors." In her narrative, Mormon sons worked to protect women even while their fathers would not.[112] This idea fit the theory that the longer a person was in Mormonism, the more indoctrinated he or she became, diminishing the possibility of change. The construction of the narrative bolstered reports that Mormonism would soon be eradicated.[113]

Offering additional support to reports of Mormonism's demise, around the time of Lee's execution another angle of the reports of old Mormons battling with young Mormons surfaced. In one version, militia member and trial witness Jim Pearce was shot by his father either for not wanting to participate in the killing or, as with Lee's son, for specifically protecting a young girl.[114] This built on Pearce's trial testimony. He focused his trial testimony on his youth and inexperience, claiming to be fourteen at the time of the massacre when in actuality he was eighteen.[115] Another account declared,

"Some of the younger men refused to join in the dreadful work. Jim Pearce was shot by his own father for protecting a girl who was crouching at his feet!" And then it provided a tale of supporting evidence: "The bullet cut a deep gash in his face, and the furrowed scar is there to-day."[116] The language is very similar to Ann Eliza Young's account, from which it likely drew. These accounts follow the pattern of specific details built on apparent first-person testimony, including markers that would suggest a primary source, and then augment the narrative with lurid details in a very functional manner. None of these additional details came specifically from John D. Lee's trials. Within the discourse of civilization, those characteristics that would not aid America on its way to its ultimate destiny would be deselected in a kind of reverse natural selection. Younger Mormons rejecting Mormonism would further its demise. As John Beadle argued, this was all part of the social evolution: "The original fanaticism wears itself out. . . . Old Mormons die; young ones grow up infidels, and the system moderates to a mild Protestantism."[117]

Though in the nineteenth century America offered multiple ideals of manhood, particularly in the liminal space of the West, Mormons could not fit the standard. Despite sharing characteristics with both models of manhood, they subverted both the militia model and the restrained model. The emphasis on the protection of women and children meant many Americans could only see Mormon failure. Lee's first trial functioned as a proving ground for reiterating nineteenth-century gender norms reinforcing popular standards by which the Latter-day Saints fell short. The rule of law, an essential element of civilization, could help heal the damage done by the Mormons. The prosecution of John D. Lee provided an interesting opportunity. If Lee's trial was commentary on Mormonism, could Lee and thereby Mormonism be redeemed and reenter civilization?

CHAPTER FOUR

Prosecuting Mormonism
*The Tyrant of the Mormon Church
and Theocratic Despotism*

When William W. Bishop arrived in Beaver, Utah, in July 1875 ready to defend his client, John D. Lee, he "found the prosecution apparently anxious for John D. Lee to turn State's evidence, in order to clear up the mystery so long obscuring the facts in the case."[1] As agents of the law, the U.S. attorneys offered Lee the possibility of redemption through confession. Bishop did not think Lee could obtain a fair trial, and he and other members of Lee's defense encouraged him to confess. Acting on his defense counsel's advice, Lee agreed to "turn state's evidence and become a witness for the prosecution." Lee "prepared a full and detailed account of the case, giving every fact connected with, preceding or following the massacre at Mountain Meadows," according to Bishop.[2] The U.S. attorneys believed that confession would allow them to prosecute the Mormon leaders they thought directly responsible. Evidence against fellow arrestee William H. Dame would be helpful, but the prosecution desired evidence that would implicate the Mormon prophet, Brigham Young. For the Mountain Meadows prosecution to redeem Mormonism as a whole, it had to reach the genesis of Mormon offense.

However, after receiving Lee's statement, U.S. Attorney William Carey rejected it, "claiming that Lee had 'not told it all.'" While the complete version of the confession is not extant, Bishop asserted that the prosecution refused to accept the statement because "John D. Lee shows, beyond the possibility of a doubt, that Brigham Young is innocent and knew nothing of the transaction until many days after the massacre occurred."[3] According to summaries of Lee's confession, Lee assigned local leaders Isaac Haight and John Higbee with responsibility for the massacre. The *Salt Lake Daily Tribune* reported that prosecutors also rejected the document because it "tells nothing to implicate [William H.] Dame, who is in custody," and in whose trial it would have been used.[4] Rather than beginning the prosecution against Dame, with Lee's confession in hand the prosecution drew a second indictment rewritten to include conspiracy and they immediately began Lee's trial. Lee had failed at his first opportunity for rehabilitation and would now be subject to the full extent of the law.

This dynamic—with the prosecution urging Lee not only to confess but to implicate others, and Lee only partly satisfying their demands—would become a theme during his first trial, which is the subject of this chapter. It would play out again in his second trial and immediately before his death, as chapter 5 will show as it continues the story. When Lee's first trial began, some people, like his defense attorney William Bishop, suspected that what the state was really interested in was adjudicating Mormonism as a whole, not just bringing Lee to justice. That suspicion was borne out as the first trial wore on and was made explicit in the prosecution's long and detailed closing arguments, which focused on the Mormon religion as a despotic, un-American system that needed to be eradicated. Lee's first trial set the tone for the public understanding of Mormonism and the dangers it posed to civilization, particularly in its embrace of its theocratic leader Brigham Young. The task the prosecutors set for themselves in Lee's trial was an ambitious one: for Mountain Meadows to be the downfall of Mormonism. To achieve that goal, they needed to prove that Brigham Young was directly involved.

Connecting Young to the Massacre

When the first reports of the massacre began to appear in California papers in October 1857, they sought to establish a clear narrative of events. Though many Americans read about the massacre as the cover story of *Harper's Weekly* in August 1859 before they read Horace Greeley's famous interview with Brigham Young on the cover a few weeks later—as depicted in figure 4.1, there were few suggestions at the time that Brigham Young knew of the slaughter.[5] One came from William Rogers, who had been recruited as an assistant to the federal Indian agent to retrieve the surviving children. In early 1860, Rogers suggested the possibility of Young's involvement. His letter, published in the avowedly anti-Mormon Utah paper the *Valley Tan*, included a secondhand report from a Paiute Indian named Jackson. Rogers reported that "after the attack had been made a white man came to their camp with a piece of paper, which, [Jackson] said, *Brigham Young had sent*, that directed them to go and help whip the emigrants."[6] Initially this report did not get much public traction, yet it would be given new life and proliferate after Lee's first trial began.

The embattled federal judges in Utah Territory already had numerous concerns that Brigham Young was a "sovereign . . . possessing an Empire in the heart of a Republic," and those concerns would persist.[7] The title "Mormon King" or "King Brigham" jarred in American ears.[8] Commentators ar-

FIGURE 4.1 Two weeks before lauded journalist Horace Greeley's interview of Brigham Young graced the front page of *Harper's Weekly*, news of the massacre colored American's perceptions of the Mormons. [Horace Greeley], "Brigham Young's Wealth, Wisdom, Wives, Etc.," *Harper's Weekly*, 3 September 1859, 561–562. Courtesy of the Library of Congress.

gued there was no place for a "supreme dictator" in America, yet Young had "founded a Kingdom within a republic and yielded a power such as no civilized king enjoys."[9] Writers hoped that the idea of an "autocracy" or an "absolute sovereign" in Utah Territory would compel their readers more fully to understand the urgency of the Mormon Problem.[10] The folk song "The Mormon King" linked Young's autocratic power with the capacity to spread violence:

Brigham Young . . . says we'll rue the day,
That e'er we came into his way,
For all of us he'll surely slay.
Out in Salt Lake City.[11]

The song melodically and sardonically argued that Young's violent potential had to be quelled or all Americans would reap the result.

Many federal officials were certain the Mormon hierarchy contradicted American ideals, but accusations against Brigham Young in regard to the massacre are almost completely absent in the voluminous correspondence documenting the early investigation.[12] While the antagonistic *Salt Lake Tribune* incessantly poked, prodded, and accused Young of nefarious actions from its inception, the majority of federal appointees did not share specific concerns of Young's involvement with leaders in Washington. Utah Territory Supreme Court judge Delana Eckels stood as the exception, writing to the U.S. attorney general, "I suspect that if an Attorney who understood his business and would try, could show that Brigham Young directed the Mountain Meadow Massacre, but no one under Mormon influence will try it."[13] Eckels claimed one of the few early attempts to prosecute the massacre, convening a grand jury in central Utah (Nephi) in 1859. A U.S. attorney seemed initially eager to prosecute those involved, but it came to little fruit. No sustained focus on Young followed the preliminary effort.[14]

The legal actions and popular narrative of the massacre never functioned independently; they were interdependent and grew more intertwined over time. The first accusations of Young that gained significant traction came from Catherine Van Valkenburg Waite (C. V. Waite) an anti-Mormon novelist, suffragist, and wife of Utah Territory Supreme Court judge Charles Waite. Ms. Waite lived with her husband in Utah for two years as he served as a federal judge. This experience and her career as an attorney and activist cemented her reliability in the minds of many Americans. In 1866, she published her sensational Brigham Young biography, *The Mormon Prophet and His Harem*, with two more editions that same year. Her considerable success with *The Mormon Prophet* enabled her to establish her own publishing company, C. V. Waite and Co. in Chicago, and continue publishing activist tomes. Ignoring any possible biblical precedent, Waite argued that Mormon polygamy came through a counterfeit revelation. Standing as a religious imposter, Young could transform nefarious goals using scripture to conceal his true intent.[15] She embodied Young's "revelations" with the words of Shakespeare's unredeemable Richard III on her title page:

> And with a piece of scripture,
> Tell them, —that God bids us do good for evil.
> And thus I clothe my naked villainy
> With old odd ends, stol'n forth of Holy Writ,
> And seem a saint, when most I play the devil.[16]

Waite was the first antipolygamy activist to include a chapter on Mountain Meadows in her polemical writing. She used Mountain Meadows as a surrogate argument for polygamy and introduced the idea of another counterfeit revelation at the origin of the massacre. Her description of Young's massacre "revelation" earned much mileage in popular sources and then in the official legal action when John D. Lee first went to trial in 1875. She imagined,

> A revelation from Brigham Young, as Great Grand Archee, or God, was despatched to President J. C. Haight, Bishop Higbee, and J. D. Lee, commanding them to raise all the forces they could muster and trust, follow those cursed gentiles (so read the revelation), attack them, disguised as Indians, and with the arrows of the Almighty make a clean sweep of them, and leave none to tell the tale; and if they need any assistance, they were commanded to hire the Indians as their allies, promising them a share of the booty. They were to be neither slothful nor negligent in their duty, and to be punctual in sending the teams back to him before winter set in, for this was the mandate of Almighty God.[17]

The invented title "Great Grand Archee" reflected a secret Mormon hierarchy possibly reminiscent of covert Masonic or early Ku Klux Klan offices. It also added idolatry to the list of Mormon sins, casting Brigham Young as God. This "revelation" included pertinent details known to Americans familiar with the massacre to produce a veneer of authenticity. Juxtaposing her conclusions with Young's counterfeit revelation, Waite elevated her narrative of Mormon atrocities in relation to the massacre again claiming their ability to "fasten conviction upon" the Mormons "by 'confirmations strong as proofs from Holy Writ.'" Beyond merely focusing on the actions of the few, Waite built her narrative of a revelation to further implicate the whole of the Mormon community in southern Utah in an act of religious violence. In her Meadows story, "many . . . from the neighboring settlements" attended a council in Cedar City, where "the revelation was read, and the destiny of the unsuspecting emigrants sealed."[18] Waite's account proliferated widely. Within two years, she offered a newly revised and expanded fifth edition (1868). It remains in print today.

A few years later, Mark Twain's *Roughing It* softened some of the standard anti-Mormon rhetoric in his description of Salt Lake City, particularly as he questioned the ubiquity of violence among the Latter-day Saints. He left the Mormon capital "a good deal confused as to what state of things existed there."[19] Was Salt Lake the tranquil place he had personally experienced, or was violence lurking in the shadows? He then explained how after his trip he read Ms. Waite's "entertaining" book and she cleared up his earlier confusion about the Mormons. Her exposé of the massacre helped him realize that Mormons were as dangerous as he previously thought his experience notwithstanding. Waite's declarations of Young's "revelation" became central to his own Mountain Meadows story in his appendix to *Roughing It*.[20] Other authors similarly expanded on Waite's notion of a revelation. In John Beadle's elaboration, the local Mormon leaders met together in a "grand Council" (including multiple bishops) to decide on the massacre. In that council "they stated that they had received a command from Salt Lake City 'to follow and attack those accursed Gentiles and let the arrows of the Almighty drink their blood.'"[21] In this manner, the story of the massacre continued to play multiple roles highlighting the physical danger of the Mormon Problem as well as the blasphemy of the Mormon counterfeit.

Several popular narratives likewise imbued Young with the draconian power to hide his accountability. Beadle conceded "the strong probability" that Young did not order the massacre. In an abortive attempt at balance, Beadle mentioned arguments of a "majority of the Mormons" that would blame the massacre on local church leaders and "claim that they acted without Brigham's knowledge." He also told the story of Young bursting into tears upon hearing of the massacre, as Beadle claimed Young's family often told. He then provided a list of what he termed "many strong proofs" of Young's guilt. Beadle wrote his *Life in Utah; Or, the Mysteries and Crimes of Mormonism* trying to capitalize on the lucrative opportunity that was the Mormon question in the nineteenth century. In his introduction, he described living in Salt Lake City in a year he called "the most despotic period of Brigham Young's rule."[22] For Beadle, the most damning evidence "more than all else, [was] the overwhelming certainty that no fact of great importance [was] ever entered upon without the advice and consent of Brigham Young."[23] Beadle and others prioritized their own existing conceptions of the Mormon leader's unquestionable power, and it became the standard in assessments of Young's relationship to the massacre.

Meanwhile, former Latter-day Saint Charles Wandell, writing under the pseudonym Argus, publicly accused Brigham Young of involvement in the massacre.[24] Historian Paul Reeve argues that the accusation came in response to a rumor that Wandell participated in the massacre.[25] Wandell encouraged participant and former Latter-day Saint bishop Philip Klingensmith to make an affidavit of his knowledge that led to the prosecution for the massacre. Early in the affidavit, Klingensmith claimed Lee possessed an order from "headquarters," though Klingensmith could not see if there was an actual written order.[26] Klingensmith's only explicit mention of Young came in the last two lines of the affidavit. They told how Lee reported the massacre to

Young as "commander in chief of the militia of the Territory of Utah."[27] It was likely Wandell himself who offered the affidavit to then U.S. attorney George C. Bates, enlarging the text of Klingensmith's affidavit by saying the massacre occurred "under the written orders of Young himself." In this new development, the order in question wasn't merely a (possibly verbal) directive from an unspecified "headquarters," but a written command from Brigham Young. Bates eagerly wrote to the U.S. solicitor general the day he received the affidavit, telling of his great discovery and explaining that he found "no reason to doubt its truth," as it could "easily be corroborated."[28]

However, corroboration apparently did not come easily, and Bates did not act against Young.[29] Despite this absence of legal action against Young, the rumors began to take effect. Young worried that he might also be arrested shortly after John D. Lee's arrest in November 1874. As such, Young sent a coded telegram instructing a close associate to put important exculpatory evidence "into a safe where it will be secure and at hand if called for."[30] Young never needed to call for it.

The Unnamed Defendant at the Bar

John D. Lee's trial in the summer of 1875 was never just a murder case in a small town on the frontier. (Figure 4.2 presents Lee's trial portrait.) As the prosecution worked to establish its case, the press spread the story of the trial far and wide, slaking a public appetite for sensational crime reports. Trial transcripts of arguments and some witnesses circulated along with considerable commentary allowing close public scrutiny of the crime "without parallel in civilized history."[31] As the trial moved forward, the *New York Times* cogently described it as a "likely . . . curiosity in criminal jurisprudence." The eighteen years that had passed since the massacre, a change in the indictments "since the trial was opened," and, most significantly, the assumption that "the entire hierarchy [of the Mormon Church] may be considered as involved in the result of this case" all exemplified this curiosity for the *Times*.[32] Few newspaper editors professed belief that Lee would be convicted, though the *Virginia Enterprise* hoped that an even greater goal could be accomplished with the trial: "There will be testimony enough before the trial is over to fasten the guilt where it belongs, and convince the people of the United States that Brigham Young and his leading captains and counselors should be hanged."[33] Much of the press followed a pattern set by Lee's prosecution, whose indictments of Young and Mormonism increased in seriousness and frequency as the trial progressed.

FIGURE 4.2
Trial portrait of John D. Lee. Courtesy of Church History Library.

As Lee's first trial began, a prosecutorial focus on Young was not immediately obvious. In his opening argument, U.S. Attorney William Carey did not begin with Young; Carey saved that until the end of the opening argument. He then proclaimed, "We shall show to you that that order was given by Brigham Young."[34] Despite what some reported, Carey was not guaranteeing the jury that he would bring evidence that Young had ordered the massacre at the Meadows. Rather, the order was to keep quiet afterward: Carey carefully claimed that Young ordered Lee not to talk about the massacre. Carey managed expectations. He promised that he would "prove to you [the jury] that the militia . . . was ordered out." He then outlined the prosecution's tenuous "hope to trace it, if possible, to the real source from whence it came in," implicitly nodding to Young as the "real source."[35]

As the case progressed, each time the prosecution attempted to "trace" the order for the massacre "to the real source," the defense balked with objections as to the pertinence of a particular line of inquiry. U.S. Attorney Robert Baskin hinted that an order from Young was the genesis of the massacre, and the source of the order was a pretend revelation—again bringing in another element from an antipolygamy novel, this time C. V. Waite's, implying Brigham Young to be the source of the massacre. Real witnesses were not always as useful as fiction. As mentioned in his original affidavit, witness Philip Klingensmith testified that two weeks after the massacre, John D. Lee reported the massacre to Brigham Young.[36] The prosecution homed in on Klingensmith's description of Young directing Lee to "take charge of" the dead emigrants' goods as "the Indian Agent."[37] His testimony only peripherally included Young.

In what became a frequently occurring process, the defense objected to the line of questioning, claiming it was not material to the case; it was both "outside the allegations in the indictment, and . . . immaterial and irrelevant."[38] In this instance and several others, Judge Boreman overruled the objections, and the defense attorneys continued to note their exceptions. Lee's defense attorney Bishop repeatedly asserted that Lee was not the real target of the prosecution. He argued, "It is plain that the government officials are after higher game than this old man," referring to Lee.[39] Baskin taunted the defense as it cross-examined Klingensmith—"It is the real criminal getting touched now."[40] Baskin's question of the "real criminal" or the "real client" implicitly brought the discussion to Young.[41] This led the *Arkansas Gazette* to report that Brigham Young would likely be "inculpated."[42] Anxious editors supplemented trial news with additional commentary to reawaken the public's fascination with the "horrible romance of the Mountain Meadows massacre."[43]

Neither side called Brigham Young or Latter-day Saint apostle George A. Smith as witnesses, though the defense wanted to use their testimony anyway.[44] The defense had a doctor in Salt Lake City swear to their poor health, and attempted to file with the court depositions that had been given in Salt Lake City.[45] The court rejected the depositions, arguing that they could not be read into evidence in a criminal case.[46] Though rejected by the court, the clerk filed the depositions, and editors published them for public consumption. The *New York Times* and other news outlets published the affidavit.[47] The Kansas *Leavenworth Commercial* saw the deposition as an ineffective "desperate effort" on the part of the Mormons "to clear Brigham Young of the Mountain Meadows massacre."[48] Though the *Salt Lake Daily Tribune* usually sided with the prosecution, this time the *Tribune* aligned itself with the defense, arguing that this attempt proved the case was "really the trial of Brigham Young and the Mormon system at the bar of the civilized world, and not merely the trial of some murderers before a jury."[49] Some newspapers considered Young's deposition to be "very damaging" to Young's "own case"—despite the lack of an official case against him.[50] Many papers had already determined his responsibility. The *Virginia Enterprise* went to the extreme, declaring, "The affidavit is as feeble as it is false . . . and [Young] is striking wildly in defense of his neck."[51] For the *Chicago Inter-Ocean*, the affidavit was not just about Young, but "seem[ed] to point unmistakably to the guilt of the whole Mormon Church in Utah."[52]

The defense quickly tired of the prosecution's attempts to make the trial about more than Lee. Lee's defense attorney W. W. Bishop argued that if the prosecution had been only concerned with convicting Lee, Assistant U.S. Attorney David P. Whedon would have argued the case. Whedon had assisted U.S. Attorney Carey for almost a year in southern Utah, where he "drew the indictment" and "commenced the prosecution against Lee." For Bishop, the federal officials—the "government"—made the decision to drag "in the church."[53] Whedon could not take on the Mormon hierarchy on his own. Bishop continued, "If it had simply been John D. Lee on trial, these legal lights would have remained in their comfortable offices in the city of Salt Lake, and when Lee was acquitted, would have contented themselves with saying 'as I expected; another evidence of the outrages against law and order committed by the Mormon Church.'"[54] Salt Lake attorney Robert N. Baskin had participated in federal efforts against the Latter-day Saints including considerable experience with polygamy prosecutions, and Carey appointed him as another assistant U.S. attorney less than a week before the trial began. As it was, "legal lights" the well-known U.S. attorney William Carey and his newly minted assistant Robert N. Baskin arrived in the outpost of Beaver, Utah, and took the reins from Whedon just days before Lee's trial.[55] Though the efforts may have been transparent to observers, that did not negate their efficiency.

Punishing Mormon Theocracy

Throughout Lee's first trial, lead defense attorney W. W. Bishop maintained his conclusion that the prosecution thought the legal proceedings a "safe occasion to blacken and vilify the character of Brigham Young . . . and others who stand high in the church."[56] The trial was "a chance for the counsel to gain notoriety"; the prosecution was "pandering to the masses."⁵⁷ Lack of evidence did not impede the prosecution's focus on Young. In fact, the spotlight on the Mormon prophet heightened and intensified as the trial went on with a dramatic culmination with the closing arguments. The locus of Baskin's passionate and long-winded—five-hour—closing argument was explicitly an attack against Young and the Mormon theocracy. The pro–Latter-day Saint *Salt Lake Daily Herald* called it "one of his characteristic, forcible, bitter speeches" in which he "embrac[ed] the opportunity for spewing out some bile."⁵⁸

The prosecution narrowed in on accusations of Young's religious power and prophetic claim. Baskin drew upon a Mormon argument that had been used to justify polygamy as a surrogate for Mountain Meadows—as demonstrated in the biblical text, it was acceptable if God commanded. He argued that the Mormon militia claimed that the order to kill "came directly by command from the Lord of heaven"—again giving C. V. Waite's claim to a revelation more mileage.⁵⁹ Baskin argued that Young claimed that the order to end the emigrants "emanated from God himself."⁶⁰ While Prosecutor Carey seemed able to fathom a God who could command Joshua to exterminate an entire people, he argued that Young could not be called a Joshua.⁶¹ Yet Baskin, like many other Americans in the nineteenth century, took issue with the violence demonstrated in the Hebrew Bible.⁶² This likewise demonstrated the problems of imbuing the Old Testament text with complete authority—another problem of which the Mormons were all too guilty.⁶³ For Baskin, the claim of a leader to speak for God egregiously affronted Christian civilization; this affront was multiplied when used to incite bloodshed. Employing the language of Christian blasphemy, he argued that a heresy lay at the foundation of Mormonism: "He [Brigham Young] is the second Jesus Christ. He speaks by authority, everything is said as seer, revelator and prophet."⁶⁴ Again intertwining multiple threads of the Meadows discourse on race and gender, Baskin maintained that White men could not have done this—it was not in their natural capacity. Only a blasphemous belief in a counterfeit prophecy could make them carry out such a brutal massacre. If Young were guilty of any part of what Baskin accused, it would reinforce the counterfeit nature of Mormonism and thereby the implicit danger of a prophet.

His religious argument then transformed into a political one. These were not merely religious concerns of heresy, Baskin warned; Young was also a "man with almost omnipotent power—greater than the czar of Russia."⁶⁵ Though he was no longer the territorial governor, the close alignment of ecclesiastical and government positions in Utah supported claims that Young still controlled the state. Baskin urged his hearers to realize that the unchecked power of the Mormon hierarchy was fundamentally incompatible with American ideals.

Where the prosecuting attorneys lacked evidence, they focused on prior assumptions, the prevailing assumption being that Brigham Young ordered the massacre. Baskin's chain of reasoning extended through a series of rhetorical jumps. As a witness, Philip Klingensmith had testified that Young ordered John D. Lee to sell the spoils from the massacre when Lee first met with Young a couple weeks after the massacre.[66] Although Klingensmith did not testify to the content of Lee's message to Young, Baskin supplied it: "There is not a man on this jury that doubts for a moment that the fact of this massacre was carried to [Young], and carried him by John D. Lee."[67] For Baskin, "the fact" is his supposition that an order required a report after it was accomplished. Baskin found inference more powerful than evidence—rather than telling Young something that he didn't know, Lee reported on how he followed through with the order given him. Baskin's assumption worked easily because at least in part his national audience maintained a belief in Young's absolute despotic power—this was already a central accusation of Brigham Young by federal officials in Utah and in the popular press.

Building upon this, Baskin ranted, "It is impossible for any man occupying that position—having power in the Mormon Church, having control of matters ecclesiastical and legislative that such an occurrence could have occurred in the country without the knowledge of it having been carried to him."[68] As Young ruled his kingdom with a ruthless hand, "no man, no bishop, nor any other person or head of the Mormon church would have dared to have taken such an important step to do such an heinous act . . . if he hadn't a direct or implied sanction of that head of the church."[69] The prosecutor worked under the assumption that Young's power was so complete that no one would be brave enough to act without his specific direction. Baskin easily argued that it was "very natural that such orders [were] given. . . . When you consider the power and authority of Brigham Young over the Mormon Church, with them the order would have been carried out."[70] Building on the perception of Young as an autocrat, Baskin's argument denied the agency of individual Mormons. The prosecution meticulously chose language in many instances not to distinguish between local leaders and general leaders of the Latter-day Saint church. In so doing, they crafted a rhetorical space that allowed reporters and readers across the country to interpret the prosecution's assumptions as established testimony.

By the end of Baskin's closing argument, he alleged, "The evidence and all the circumstances show that the order made by Brigham Young was actually carried out—an order which sent seventeen little children, whose parents had been ruthlessly murdered, out upon the cold charities of the world."[71] Baskin did not have testimony that Young had ordered the massacre itself. Yet his accusations fueled even broader charges, as Baskin verbally "arraigned" Young at least a half dozen different times during his closing argument. This informal arraignment included "first as an accessory of this murder, because considering the power he had over this people, the position in the territory he had over them."[72] Then Baskin arraigned Young "as having been accessory before the fact" for "quietly" sitting by as "little children [were] made orphans."[73] His verbal arraignment moreover included "accessory to the robbery of these infant children."[74] Finally, he "arraign[ed] this iniquitous system, and leaders of the church," though he consistently assured the jury that this did not involve individual members of the Latter-day Saint church.[75] John D. Lee, the defendant, sat at the bar, all but forgotten.

Undoing Mormon Theocracy

Baskin held little back in his condemnation of Young and clearly struggled to value Latter-day Saint belief. However, in a potentially pragmatic effort, individual Latter-day Saint jury members received considerable positive attention in Baskin's closing argument. Fending off accusations from the defense that his prosecution was a "religious crusade" against the Mormon people, Baskin argued that it was not a malevolent desire to persecute the Saints for their belief in a prophet but "more of a tendency to mercy." He framed his effort as salvific or perhaps even a form of proselytizing—he and Carey only wished to show the Saints the evidence and save them from "unscrupulous and fanatical leaders in the territory." Baskin structured his prosecutorial efforts as a "merciful" opportunity for Latter-day Saint jury members to "throw off the shackles . . . assert [their] individuality and lop off the faults of the Mormon church." He asked rhetorically, "Is that persecution?"[76] In his zeal, Baskin seemed unable to accept that American men could willfully choose to become (or remain) Latter-day Saints. A "good citizen, an honest man, a law-abiding man" would take advantage of the opportunity offered him—he would throw off Mormon oppression. He persisted in this possibility, telling the jurors, "You can do it. You have in your power to lop off these faults."[77]

Baskin's proclaimed desire was not only reformatory. He interpreted the power of jurors as having the potential to "strike down" Mormon leaders.[78] If the jury chose a guilty verdict, it would not only find the individual, Lee, responsible for his crime but also become part of a greater cause. The law had the power to rectify the injury Mormonism had made on civilization. The discourse of civilization was powerful: civilization could rehabilitate savagery, regain Whiteness, restore manhood, and bring liberty to Utah. Just as Judge Boreman had given the grand jury that indicted Lee and the eight others an opportunity, Baskin offered the jury the power to restore civilization through law. The nation would "rejoice that the supremacy of law has been established and asserted" and "that organization [of the Mormon Church had] been overturned."[79]

Baskin gambled that the jury would not choose to participate in the avenue of Mormon redemption he offered them, which was not a risky bet. Lee's first trial proceeded without any direct testimony of Lee murdering anyone, and the trial ended. Though they deliberated for two days, the jury was split, and they could not be reconciled. They ended as a hung jury.[80] With this disappointing result, Baskin lost the courtroom battle but won the war: a hung jury demonstrated the Mormons' rejection of the offer of civilized redemption, bolstering Baskin's claims that Mormons were not capable of acting as full citizens.

In the *Salt Lake Daily Tribune*, editor Frederick Lockley would later blame the lack of a verdict on inhibited Mormon jurors, yet Baskin's closing argument did not allow space for a juror to both remain a believing Latter-day Saint and find John D. Lee guilty. Baskin had argued that a vote to convict Lee was simultaneously a vote to indict the Latter-day Saint hierarchy, and he rightly surmised that this would be a step too far for the jurors. Baskin staked his efforts on the dual prospects of expanding a salacious account of the massacre and the Mormon hierarchy as he hoped for increased federal intervention and further legislative censure. Federal officials could use the hung jury to corroborate Baskin's earlier claim that the Poland Act would not be enough to bring the rule of law to civilize the Mormon territory. The fact that the trial ended in a hung jury provided political capital for Baskin and others who were primarily interested in putting Mormonism on trial, not just John D. Lee.

Despite the strident efforts of the prosecution, its attorneys could not directly implicate Young and other members of his hierarchy, or even convict Lee on their first attempt. Baskin later admitted, "There was no direct evidence in the trials of Lee, nor is it stated in Lee's confession, that any order was given either by Brigham or [George A.] Smith to massacre the emigrants."[81] Judge John Cradlebaugh, who had investigated the massacre in 1859, later similarly conceded, "There have been many theories advanced for this slaughter, and many charges have been made that have seriously implicated Brigham Young as being the instigator, though there is no proof that sustains it."[82] In spite of the lack of evidence, the U.S. attorneys ensured that Young's involvement became a central element of John D. Lee's first trial and its enduring legacy.

Insinuations Transformed into a Narrative of Guilt

The narrative presented by the prosecuting attorneys at Lee's first trial, especially in the more strident closing arguments, became the dominant narrative of the Meadows. The public believed that John D. Lee was guilty, but the guilt of Brigham Young and those who supported him always superseded Lee's culpability. Publishing her exposé just a few months after Lee's first trial, Ann Eliza Young, Brigham Young's former wife, mustered only the slightest bit more restraint than many sensationalized accounts in her assessment of Young's involvement. She did not know "Young's connection with the massacre itself, — whether it was done at his instigation or merely with his connivance," but she nonetheless argued for his accountability through his theocracy, claiming that "he was, to all intents and purposes, the murderer of these people, and should be held responsible for their lives."[83] Many were broader in their accusations. The Fort Smith, Arkansas, *Tri-Weekly New Era* declared, "It is believed by a greater portion of the citizens of the United States, that the massacre was but the result of Brigham Young's orders" and that "the criminality of Brigham Young and other high dignitaries of the Mormon Church might easily be established."[84] "As to Brigham's guilt," Connecticut's *Hartford Daily Courant* observed, "the evidence accumulated."[85]

CHAPTER FIVE

One Punishment Is Not Enough
Lee's Second Trial, Execution, and Aftermath

Before the closing arguments in Lee's first trial even began, the *St. Louis Republican* already predicted the end—it didn't believe Lee would be convicted. The *Republican* laid out its evidence and declared that "unanimous public sentiment demands that Brigham Young be brought without further delay. The blood shed eighteen years ago cries out for vengeance."[1] The prosecution had already achieved its goal. Baskin's assault of a closing argument would only further cement those inclinations. As we have seen, affixing responsibility for the massacre on Young had not been automatic when the massacre occurred in 1857; it took two decades for the blame to be securely fastened on Young in the popular mind—but the first trial had done its work. The second trial would not derail that narrative. That belief would further expand in the two years between John D. Lee's first trial and Brigham Young's death, and the narrative of Young's guilt became fixed. Once fixed, it would stay. It would endure longer than the prevailing discourse of civilization to which it initially belonged.

This chapter will consider how the narrative of Brigham Young's involvement with the massacre stretched in the public imagination in the months before, during, and after John D. Lee's second trial. In this period, Young's complicity in the massacre developed from an insinuation to a given. Lee's first trial planted a seed that quickly took root in the popular mind and shifted the narrative of blame, and his second trial and subsequent execution cemented that narrative. This chapter will assess how the press extended Young's role in the massacre after Lee's first trial. Though none of the threads of Mountain Meadows discourse functioned independently, concerns over policing race and gender in the project of White civilization generally heightened social concerns about the chosen moral decay of the Mormons and elicited an emotive response, whereas the focus on a prophet practically highlighted both political and religious concerns. All asked important questions about the place of the Latter-day Saints and other minorities in the American project of building civilization. The lack of prosecution of the Mormon Prophet served the narrative more effectively than would a prosecution.

Lee's Second Trial and the Push for a Confession

A year after his first trial ended in a hung jury, John D. Lee found himself again before the bar. Initially it did not appear that he would be alone this time. In April 1876, subpoenas were issued for the cases against Lee, William Dame (again), and George W. Adair Jr., all of whom were in jail. However, a flurry of changes in the U.S. attorney's office left their prosecution hanging, and Judge Boreman released the prisoners on bond after their attorneys pressed for a trial—Lee and Dame had been in jail for a year and a half, Adair for about six months. Then, in September, the new U.S. attorney was ready to begin. In his first act, the pragmatic Sumner Howard promptly arrested Ellott Willden, another indicted massacre participant, and gave notice to George Adair Jr. to prepare for his own trial. Meanwhile, Howard turned his attention to Dame and Lee. Howard then quashed the joint indictment for conspiracy against Dame because of a lack of evidence. (His individual indictment was dismissed in August 1875 because of a technicality.) Dame was free the same day Lee's second trial began.[2]

Under the prosecutorial leadership of Howard, Lee's second trial could not have proceeded more differently than the first. Absent most of the national fanfare present during the first trial, only local papers consistently reported on the details of the trial. The first trial took fourteen days, and its trial transcripts run 3,400 pages. In contrast, the second trial took five days, and its transcripts run about 600 pages. The jury empaneled was entirely made up of Latter-day Saints. As soon as Howard agreed to the jury, speculations began to spread that Howard had an agreement with church leaders in Salt Lake—they would work together to "hang Lee."[3] Howard explicitly stated his intention to leave the larger issues of the Mormon Question alone and focus on prosecuting Lee.

Seven witnesses were called to the stand. Only one had been previously called in Lee's first trial. Unlike the first trial, witnesses focused their testimony on the actions of Lee. Massacre participants Samuel Knight and Samuel McMurdie both testified that they saw Lee murder emigrants. (In the first trial, no one testified to Lee killing anyone.) The prosecution no longer needed the indictment for conspiracy; they had direct testimony of Lee's guilt. At one point, Howard diverged from the witness he was questioning, to enter his assessment of the involvement of Brigham Young and other church authorities into the record. He told the story of how he began his preparation looking at all possible guilty parties, but after his three months of preparation, he now "exonerated the authorities from the head of the church down, Brigham Young down to the authorities at Cedar City." He stated his goal was to show "whose hands were red"—"to prove that [Lee] committed the act."[4]

Then, after the prosecution finished with its witnesses, in a surprising (and potentially derelict) move, Lee's attorneys rested their case without calling a single witness of their own to the stand. Nor did they impeach any of the prosecution's witnesses.[5] Defense attorney Bishop later defended this move, claiming his confidence that any one of several technicalities would be enough to release Lee. After a Sunday adjournment, closing arguments began on Monday belaboring the specifics for longer than did the witnesses. The prosecution reviewed the witnesses, and the defense attorneys threw out a litany of theories that might exonerate Lee. After another adjournment, William Bishop's closing argument harangued those witnesses who testified to Lee's guilt because they too were guilty. He posited that the witnesses were in league with the prosecution to remove accountability from the people of southern Utah and place it on Lee.[6]

Sumner Howard's three-and-a-half-hour closing argument had a little more in common with the first trial as he, too, placed the burden of Mormondom on the jury's shoulders. He agreed with Bishop that "the territory of Utah [was] looked upon with suspicion and derision" because of the massacre. He told the jury it was not their fault, but it would be their fault as well as his own "if justice [was] not done to the guilty party." He continued, "There never was a time in the history of this or any other country where the reputation and standing of a territory or city or a community was so fully within the hands of 12 men." He reminded them that he had examined every evidence "from the top to the bottom" determined to "place the responsibility of that crime where it belonged." It was now in their hands and he trusted that they would "act honestly and justly."[7]

Judge Jacob Boreman didn't expect the trial to end so quickly and needed extra time to prepare the jury instructions. After a slow start the following day, Wednesday, 20 September, the jury began their deliberations at 11:45 A.M. They deliberated for three and a half hours before returning the verdict: Lee was found guilty of murder in the first degree. The defense asked for ten days to prepare its appeal.[8]

In contrast to the particulars of the trial, the end of the trial captured the country's attention. Lee's verdict was not just a local affair, as people from around the United States waited for Lee's reaction. In the West, the defendant's reaction to a verdict and sentence were critical to the public acceptance of the public reformation of the individual.[9] The possibility that Lee could be rehabilitated offered the promise that all Mormons could be redeemed and choose to return to civilization. This focus on the importance of a criminal's confession had a long history. In the seventeenth century, Protestant ministers used popular execution sermons to detail the potentially redemptive path of one condemned to die. Daniel Cohen argues that the decline in these execution sermons was a part of a larger downturn in ministerial sovereignty in the early republic, as the power of the clergy diminished and was transferred to the bar.[10] Confession and execution continued to play a clear role in how a nineteenth-century public wanted murderers to rehabilitate themselves, regain their manhood, and meet the demands of eternal justice. By the time of Lee's conviction in 1876, the legal system offered the redemptive path. Confession provided an opportunity to become right before God and Christian civilization. Lee's redemption was never just about him. As with much of the Mountain Meadows prosecution, particularly in his first trial, it was never just about the individual perpetrators. Lee and other massacre participants were offered an opportunity to expand the responsibility beyond the local leaders already indicted.

For most convicted murders in the nineteenth-century American West, the delivery of a guilty verdict provided an opportunity for the American public to evaluate the individual who transgressed the legal boundaries set by civilization. Reinforcing the slippery nature of gender ideals, executions had their own standard of manliness.[11] As such, Lee's performance at the verdict and then at the sentencing was quickly prepared for public display and digestion. An exposé of those above him could have been counted to Lee's credit and the public saga of redemption, as could the story of Lee taking the collective blame for the actions of others. It soon became clear that the public was disappointed in his stoic response. San Francisco's *Daily Morning Call* reported that "Lee's face betrayed no sign of emotion."[12] The *Call* later expanded its description: "He never flinched, he never moved a muscle, but sitting erect and immovable as a marble statue, eyed the jurymen like a hawk." In general, such a cool response to a guilty verdict was considered manly. Lee responded to his sentencing steady and "erect" and answered "in a clear, firm voice," which should have satisfied some of the expectations for civilized manhood.[13]

Though Lee evinced coolness in the public courtroom, some sources countered with rumors of extreme behaviors in private—returning the narrative to an emphasis on Lee's duplicity. The antagonistic *Salt Lake Daily Tribune*'s columnist stated that while "not a feature of the old culprit's [Lee's] face moved" upon hearing the verdict, it was a different story behind closed doors:

"He was soon afterwards heard to boast of his complacency in listening to the words which stamped him a murderer and recommended him to the hangman."[14] The Latter-day Saint press similarly saw an unmanly and unrepentant convict. Though he did not initially show it, they reported, the verdict upset him and his behavior became erratic: "At times he warmly threatens to expose the whole story of the killing at the Meadows and how it was brought about, and again he is sullen and uncommunicative. He is mad and sad by turns."[15]

Lee responded similarly to the sentencing ten days later. The morning of 10 October 1876, Judge Boreman sentenced Lee to death and scheduled his execution for 26 January 1877. He immediately "asked to be executed by being shot."[16] His trial was over. No boasting was present in public as he accepted his sentence, but it did not appear to help the public opinion of Lee. However, Boreman was not done. Annoyed that Lee hadn't been convicted in the first trial when he believed "the evidence of guilt were plain," he used the opportunity to express the surety of Brigham Young's guilt—"a vast conspiracy extending from Salt Lake City to the bloody massacre field"—and to rail against the church.[17]

As Lee's lead attorney, William W. Bishop approached Lee's appeal from many different possible angles. He had already tried a plea in abeyance to end the trial before the verdict to no success. He then filed a motion for a new trial a week after the verdict likewise to no avail. Further preparation would require significant work, and Bishop wanted financial compensation. He told Lee his lack of funds would inhibit his ability to go to Salt Lake and present the appeal to the territorial supreme court, but he could send a brief. Lee scrambled for money to pay Bishop. He promised Bishop his memoir and continued to try to gather funds. Bishop's repeated pecuniary pleas to Lee could provide a rationale for the potentially lackluster performance in Lee's second trial. However, the memoir provided added incentive, and eventually Lee found the money for the appeal. When Lee was finally able to find a loan, Bishop headed to Salt Lake to argue the appeal.[18]

The appeal was made before the three federal district judges in the territory, including Judge Boreman, who presided over Lee's two trials in the second district. Though Bishop submitted a long list of exceptions, his central argument focused on Boreman's actions. He argued that Boreman's charge to the jury prejudiced the jury against his client and hindered a fair trial. Unsurprisingly, Judge Boreman and the other justices rejected the appeal.[19] Bishop's report to his client reaffirmed that he had done "all he knew how to do." However, "we had the prejudice of civilization to contend with."[20] Bishop's efforts were not enough.

Facing his execution after the Utah Territory Supreme Court rejected his appeal, Lee searched for an escape. As portrayed in figure 5.1, he expressed to U.S. Attorney Howard that he was once again willing to confess—"to write a 'statement of the Mountain Meadows massacre and other Church crimes.'" Howard reminded Lee that earlier prosecutors had rejected his pretrial statement "because they did not believe he told the truth." Lee replied "that he did not do before his first trial as he would have done if he had supposed the Church was going to sacrifice him and send perjured witnesses to swear his life away."[21] In the performance of confession, this could be a positive opportunity for Lee to unburden all he knew before the state. Once again, newspaper editors were excited at the prospect that rather than dying "without divulging anything," Lee would finally tell the full story. According to the *Sacramento Daily Record-Union*, Lee delivered his written statement to Howard, "detailing with much minuteness the story of the massacre." The press presumed that Lee would still "be far short of the whole truth" and did not believe Lee's information would be enough to indict Young.[22] Both the media and the prosecution believed that Young was the origin of the massacre and would not accept a lesser version of the truth.

The Virginia City *Enterprise* also reported that Lee was finally "divulging, with minuteness, the dreadful story of the Mountain Meadows Massacre." Though the replication of "minuteness" highlights nineteenth-century newspapers' custom of appropriating articles of interest from other newspapers often without citation, the *Enterprise* constructed its own analysis. For its editors, the timing of Lee's confession was essential and gave them hope. Now Lee truly stood before God without hope of an earthly suspension to his crimes. They argued that he was now ready to "implicate many pillars of the Mormon Church, including, perhaps, Brigham Young himself." Lee still had the opportunity to accept the restitution civilization offered and could help Christian civilization as it searched for justice. The newspaper once again saw a glimmer of hope that despite the "nearly twenty years since the massacre . . . there is a strong probability that others besides Lee will be exposed and brought to deserved punishment."[23]

However, it came to naught. As prosecutors had done with Lee's earlier statement, Howard also rejected this one, telling him that "every man implicated . . . was either dead or had absconded, or that better proof existed against them than . . . [Lee] could furnish."[24] Moreover, Howard said

FIGURE 5.1 John D. Lee was front page news again as he wrote his confession for the last time. *Frank Leslie's Illustrated Newspaper*, 7 April 1877. The same engravings were sometimes used multiple times. See Stenhouse, *"Tell It All,"* (1878), 632. Courtesy of L. Tom Perry Special Collections, Harold B. Lee Library, Brigham Young University, Provo.

Lee "contradicts many unimpeachable witnesses, and denies facts" that had been established in the trials against him.[25] For those who read Prosecutor Howard's words and agreed, Lee was not acting as a penitent headed for a reckoning before God and Christian society. He was not playing the role that the public demanded.

The Place of Punishment

Notwithstanding John D. Lee's efforts to overturn his conviction in the winter of 1877 and submit petitions for clemency with more than 500 signatures that spring, he was slated to be executed. At the Meadows on 23 March, Lee was given his final opportunity to admit his guilt and perform as the waiting public expected. To follow the pattern of a manly execution, he would have to admit his guilt, accept the verdict, and forgive those who killed him. The officers of the law crafted Lee's death as a spectacle laden with meaning as they planned to execute him at the place of his crime. They had offered Lee multiple opportunities to "tell it all," and they still did not believe that he had advanced the whole truth. Although vigilante lynch mobs often brought their victims to the place of their original offense, there was no understood precedent within the rule of law to bring crime and punishment together. The papers speculated at the rationale — perhaps the field of the massacre would finally elicit complete remorse.

As the prologue pictured, on the morning of 23 March, John D. Lee sat on the edge of his coffin looking out at the Mountain Meadows valley that was the site of the massacre twenty years earlier. There he was to bear the weight of Mormon transgressions against civilization. Through the rite of execution, the American system of law now could further rehabilitate the portion of civilization Lee's actions damaged. This became emblematic of the redemptive possibility for all Mormons. Americans questioned whether Mormons in general could be rehabilitated to meet the standards of civilization or whether extermination was the only action that could quell the Mormons — did the ulcer need to be removed?

Fearing retaliation from Lee's numerous sons, the army met Lee at the Meadows.[26] The officers of the law and a Methodist minister arrived with Lee. Most Western executions were still public events; however, in this instance they worked to keep this from the public. Not only was the public not invited, but the organizers also kept private the location, except from the press at the last minute; moved Lee from the jail a day earlier than originally planned; and then traveled 100 miles of difficult road to the Meadows. Despite the efforts of federal officials aided by the army, the word circulated, and a few hundred gathered a distance away from the appointed spot. This execution did not involve the general fanfare and carnival atmosphere of public executions.[27] Yet even in its sober decorum, the execution remained a performative event for those present and for the larger country through newspaper reports, pamphlets, books, and images. As with lynching, much of the spectacle was transmitted in the sharing of the event, particularly in lurid photographs and detailed descriptions. Circulating the images and particulars of the execution "expand[ed] the act of witnessing" and convinced the public that justice had been met.[28]

As the executioners prepared for Lee, two photographers correspondingly readied themselves to photograph his last minutes. James Fennemore, a local photographer, iconically photographed Lee sitting atop his coffin at the place of his crime as well as Lee's body in his coffin minutes after his execution. At least two of Fennemore's photographs shown in figure 5.2 were made into stereographic prints to be disseminated alongside lynching images and postcards of scenic vacation spots. Both photographers sold pictures of Lee's execution to newspapers across the country and advertised them to interested individuals desiring their own "good picture" of the condemned man.[29] As reproduced in figure 5.3, several of the photographs would be made into engravings and published in a *Frank Leslie's Illustrated* special supplement issue for Lee's execution with multiple action images to bring the eager public to the event.

Josiah Rogerson, a court reporter, took shorthand of Lee's last words: "I feel resigned to my fate. I feel as calm as a summer morn. I have done nothing adversely wrong. My conscience is clear before God and man. I am ready to meet my Redeemer and those who have gone before me behind the veil."[30] The reporter climbed a telegraph pole, set up a temporary telegraph office, and sent Lee's final statement around the world instantaneously.[31] Coastal newspapers in the east and west were "red-hot over the massacre," as were those from small towns, like the Virginia City, Nevada's *Enterprise*. Competing papers sold thousands of extra copies of the issues reporting Lee's execution. Reporters would add supplemental descriptions of Lee's last minutes. The *Salt Lake Daily Tribune* detailed that "while walking to his coffin, he seemed to grow weaker, and as he approached it, he leaned heavily on the arm of Rev. Mr. Stokes. He pulled off his overcoat, and sat on the lid of the coffin, facing the wagons where the executioners were stationed."[32] The minister was there to help Lee in his path of potential reconciliation. It is unknown who requested Stokes—the minister father of the federal

FIGURE 5.2A&B Like the image of John D. Lee sitting on his coffin that began the book, James Fennemore's photographs of Lee provided visual evidence for an eager public. Fennemore sold the images as cabinet cards to individuals as well as to various newspapers ready to commission an engraving of the photograph that could be reproduced in their pages. Fennemore, "John D. Lee at Fort Cameron, Utah, circa 1877," and "J. D. Lee in Coffin." Courtesy of the Church History Library.

Supplement to Frank Leslie's Illustrated Newspaper

No. 1,124—Vol. XLIV.] NEW YORK, APRIL 14, 1877. [SUPPLEMENT GRATIS.

JUSTICE AT LAST!
EXECUTION OF JOHN D. LEE
FOR COMPLICITY IN THE MOUNTAIN MEADOWS MASSACRE.

THE circumstances of the terrible Utah tragedy of twenty years ago, known as the Mountain Meadows Massacre, are familiar to our readers, as well as the fact of the Mormon elder, John D. Lee having atoned for his complicity in the affair, on March 23d, by his life. The details of this summary, if somewhat tardy, vindication of justice, have been published, with their terribly dramatic accompaniments. The proceedings attending Lee's execution were conducted with appropriate gravity and decorum. It had been determined by the authorities that the execution should take place on the spot where the massacre had occurred, and, accordingly, the prisoner was conveyed, on Wednesday, March 21st, from his prison in Beaver City, the subject of our illustration last week, to the hill-surrounded plain, known as Mountain Meadows. He was in the custody of Marshal Nelson, with an armed guard. The party camped out on Thursday night, and, after making several brief halts along the road, reached Mountain Meadows about ten o'clock, on Friday, the 23d.

SCENE OF THE MASSACRE.

No more dreary scene can be imagined than those Mountain Meadows. From the point of the massacre to the emigrant-camp measures a distance of about a mile and a half. The meadows are cut up into deep gullies and covered with sage brush and scrub oak. At the lower part, where the emigrants were encamped, is seen Murderers' Spring, the point where the first acts of the massacre were perpetrated. This spring was twenty years ago on a level with the surrounding country; but it has since been washed until it forms a terrible gulch some twenty feet in depth and eight or ten rods wide.

Coming down to the easterly bank of this ravine is the monument of loose stones erected by Lieutenant Price about thirteen years ago. Some of these stones have slid down the declivity. The ravine monument is oblong in outline and about twenty feet in length, being some three feet high. Under the monument at the time of its erection were placed all the bones that could be obtained on the field; but on removing some of the stones, down to the level of the earth, no trace of bones was discovered.

Counting the military escort, the marshal and his deputies, and a few officials, there were probably eighty persons present. A singular feature was the presence of a photographer, who accompanied the solemn band, provided with his camera and paraphernalia, for the purpose of taking pictures of Lee in his last moments, and of the scene of the execution. As soon as the party arrived at the scene of the massacre a halt was called and Lee was ordered to descend from the wagon in which he rode. Before the arrangements for his execution were completed Lee coolly pointed out to Marshal Nelson some points in the vicinity, with a view evidently of showing the movements of the ill-fated people previous to their being so cruelly massacred. The civilians accompanying the officers were still kept back for a time. Some of the soldiers were posted on the adjoining hills to guard against surprise from any quarter.

CONCEALING THE FIRING SQUAD.

The wagons were meanwhile placed in line near

JOHN D. LEE, THE MORMON ELDER, SHOT, MARCH 23D, FOR COMPLICITY IN THE MOUNTAIN MEADOWS MASSACRE—TAKEN JUST BEFORE HIS EXECUTION.

the monument and the army blankets fastened over the wheels. Behind this improvised screen the squad of men who had been appointed to shoot Lee were to be stationed. The purpose of this concealment of the firing party was to prevent the men composing it from being seen by any one, there being a reasonable fear that some of the numerous relatives of Lee might wreak vengeance on the heads of his executioners.

The boards of which the coffin was to be formed were next unloaded from a wagon and the carpenters began to nail them together. It was a rough pine box. While it was being made Lee sat at some distance away with Marshal Nelson, intently watching the scene around him.

The civilians, and those specially invited as witnesses, were allowed to come within the military inclosure. All of the others were allowed to witness the proceedings from a considerable distance east of the ravine. At Murderers' Spring there were only some twenty-five or thirty persons gathered from the neighboring settlements, for the time and place of the shooting had been very sensibly kept private.

Marshal Nelson then read the order and sentence of the Court, directing the Marshal of the Territory to conduct his prisoner from the place where he was confined to the place of execution, and then to see that he was shot to death. The marshal read the order in a clear tone, his words being audible to every one present. As he concluded the reading he asked Lee if he had anything to say before the sentence of the law was carried out. Lee looked up quickly, and noticing Mr. Fennimore, the photographer, in the act of fixing up his canvas preparatory to taking a photograph of the prisoner, pointed with his finger towards him and said : " I wish to

UTAH.—THE MOUNTAIN MEADOWS MASSACRE.—THE BODY OF THE MORMON ELDER, JOHN D. LEE, DEPOSITED IN ITS COFFIN IMMEDIATELY AFTER HIS EXECUTION, MARCH 23D.—FROM A PHOTOGRAPH, TAKEN EXPRESSLY FOR THIS PAPER, BY FENNIMORE, BEAVER CITY.

FIGURE 5.3A&B Only one of many reproductions of Fennemore's images, *Frank Leslie's Illustrated Magazine* published a special issue devoted to Lee's execution as well as another keepsake supplement documenting the execution in both their English and German editions. The publishers created engravings from Fennemore's images as well as live action engravings that transported the public to the event. "Justice At Last!," *Frank Leslie's Illustrated Newspaper*, 14 April 1877 and "Die Hinrichtung des Mormonen Lee," *Frank Leslie's Illustrite Zeitung*, 21 April 1877. Courtesy of L. Tom Perry Special Collections, Harold B. Lee Library, Brigham Young University, Provo.

marshal — but if federal authorities were hoping for a full confession implicating Latter-day Saint leaders, they would consider a Saint a hindrance to that end. Newspapers consistently mentioned Stokes's Methodist ministerial affiliation. A Mormon leader would block the retributive and Christian redemptive narrative from playing out in front of civilization — a heretical religion responsible for the crime could not act as the representative for God and civilization.

The papers reported Lee's composed demeanor. As Marshal William Nelson read the sentence of death, Lee listened "in a rather abstracted way, looking first in one direction and then in another. . . . After Marshal Nelson read the court order, he asked Lee if he had anything to say before the execution was carried into effect."[33] Lee's final statement was religious in tone, affirming that he was "not an infidel" and had "not denied God or his mercy," but was "a strong believer in these things." He continued, "I declare my innocence of ever doing anything designedly wrong in this affair," and said that the evidence against him was "false as the Hinges of Hell" — though the night before, he had privately confessed to killing "five emigrants possibly six."[34] Lee refused to reject Mormonism, announcing that he "believe[d] in the gospel that was taught in its purity and introduced by Joseph Smith in former days." Regardless of Lee's professed faith in Mormonism and his relationship with Brigham Young, Lee explicitly denounced the Mormon leader, saying that Young "was leading the people astray" and blaming him for his execution.[35] But when given the opportunity to charge Young with responsibility for the massacre, Lee refused.

Executions were set up to encourage the murderer to play the part of the sinner ready to admit guilt and forgive those participating in his death; ultimately Lee did not perform the role as desired. On the one hand, his last words were unambiguously religious in tone, he remained cool and calm in demeanor, and he declared the betrayal he felt from Brigham Young, all of which could work in the expected narrative. Yet when offered the opportunity to be accountable for his actions or at last finally divulge the supposed higher authoritative source of his orders, Lee died without meeting the demands of American civilization. Lee went to his death proclaiming that he was killed in a "cowardly way," thereby offering his own counternarrative of manhood.[36]

The vast attention of the popular press to Lee's execution gave the American public repeated opportunities to evaluate Lee's final performance, though their verdict was split. Some believed his assessment that he was a scapegoat for the Mormon Church — that he was sacrificed for others.[37] Others saw a defiant and unrepentant Lee. The "hardened criminal as he was, said, with a felon's death staring him in the face, that he was as well satisfied with the prospects of his fate as he had been in twenty years."[38] Ultimately, Lee's death satiated very few individuals. Though a mostly Latter-day Saint grand jury had originally indicted Lee and a wholly Latter-day Saint jury had finally convicted him, it was not enough to rid Latter-day Saints of the Mountain Meadows stain. After the hype surrounding Lee's execution died down, many saw an opportunity for those most responsible to be then brought to justice — particularly Brigham Young. (It was likely that this was U.S. Attorney Sumner Howard's plan.) The agents of the law would hold on to the possibility of further Mountain Meadows legal action for almost another twenty years as they maintained the search of Mormon reform. Howard continued the cases of indicted massacre participants George W. Adair and Ellott Willden for three years before he dismissed them in 1879.[39] The last Mountain Meadows indictment to be dropped would be that of John M. Higbee, the leader on the massacre field who gave the final order to shoot. On the run for years, Higbee was sixty-nine when his indictment was dismissed at Utah statehood in 1896, nearly forty years after the massacre. Massacre participant William Stewart and instigator Isaac Haight would be on the run for the rest of their lives. Americans had given Mormons multiple occasions to reform themselves and be redeemed, but the Mormons never fully accepted what was offered them.

Creating a "Useful and Interesting" Confession

In life, John D. Lee had multiple offers from different individuals to publish his story. After his conviction, Lee consistently searched for funds to support his continuing defense. As noted previously, Bishop wrote him detailing his lack of funds and petitioning Lee to pay him in form of his autobiography. When funds for his appeal were not forthcoming, Lee agreed that he would write his autobiography for his defense attorney, Bishop, as a form of payment for his legal services and in hope that any residual royalties would go to his family. In the last months of his life Lee's manuscript was slow going, and Bishop consistently prodded him to write more about the Utah period of his life—particularly about the massacre. Bishop feared that Lee would be executed before he could finish and that Lee's story would not be as valuable without what Bishop considered the most important part.[40] Before Lee's execution, Bishop wrote to Lee that he would elaborate upon Lee's autobiographical writings so as to "make the story useful and interesting" to the public.[41]

Though Bishop left Lee without a much of a defense in his second trial and isolated after his conviction with little support other than U.S. Attorney Sumner Howard and Marshal William Nelson, Bishop felt clearly betrayed when Lee also offered Howard a confession for publication just prior to his execution. In March 1877, just two weeks before Lee's scheduled execution, Bishop again lamented that Lee had not yet written about his life in Utah, specifically the Mormon Reformation and the massacre. He continued, "Your confession given to Howard is having a bad effect so far as the sale of your writings are concerned but by giving me your history during your life in Utah I can make the thing work all right yet I think."[42] Though it was not yet public, the confession already negatively affected Bishop's publishing prospects. Bishop's attempt to "make things work all right" was twofold. Firstly, he preempted Howard and published an altered version of Lee's July 1875 confession in the days leading up to Lee's execution. Bishop's version directly incriminated Brigham Young. Secondly, he altered Lee's memoir sensationally, elaborating Lee's words to heighten the level of Mormon transgressions against civilization—particularly the accountability of Young and other Latter-day Saint leaders.[43]

Bishop sold his version of Lee's confession for $750 to several papers, promising them exclusives in their states. Costing 25 cents, Barclay and Co. of Philadelphia published the Bishop confession in pamphlet form. That pamphlet went through two English editions in 1877 plus another in German, and then another in 1882.[44] Moreover, the Old Franklin Publishing House in Philadelphia published another pamphlet of Lee's confession in both English and French that touted the "implication of Brigham Young."[45] The day after Lee's execution, the *Sacramento Daily Record-Union* and the *San Francisco Daily Bulletin* both published Howard's version of "Lee's Last Confession."[46] Citing these papers as their source, a number of other newspapers also quickly published the confession before the end of the day. During the next week, numerous other newspapers across the nation likewise republished this confession.[47]

U.S. newspapers battled over which was the "right" version. The main difference between the two confessions was the accountability placed on Brigham Young and other Latter-day Saint leaders. In contrast to Bishop's earlier claim that Lee's confession did nothing to implicate Young and the Howard confession's lack of incriminating material on Young, Bishop's second confession proclaimed that the "massacre was the result of the direct teachings of Brigham Young, and it was done by the orders of those high in authority in the Mormon community."[48] In Bishop's version, Young frequently ordered Mormon violence. Mountain Meadows became further evidence of the perception of ubiquitous Mormon savagery. Bishop made "the thing work out right" as he altered Lee's confessional text prior to publication. Since Lee did not give him the narrative he desired, he altered the manuscript to match the discourse the nation expected.[49] The *Ogden Junction* labeled Bishop's role in the confession, titling its response "A little Lee and a little lawyer."[50] After considerable debates as to the veracity of the different confessions, many Americans chose the narrative they desired—the one that implicated Brigham Young.

The day of Lee's execution, the *Eureka Republican* began to advertise Lee's more complete autobiographical writings that Bishop would also publish in book form five months after Lee's death.[51] What became *Mormonism Unveiled: The Life and Confessions of John D. Lee and the Complete Life of Brigham Young* went through a dozen editions before the end of the nineteenth century. The publication of *Mormonism Unveiled* gave the public what Lee had never offered while alive: it argued for Brigham Young's guilt and further heightened the complicity of the Mormon hierarchy in the massacre and widespread Mormon violence. Bishop chose to share the title of the first anti-Mormon book published in 1834: *Mormonism Unvailed* [sic].[52] Like its predecessor, the full title revealed the broadened scope of its narrative: *Mormonism Unveiled; Including the Remarkable Life and Confessions of the Late Mormon Bishop, John D. Lee; (Written by Himself.) and Complete Life of Brigham Young, Embracing a History of Mormonism from its Inception Down to the Present Time, with An Exposition of the Secret History, Signs, Symbols, and Crimes of the Mormon Church. Also the Mountain Meadows Massacre*. As depicted in figure 5.4, the cover of the 1882 edition literally pulled back the curtain on Mormonism. More exposé than history, the book unequivocally placed the responsibility for the massacre on Young and church leaders. The crime "without a parallel . . . was done by a band of fanatics, who had no cause of complaint against the emigrants except that the authorities of the Mormon Church had decided that all the emigrants who were old enough to talk, should die—revenge for alleged insults to Brigham Young, and the booty of the plundered train being the inciting causes of the massacre."[53]

Under scrutiny, it is clear that the original manuscript was altered. Not unlike *The Confessions of Nat Turner* which are now understood to be heavily edited by the White pro-slavery attorney who provided them, evidence demonstrates that Bishop added sensationalized and erroneous details to the manuscript.[54] As published, *Mormonism Unveiled* included contradictory statements, shifts in "tone and sentiment," clear embellishments, obvious

FIGURE 5.4 This 1888 edition of *Mormonism Unveiled* pulls back the curtain on Lee, Young, polygamy, and Mormon violence—its title and content expanded over years. *Mormonism Unveiled: Confessions of John D. Lee and Brigham Young* (Lewisburg, Pa.: S. T. Buck, Son and Co., 1882). Courtesy of L. Tom Perry Special Collections, Harold B. Lee Library, Brigham Young University, Provo.

errors of Latter-day Saint history and doctrine, and significant inconsistencies. Examples such as incorrect ecclesiastical titles that would go unnoticed by an outsider glare to an insider. Those inconsistencies appear perhaps most stark when comparing Lee's religious experience with extremely detailed descriptions of Mormon violence.[55] Early twentieth-century Mountain Meadows author Birney Hoffman concluded, "The evidence is strong—although entirely circumstantial in its nature—that certain portions of that narrative were skillfully altered after Lee's death so that the volume could be employed as a weapon against the Mormon Church."[56] Despite these warnings, the volume continues today to be often used as an uncontested primary source.[57]

Overall, Bishop's embellishments expanded the responsibility for the massacre by heightening the accountability of Mormon leaders—particularly by claiming a role for Brigham Young and apostle and former Utah militia general George A. Smith. Bishop's version also transcended Mountain Meadows, asserting these religious leaders' collusion in a host of other claimed Mormon atrocities. Lee had the opportunity to inculpate Brigham Young multiple times in life to aid himself, yet he did not.[58] The only times his writings blamed the massacre on Young were in those edited by Bishop's hand after Lee's death. Though Lee himself had not acted as the public anticipated by earning redemption from American citizens and inculpating Young in the massacre, his attorney stepped in after Lee's death. Bishop provided the narrative the public desired, and the public responded in kind buying the book in droves.

Brigham Young's Death and Legacy

Unsubstantiated popular accounts of damning new evidence continued to surface after Lee's death, all claiming to tie Brigham Young irrefutably to the massacre. Yet the promised "evidence" never yielded action from the federal officials in Utah against Young—or seemed to even exist. The month after Lee's execution, the *Dallas Weekly Herald* reported that Mormons were "secretly arming themselves" to protect Young from arrest for "complicity with the Mountain Meadows Massacre."[59]

Yet Young, then in his mid-seventies, was never charged. A cabinet card of Young in the 1870s is pictured in figure 5.5. Five months after John D. Lee's execution, Brigham Young died on 29 August 1877. As it published news of his death, the Baptist *Chicago Standard* declared that Young had "never been less than the tyrant of the Mormon church." The commentary then directly turned to the massacre, declaring, "If there does not cleave his soul today the deadly crime of wholesale murder in the massacre of Mountain Meadow [sic], there will forever, probably, cleave to his name the guilt of that awful slaughter, in the conviction of the American people." Unsure that God would hold Young accountable for the Mountain Meadows Massacre, the article editorialized that the American people would continue to hold him responsible—"probably" forever—and regretted that Americans had missed an opportunity to convict him before the "bar of human justice." Rather than merely supplanting ministerial power with that of the law, this editor demonstrated more faith in the American justice system than in divine justice. The editor seemed sure that the legal system could have fixed Young's damage to America if given the opportunity—if only Young been tried for the massacre "and the involved iniquities that defame his memory and disgrace his name."[60]

FIGURE 5.5 Between Lee's first trial and his second trial, the narrative of Young's participation in the massacre transformed from an insinuation to a full-blown narrative of guilt. Utah Series, President B. Young, cabinet card, taken by C. R. Savage, Salt Lake City, Utah, [1870?], Marian S. Carson Collection. Courtesy of the Library of Congress.

Even after Young's death, a number of authors continued to claim to have fresh evidence that demonstrated Young's responsibility. The *Chicago Daily Tribune* maintained his death released him from the moral "onus" of the massacre he had borne "for many years" but that if he had lived, the "onus of that massacre would [finally] have been fixed on him legally." The *Tribune* further asserted, "There has been a growing determination on the part of the Government lately to bring the old man to justice."[61] The *Daily Courant* claimed, "A Mr. L C Hughes published in the Tucson (A[rizona] T[erritory]) Star, March 27th, the special order for the massacre which was issued in 1858. The original of this order is in Hughes's possession, together with three affidavits accompanying it."[62] (The massacre occurred in 1857, not 1858.) In an alternate version, "it was dated April 19, 1858" (eight months late) and had come through Judge John Titus.[63] Baptist author Martin Oswalt assured his readers that "five true bills were secured against Young, but as his death occurred soon after, he was never brought to trial."[64] The *American Messenger* did not believe Young's death was enough. Its editors argued that "indictments brought against the Mormon Chief for inciting and directing the Mountain Meadows Massacre so involved his system" that the path of justice was to prosecute the "indictments . . . against the remaining officials at St. Lake City."[65] No such indictments or affidavits were published or are extant among voluminous court records.

The lack of official evidence did not do much to deter public opinion. Convinced of Young's guilt, most American editors assumed that God sided with them in their search for justice but lamented their inability to convict the Mormon prophet.[66] Though the *Chicago Standard* editor did not specify whom he might include in his category of "Americans" who would hold Young responsible for the massacre forever, the editor of the *Cherokee Advocate* felt it an important message to republish the claim for both his English-speaking and Cherokee-speaking audiences in Oklahoma. Many American news editors would similarly address Young's accountability in the massacre in the days following his death. The *Chicago Standard* proved to be prophetic—after John D. Lee, Brigham Young received the lion's share of popular scrutiny regarding the Mountain Meadows Massacre in the last quarter of the nineteenth century and has continued to be a primary target of popular condemnation into the present day.[67] As a result, recent Young biographer John Turner accurately calls the massacre a "dark stain . . . left on Young's reputation" and legacy.[68]

At his death, the *New York Tribune* reminded Americans "that Justice is used to being cheated, and would hardly believe her unaccustomed eyes if she would get the best of a bargain. Let it be remembered too, that the Prophet has gone with his bloody hands beyond our jurisdiction."[69] As it was, his death offered an opportunity for America to learn from its mistakes. For New York City's Congregationalist *Independent*, "Mormonism, next to slavery, [was] the crowning disgrace of [the] nation."[70] Its editors lamented that Brigham Young, "a coarse brutal tyrant," would die peacefully in his bed rather than being "shot, like Bishop Lee, who was no more guilty of the Mountain Meadows Massacre."[71] The editor loquaciously and dramatically declared the failure of America to let Young die without experiencing the weight of punitive action. Had Young, like Lee, been convicted in a court of law, the American people could have celebrated, remedying the damage he had committed against civilization. Americans inherently possessed a duty to guard against moral threats, and for the *Independent*, anything short of "punishing the man and crushing his system . . . dishonored our laws, as well as our civilization."[72]

The press continued to conflate expectations of ubiquitous Mormon violence with the Saints' defiance of American marriage conventions. Hartford, Connecticut's *Christian Secretary* reported that Brigham Young "introduced polygamy, and ruled with a strong hand, instigating or favoring at least, to further his interests, such crimes as the Mountain Meadow [sic] massacre."[73] Other news outlets followed suit, reinforcing the American public's image of Brigham Young with the themes of violence and polygamy through coercion. For the *Maine Farmer*, Young "ruled his followers by their strongest passions, and [with] his unscrupulous readiness to shed human blood, he held absolute dominion over them."[74]

The massacre played a consequential role in Young's obituaries around the nation. For some newspapers, the massacre was just one on a laundry list of Young's offenses.[75] Most sources assumed that he had ordered the massacre; as the *Chicago Daily Tribune* put it, it was "more than suspected that he was in part responsible for the horrible Mountain Meadows massacre."[76] Another *Tribune* article considered Mountain Meadows the "most terrible and notorious" of Young's crimes, but only one among many. Young's leadership, it stated, had resulted in "dark and bloody pages in the history of the Mormon occupation of Utah."[77]

The late nineteenth century featured a number of premature predictions of Mormonism's demise, as many observers argued that immigration or the railroad or various other events would sweep Mormonism out of Utah.[78] Young's death similarly became an occasion to predict the oncoming collapse of the religion.[79] A wide array of reports saw the massacre as part of the damning evidence that would put Mormonism at death's door. The *New York Tribune* proclaimed that Lee's execution "proved conclusively that the temporal power in Utah is no longer in the hands of the Latter Day Saints" despite all of Young's work.[80] Young's death "shattered the last pillar of this monstrous faith" for others.[81] For some it did not matter whether Young lived or died. If civilization were moving forward, then lesser forms of barbarity and savagery would be swept away. First, however, the narrative of Mormon guilt needed to be broadened beyond Brigham Young.

Expanding Accountability: A Multiplicity of Mormon Bishops

For many Americans, the presence of a Mormon prophet was antithetical to American ideals, but the threat of Mormon theocracy was not limited to just one man. It also included those in the prophet's inner circle. According to the *New York Times*, "the power of the Mormon hierarchy was employed to suppress the truth" of what happened at Mountain Meadows.[82] Accounts enlarged the scope of their focus to include other perpetrators besides just Young and Lee. In doing so, they sometimes fabricated ecclesiastical offices (such as Waite's Great Grand Archee) or used actual Mormon priesthood offices to focus on the undemocratic function of the Mormon church. In one account, Mormons "murdered . . . at the command of fanatical priests after the order of Melchizedek."[83] There was a similar emphasis on "grand councils" that came together to plan the massacre, and a virtually omnipresent focus on the office of bishop.[84]

In the title of Lee's autobiography, William Bishop labeled Lee a Mormon bishop—*Mormonism Unveiled; or, the Life and Confessions of Late Bishop, John D. Lee*. This was not the first source to nominate Lee a bishop. However, with his intimate knowledge of Lee, Bishop, Lee's defense attorney, knew Lee had never been a Latter-day Saint bishop. Lee had previously been a local lay ecclesiastical leader of the Saints' Branch in Harmony—a branch president, but not a bishop.[85] More than merely a semantic difference or misinformation, the title "bishop" carried the punitive weight of nineteenth-century antihierarchical thought frequently evidenced in American anti-Catholicism. The *Sacramento Record* saw Mormonism as a second, even more tyrannical, Vatican, "a power more autocratic than Rome," and did not understand why there was such hesitation to censure Mormon leaders who were "claim[ing] supreme allegiance" from adherents.[86] Though a Mormon bishop is not the hierarchical equivalent of a Catholic bishop, the implied relationship was clear.

In the burgeoning popular narrative, there were bishops all over the massacre field, including John M. Higbee, Isaac Haight, and William Stewart, the first to kill after chasing the two escaping emigrant men.[87] In Beadle's account, two Mormon bishops, Lee and Haight, met with the emigrants on the massacre field to convince them to give up their weapons, thereby opening the way for the massacre.[88] Though Isaac Haight and William Dame were involved in the decision that initiated the massacre, neither was present at Mountain Meadows during the massacre. Moreover, both were Latter-day Saint stake presidents (above the office of bishop in the Saints' hierarchy) and militia leaders, not bishops. The only current bishop at the Meadows who was directly involved in the massacre, Cedar City bishop and early confessor Philip Klingensmith, was conspicuously absent from the accounts. His status as a former Latter-day Saint who had decided to turn state's evidence limited the usability of his former title.

Moreover, a variety of different sources placed other members of the Latter-day Saint hierarchy or prominent politicians on the massacre field despite a complete absence of evidence associating them with the massacre. Ann Eliza Young situated Daniel H. Wells, a member of Young's First Presidency and lieutenant-general of the Nauvoo Legion, at the massacre, claiming he had killed "one of these babes with his own official hand."[89] Frank Triplett chose LDS apostle and Utah territorial congressional delegate

George Q. Cannon as a possible accessory after the fact "if not an adviser" of the massacre.[90] Abram Gash later picked up prosecutor Baskin's suggestion that William Hooper, another territorial congressional delegate from Utah, received the emigrants' cattle from the massacre spoils.[91]

These efforts to implicate Latter-day Saints who held ecclesiastical or governmental authority revealed that Americans' desire to prosecute Mormonism had not been quenched with the execution of Lee or the death of Young. If the Mountain Meadows Massacre was emblematic of Mormon sin, then all Mormons bore guilt, particularly those in authority. Beyond cattle, rewards and penalties were also depicted as one of the ways Young maintained allegiances within his hierarchy. Tales abounded of Mountain Meadows leaders receiving more young polygamous wives "as a reward for their valor" on the massacre field.[92] The *Chicago Daily Tribune* reported that Young had rewarded Lee, Haight, and Higbee with wives.[93] *Zion's Herald* assured its readers, "Special heavenly favors were promised to those men who took part in the affair."[94] In the same vein, the penalties for disobedience were detailed in graphic horror as a stock element of anti-Mormon tomes. Ann Eliza Young dramatically revealed, "Brigham's law was not to be broken, and the person who should venture to disregard it pronounced his own death sentence."[95]

The *New York Times* asserted Mormonism held "two cardinal principles": the infallibility of priestly leaders and a commitment to destroying all enemies of the true faith.[96] Violence sprang from these cardinal principles, which were maintained by devotion to fanatical oaths. Grisly tales of blood oaths in LDS temple rites were already an element of sensational anti-Mormon literature; some Mountain Meadows accounts built on the theme dramatically and continued to expand elaborately over time. In the anonymously authored *Crimes of the Latter Day Saints in Utah by a Mormon of 1831*, the writer's anonymity heightened the element of fear present in the narrative with the implication that it was dangerous for a Mormon to speak out against Mormonism.[97] In this purported first-person narrative, the decision to massacre the emigrants was made long before the train even arrived in Utah. Mormons disguised as Indians followed the Arkansas train across the plains and attacked them twice unsuccessfully. The emigrants shot one of the disguised Mormons in the thigh, and in his anger, he signed a pledge with blood from his wound. He drew enough blood with a fountain pen to write an oath in blood. These pretend "Indians" then participated in a Mormon "ritual." They drew "bowie knives, and placeing [sic] the blades in contact, so that the points were aimed at the written agreement," they then "repeated in unison the words, 'By God' three times, and the 'Mountain Meadow Massacre' was 'done all but doing,' as the Chief laughingly said."[98] Foreign, savage, and blasphemous oaths demonstrated the heathen nature of Mormonism as well as insinuating the inability of Mormons to be true to their oaths as American citizens.

The expanding claims of Mormon guilt found a wide audience of readers in the late 1870s, though the particular culpability of Brigham Young continued as a central theme. The *New York Times* exemplified a consistent strain of scandal surrounding Young when it argued, "Brigham Young's connection with the massacre has never been judicially established, though there is no doubt that a strong feeling has always existed in the public mind that the unfortunate emigrants met their cruel fate by his orders."[99] However, the *Times* editor's memory failed. Young's involvement had not always been assumed, and it was not until John D. Lee's first trial that belief in Young's direct involvement in the massacre at Mountain Meadows became commonly accepted. However, it would endure. It became the prosecution's most enduring success.

Epilogue
Ex Uno Disce Omnes

When Catherine V. Waite included a chapter on the Mountain Meadows Massacre in her uber-successful 1866 antipolygamy book *The Mormon Prophet and His Harem*, she defended her choice with the Latin phrase *ex uno disce omnes*—from one person learn all persons (from one we can judge the rest).[1] Though Waite's book centered on Mormon theocracy and polygamy, she saw the Mountain Meadows Massacre as the exemplar of Mormon sin, the singular example that allowed Americans to know all they needed to know about the Mormons. Waite wielded the massacre narrative to both heighten the Mormon Problem and encourage action against the Latter-day Saints. The Mormon Question demonstrated some of the limits to *e pluribus unum*; were the many to become one, the limits of Americanness had to be carefully circumscribed. Over time, the massacre narrative became a protean tool, moldable to a multitude of different problems to reinforce the limits of difference within the American project and encourage action against the Mormons. There was no need to enumerate all of the religion's crimes; the Mountain Meadows Massacre was emblematic of the rest.

The foundation of the popular narrative was in a sufficiently terrible event. Historians do not dispute most basic details of the massacre. With the discourse of civilization as text, a popular Mountain Meadows narrative unfurled with great alacrity in predictable directions for postbellum Americans defining White civilization, citizenship, and Americanness with few objections other than from the Latter-day Saints themselves. Within the massacre discourse, the narratives of Mormon savagery, contested Whiteness and exceptionalism, repudiated manhood, and despotic theocracy demonstrated the American boundaries of civilization, with the Mormons clearly positioned beyond those limits. As with many of the nineteenth-century authors enamored with the massacre story, motivations were often more complex than mere lucre, though profitability certainly added to its appeal.

As a public sensation, John D. Lee's first trial built on the elements of the popular discourse, reinforced it, and expanded it, igniting already present fervor against the Mormons even as trial testimony offered important facts to establish the particulars of the massacre. Mormons could either throw off their dangerous religion or be expelled from the American empire so civilization's incursions could be healed. John D. Lee's execution did not satiate the public yearning for justice. Though the narrative was generally focused on the punishment of the guilty participants at Mountain Meadows, a lack of punishment also served the narrative, perhaps even more effectively. Despite years of continuing cases against other indicted massacre participants and official talk of a continuing prosecution, nothing substantial would be accomplished through legal channels after John D. Lee's execution. The absence of a comprehensive Mountain Meadows prosecution left yet another gap in which the popular narrative sprouted and then flourished. For the more bellicose authors, the blustering developed into 1870s calls for Mormon extermination. Similar calls had been heard in the immediate aftermath of the massacre, but the popular response surged even more forcefully with Lee's execution in 1877 and when Brigham Young died later that year.

Strident and harrowing discourse further separated Mormons from White civilization, yet they were still considered part of it. Despite threatening rhetoric, the only state action against the Mormons would be legislative. Onerous legislative strictures—as Patrick Mason coined, "disciplinary democracy"—gave Latter-day Saints the opportunity to reform and return to civilization.[2] Yet in the latter half of the nineteenth century, the extreme rhetoric against Mormons was not backed up with violence, expulsion, or eradication, despite an ingrained American tradition of violently dealing with minorities. The Saints shared experiences with other minority groups likewise racialized, disenfranchised, and ostracized. However, as Angela Pulley Hudson reminds us, "there is no Mormon Trail of Tears."[3] At a time when much of America focused on "reforging the white republic" and defining the relationship between citizens and their government after the Civil War, the Saints ended up better off than Black and native peoples who were lynched and exterminated.[4] If the Mormons were initially White, then they still had the potential to change. Despite calls for vigilantism against the Mormons and individual violence against Latter-day Saints in the South, most of the violent bombast lingered solely to encourage government action.[5] White privilege existed even amid severe prejudice and harsh rhetoric.

In 1889, as the prolific historian Hubert H. Bancroft published his *History of Utah: 1540–1886*, he acknowledged that it was "largely a history of the Mormons, these being the first white people to settle in the country." There was value in their Whiteness. In contrast to the many sensational accounts of the Mormons, Bancroft—or his assistant Alfred Bates, whose work he quoted without attribution—endeavored "in a spirit of equity to present both sides, leaving the reader to draw his own conclusions." The massacre earned a chapter in Bancroft's history and resulted in an attempt at balance that would remain a central massacre source for decades.[6] Bancroft's moderating tone both reflected and contributed to a broader softening of rhetoric against the Saints. Then after decades of increasingly severe congressional censures on the Latter-day Saint Church and widespread prosecution of its people, Church president Wilford Woodruff announced a disavowal of polygamy in 1890. After the renunciation, Utah gained statehood in 1896. The official legal action for the massacre ended at Utah statehood after nearly forty years.

However, Mountain Meadows narratives continued to thrive on embellished fictional elements as they told the story of the Meadows. Moreover, the novels published near the turn of the century novels provided a particularly effective medium to weave in all the threads of the Mountain Meadows discourse. In 1899, former Utah attorney Abram Gash published *The False Star*, a novel that found its heart in Mountain Meadows and the prosecution for the massacre. Gash was one of a long line of Utah federal appointees who sought to warn the country of the Mormon menace as lucratively as possible. Part of a significant strain of novels based on rumors of surviving children who were not returned to their families in 1859, the center of the story is a little girl in a white dress pictured on the frontispiece and in figure 6.1. In Gash's narrative, when the Mormons raised a white flag on the massacre field to parley with the emigrants, one emigrant held up a "little baby girl, dressed in white" as their white flag.[7] The beautiful girl was saved from the massacre but had not been returned with the other children. She was held back for nefarious polygamic intentions and adopted by a Mormon family. Predictably, the moralistic and winding romance focused on overt themes of danger mirroring earlier Mountain Meadows narrative tropes. The little girl in the white dress stood emblematic of why civilization needed to be guarded and circumscribed, playing a role not unlike the figure of female purity in John Nast's popular painting *American Progress*. However, ultimately the little girl could see through the deception. She ran away from a hoary bishop attempting to court her and married her (age-appropriate) love. Together they escaped shadowy southern Utah for the golden state of California—the promised land.

A few years later, author Harry Leon Wilson, one of Bancroft's former assistants, published another novel, *The Lions of the Lord*. Wilson quit his job at the popular magazine *Puck* to write *Lions*, his second book. Both Bancroft and *Puck* had spent considerable time publishing about the Latter-day Saints, and Wilson stuck with what he knew. *The Lions of the Lord*'s main character,

THE FLAG OF TRUCE AT MOUNTAIN MEADOW.

FIGURE 6.1 In this fictional retelling of the massacre, a little girl in a white dress became the flag of truce and then the romantic protagonist seeking to break free from the confines of Mormonism. Gash, *False Star*, frontispiece. Courtesy of L. Tom Perry Special Collections, Harold B. Lee Library, Brigham Young University, Provo.

Joel Rae, is born a Latter-day Saint and is a devoted follower. Some of Bancroft's efforts at balance are manifest in the compassion shown his Mormon protagonist and the level of detail included in this "romance in a romance." However, the larger narrative continued multiple elements of the discourse centered on young Mormons reforming or leaving Mormonism.[8] Pretended "heavenly sanction," participation in the massacre, and a found Bible of a former love and massacre victim led to authentic divine sanction for Joel Rae on the massacre field—"a flood of light seemed to shine upon his mind." This was the beginning of Rae's long journey out of Utah and Mormonism. The narrative ends hopeful that Joel Rae is not the only one who might take up that journey—certainly this should be Mormonism's death knell. Novels employing the narrative of the massacre continued to increase, as did dime novels. Some of those dime novels included a new incarnation of Buffalo Bill's Wild West Show, *The Buffalo Bill Stories*. (This life for Buffalo Bill's stories would endure through the 1960s.)[9]

Resurrecting Lee's Confessions

As demonstrated by another major controversy a decade later, the Mormon Question would not be definitively answered in the nineteenth century.[10] From 1903 to 1907, a broad coalition of Protestant organizations challenged the seating of Reed Smoot, a Latter-day Saint apostle who had recently been elected as a U.S. senator from Utah. The popular press revived the Mountain Meadows narrative with much zeal. One such illustration is found in figure 6.2. Kathleen Flake notes that it did not affect the congressional debates directly; it merely provided grist for the sensational newspaper campaign.[11] However, the grist multiplied.[12]

In early 1905, a *Washington Times* magazine headline read, "How 1,500,000 American Women Are Fighting Mormonism." The article profiled the work of the National League of Women's Organizations against the Mormons. They were among those who originally petitioned the Senate for an investigation of Reed Smoot and engaged an attorney to join in the fight against Smoot's seating. As part of that historical moment, journalist Alfred Henry Lewis resurrected John D. Lee's confessions almost thirty years after their original publication with *The Mormon Menace*. The National League of Women's Organizations published the first edition of Lewis's "powerful arraignment of Mormonism," and any proceeds from the sale of the books were to go to "protecting the country from the treasonable teachings and practice of Mormonism."[13] Lewis also published an abridged version in pamphlet

FIGURE 6.2 In this *Puck* cartoon, a bearded patriarch donning his "Mormon Hierarchy" hat drops his Reed Smoot puppet through the Senate door. The patriarch's patchwork coat incorporated a polygamy sleeve, while the lower flank of the coat exemplified rumors of Mormon violence. The Mountain Meadows Massacre patch on his thigh reminds the reader of not only the violent potential of the Mormons, but their violent history. "The Real Objection to Smoot," *Puck*, 27 April 1904. Courtesy of the Library of Congress.

form. He asserted that "in the name of Mormon safety," Brigham Young had suppressed Lee's *Confessions* when originally published. Ignoring the dozens of editions of *Mormonism Unveiled* published between 1877 and 1905, Lewis asserted that he had obtained this rare, buried confession in order to bring it before the reading public. "At least two volumes escaped," wrote Lewis. "These have been placed in my hand by certain patriotic influences." Though the book's chapters appear nearly unaltered from *Mormonism Unveiled*, Lewis claimed he could not publish the text as originally produced. Rather, like those before him and those who would follow, it was his duty to expurgate "much that was shocking and atrocious," making the volume fit for "modest ears and eyes."[14] Mountain Meadows still represented Mormonism as a whole. Young was no different than the current Church president, Joseph F. Smith—"a black kitten makes a black cat."[15]

As the congressional debates over the seating of senator-elect Smoot finally waned in 1907, Arkansas senator James H. Berry argued against allowing Smoot to take up his elected role. Berry pulled out the Mountain Meadows narrative in a last-ditch effort, but it failed.[16] After four long years of testimony, the Senate finally voted to seat Smoot. Yet Alfred Henry Lewis's concern only heightened when the controversy over Smoot quelled. A few years later, Lewis wrote another Mormon exposé, a three-part series for *Cosmopolitan* magazine titled "The Viper on the Hearth."[17] Parroting U.S. Attorney General Charles Devens's argument in the Supreme Court polygamy test case, *Reynolds*, decades earlier, Lewis argued that massacres like Mountain Meadows would happen "in every corner" of America if Mormons were given the chance.[18] If left alone, as the Latter-day Saints wanted and America seemed to be content to do, then the "Mormon Church might in any campaign be easily strong enough to make or mar a White House."[19] A century later, some might consider Lewis prophetic.

Modulating the Narrative

In the post-Smoot years, the American public was not suddenly wholeheartedly supportive of the Mormons, but many were now willing to reserve judgment. The Mountain Meadows story would continue to be resurrected as a potent anti-Mormon tool that doubled as entertainment—as with Jack London's 1921 Mountain Meadows narrative in *The Star Rover* we discussed in the introduction. Mormons were still considered deceptive, and some authors would continue to warn Americans to be wary. But for the most part, America and the Mormons settled into an uneasy truce.

Cristine Hutchinson-Jones labels 1917 to 1942 a period of "moderating stereotypes" for Mormonism in the American mind. The image of Latter-day Saints began to fluctuate as Americans came together to celebrate pioneer spirit and revel in patriotism for wars won. Representations of Mormonism began to shift between wholly negative to more pragmatic and sometimes even positive assessments.[20] The narrative of Mountain Meadows would likewise begin to evolve, if ever so slightly. The 1930s marked the beginning of a movement toward a more nuanced view of the massacre. Though authors were still repeating some significant tropes of the sensational narrative, they were also beginning to place the massacre in its larger American context. Past persecutions of the Mormons became important to the narrative, and—building on Bancroft's lead—the narrative no longer blamed all Latter-day Saints for the actions of a few. The extreme sensationalism of the latter part of the nineteenth and early twentieth centuries was left behind, at least for some. These changes began to allow Mountain Meadows to recede into the larger myth of the American West.[21] Then, in 1950, Juanita Brooks published the most complete history of the event to date, *The Mountain Meadows Massacre*. A Latter-day Saint teacher from southern Utah, Brooks felt a compulsion pushing her to work on the massacre. Denied access by the church to some sources, nevertheless Brooks crafted a thorough account of the massacre. Her work would stand as the history of the Meadows for more than a half century.[22]

A Twenty-First-Century Return

Replicating the historical popularity of the Mountain Meadows Massacre, the massacre has been a recent popular topic of attention with yet another gush of books, both history and exposé, as well as entertainment through television, novels, and film produced since the turn of the twenty-first century. As of this writing, Latter-day Saints have transitioned from an Other not capable of American citizenship to the epitome of American patriotism for some—yet the attention to Mountain Meadows endures. Some of the works have been historical attempts to better understand a contested narrative, but others have wielded Mountain Meadows as a weapon in anti-Mormon works. It has once again become a foundation for fictional forays and a consistent element in new political tomes. For some, the general shape of the Mountain Meadows Massacre narrative has not changed, nor has the desire to use the Meadows as shorthand for larger issues with Mormonism.[23]

In 2002, the *New York Times* ran a subline that looked like it was straight out of the nineteenth century: "New Accusations that Brigham Young

Himself Ordered an 1857 Massacre of Pioneers."[24] The article considered two new histories whose indictment of Young for the massacre hadn't changed much from the nineteenth century: Will Bagley's *Blood of the Prophets: Brigham Young and the Massacre at Mountain Meadows* and Sally Denton's *American Massacre: The Tragedy at Mountain Meadows* which relied on Bagley's work. For Bagley, Brigham Young drenched nineteenth-century Utah in blood as the mastermind behind the massacre. Denton likewise saw Young at the center of the massacre, though she focused on greed as the impetus for the massacre. Both write a compelling story as they spend their time replaying nineteenth-century tropes about the massacre.[25]

One of the most successful to date, Jon Krakauer's *Under the Banner of Heaven: A Story of Violent Faith*, was on the *New York Times* bestseller list for months when published in 2003, and sales remain steady two decades after its publication. (A limited television series based on the book appeared in the spring of 2022.)[26] Krakauer weaves together a dazzling litany of sensational Mormon-adjacent moments: the grisly 1984 Utah murders of a young mother and her baby by two fundamentalist Mormon brothers and political extremists, earlier excommunicated by the Latter-day Saints; the 2002 kidnapping of Elizabeth Smart; and fundamentalist polygamy—with a walk-through Mormon history, including a chapter on the massacre. Written in the aftermath of 9/11, he uses the narrative to point to the deficiencies of all religion, particularly religion's capacity for extremism, and to implicitly warn against a specific Mormon inclination to violence.[27] The narrative of the massacre remains a flexible tool ready to morph to address a wide spectrum of concerns.

The massacre narrative continues to flourish for a variety of reasons. Today Latter-day Saint politicians are common on the national stage, but in 2008 the threat of a Latter-day Saint U.S. presidential candidate was relatively new. Then the presence of an actual Latter-day Saint presidential candidate in 2012 gave the Mountain Meadows narrative additional new life.[28] The rise of digital printing expanded that rise, giving many individuals wary of the Mormons a personal megaphone. For some, the massacre remains the primary signal of Mormon heresy disguised as a political threat.[29] For others, it still exemplifies the possibility for Mormon violence and religious extremism—the conspicuous 9/11 date of the massacre emboldens labels of domestic terrorism and engenders more suspicion.[30] For one commentator, the massacre provides clear evidence of the Mormon potential for theological radicalism and underscores the need to amend the U.S. Constitution and establish a religious test for office in the United States.[31] Another author finds the source of xenophobic Arizona immigration laws in the legacy of the massacre.[32]

In response to some of these accounts, beginning in 2001 the LDS Church demonstrated a willingness to examine the massacre in detail for the first time. With massive institutional support, two church historians and a Brigham Young University professor published *Massacre at Mountain Meadows: An American Tragedy* in 2008. Richard Turley, one of the authors and then managing director of the Church History Department for the Latter-day Saints, called Mountain Meadows "the darkest chapter in Latter-day Saint history." He proposed that "candid evaluation of that tragedy can produce catharsis—a cleansing spiritual renewal among those who still feel the wounds from this mid-nineteenth century event." He added that the authors (and presumably the larger institutional church) were "anxious to tell the story of the massacre fully and completely." Another historian suggested that "despite the suspicion and guilt that still linger[ed] among a few descendants on both sides [of the massacre], an environment now exists where honest inquiry can take place."[33] It had been more than a century since any explicit church-sponsored confrontation of Mountain Meadows.[34]

On 11 September 2007, the one-hundred-and-fiftieth anniversary of the massacre, the Church participated with hundreds of descendants of both massacre victims and perpetrators in a memorial for the massacre. Latter-day Saint apostle Henry B. Eyring spoke of the support and freedom given to the *Massacre at Mountain Meadows* authors to uncover the history of the massacre. He then spoke of the massacre, "The truth, as we have come to know it, saddens us deeply. The gospel of Jesus Christ that we espouse, abhors the cold-blooded killing of men, women, and children. Indeed, it advocates peace and forgiveness. What was done here long ago by members of our Church represents a terrible and inexcusable departure from Christian teaching and conduct. We cannot change what happened, but we can remember and honor those who were killed here." And offered an apology: "We express profound regret for the massacre carried out in this valley 150 years ago today and for the undue and untold suffering experienced by the victims then and by their relatives to the present time." He continued, "A separate expression of regret is owed to the Paiute people who have unjustly borne for too long the principal blame for what occurred during the massacre. Although the extent of their involvement is disputed, it is believed they would not have participated without the direction and stimulus provided by local Church leaders and members." This stands in stark contrast to the efforts of the Church to deny, ignore, or work to cover up the massacre in the nineteenth century, but will it change the popular narrative of the massacre?

THE CONTEXT HAS TRANSFORMED over the last century. In salacious nineteenth-century novels and melodramas, writers racialized Mormon savagery and contested the nature of Mormon Whiteness; today, perhaps Mitt Romney is too White.[35] However, some elements have modulated along with popular discourse. An implicit part of some earlier critiques was that Mormons looked acceptable, but behind that familiarity lay something or someone dangerous. This thread of Mormon duplicity endures. Mitt Romney could now be also considered *too* nice. Even the story of Broadway's *Book of Mormon* musical revolves around Mormon "niceness." Questioning Mormon religiosity and Mormon Americanness is a well-established pastime. The circumstances may be different, and some of the extensive grammar of a nineteenth-century discourse of civilization lost, but these sources suggest that Mountain Meadows continues to be a malleable tool employed by some to warn against the Mormons.

In the fall of 2007, the motion picture *September Dawn* was released, depicting angelic emigrants, snarling Mormons, and secret Mormon temple rituals. There was also a "romance within a romance" — once more a couple found love in the middle of the Mountain Meadows Massacre, proclaiming a "time to die in the name of God."[36] The film's cloning of anti-Mormon novels of more than a century earlier did not play well. Critics panned its heavy-handedness and anachronisms. The *New York Post*'s Kyle Smith asked, "Why does this film even exist?" Unimpressed by the hackneyed tale, Roger Ebert noted that the "strange, unpleasant movie" was "at pains to point out that on another Sept. 11, another massacre again took place, again spawned by religion." He added, "If there is a blessing it is that the film is so bad."[37]

In contrast, Netflix's 2018 limited series *Godless* offers compelling and nuanced storytelling augmented by gorgeous cinematography, and it met with a much-improved reception. Instantly recognizable as a Western, *Godless* opens to a bloody 1884 scene of a vengeful fictional massacre which laid waste the town of Creede, Colorado. The camera narrows the wide-angle shot to focus on a seventeen-year-old girl, the sole survivor of the atrocity, singing a plaintive melody, "It Is a Mystery in My Soul," as she cradles a dead man in her lap.[38] A stolid marshal drops to his knees at the sight of a young boy's lifeless body hanged on a pipe filler. So thorough was the perpetrators' quest for vengeance on a city that was about to hang two of their train-robbing comrades that they slaughtered the whole town—men, women, and children. This is a violent West of carnage and mayhem.[39]

The antagonist, Frank Griffin, and his band of rogues have been terrorizing Colorado as they move across the state robbing mining operations. Griffin is often mistaken for a preacher with his cadence of scripture, his clerical collar, and his flat-brimmed hat despite his "unusual" thoughts on religion—including that the original Garden of Eden was in Missouri. Griffin views himself as a visionary prophet who has seen his own death. In an astonishing breach, a church congregation sings the hymn "Nearer My God to Thee," and Griffin barges into the service on his horse, replacing the preacher on the dais (still on his horse), and questioning the congregants' righteousness as he brazenly demands their loyalty.[40] He consistently recites from "the good book"—but it isn't usually the Bible he's quoting. Feigning markers of religiosity and kindness, he shields his most menacing actions.

Though the audience may be unaware, Griffin's story is intricately connected to the Mountain Meadows Massacre—it is the source of his evil. The foundational elements of *Godless* appear as a meticulously tailored and moving expansion of many of the popular tales of the Mormon massacre that once swirled throughout the United States and beyond. In the story, Griffin's counterfeit religion of violence must be eradicated for the mythic West to thrive. The most significant difference here is that Scott Frank wrote *Godless* not in the nineteenth century, but in the twenty-first. Overthrowing Griffin and his violent stranglehold on the land becomes the central goal of the narrative—one that allows all outside his gang to unite against a common foe. NPR's Terry Gross called Griffin "a great villain," and the series earned twelve Emmy nominations and three wins.[41]

The context of this Mountain Meadows story has changed, but facets of the discourse of civilization remain embedded in the American experience. In this view, Mormons still need to be punished. *Godless* offers nuance in aspects of the Western genre but not in its indictment of the Mormons. Though it is more than a century and a half removed from the original event and absent the heavy-handedness of its predecessors, ultimately the discourse tells the same story: Mormonism is not true religion, not true Christianity, and something dangerous lurks behind the feigned niceness. However, this time it is subtle—the word "Mormon" is never uttered. In the second episode, the story reveals that as a child, Griffin had "come up west on a wagon train." Things were "going just fine" until the party reached a place called Mountain Meadows in Utah Territory. There his "mammy and pappy and most everybody else" were massacred "by Indians, it looked like"—until their war paint washed off in the creek. These were not Indians, but men "from Salt Lake . . . men of religion, they say." The Mormons orphaned Griffin in the 1857 Mountain Meadows Massacre.[42]

Rather than being returned to extended family with the rest of the orphaned children, Frank survived the massacre to be adopted by Mormon leader Isaac Haight, his "new pappy." Haight, who played a central role in murdering Frank's parents, preached a counterfeit gospel that "required blood to purify." On the massacre field, Haight preached that killing the emigrant company would offer "eternal salvation" to the murdered Gentiles—their slaughter was a "means of grace." The fake religion of Mormonism caused White men to devolve from civilization to become savages. Mormons were "playing Indian" by raping women, smashing babies' heads on wagon wheels, stealing gold and cattle, and wearing war paint. Rather than hating the man who murdered his family, Frank "learned to love" Haight and his counterfeit teachings of love with "a stick and a bullwhip and a knife."

What was not obvious to most viewers is how *Godless* replayed nineteenth- and early twentieth-century concerns of American identity, authentic religion, Christian boundaries, and the dangers of Mormonism. The Mountain Meadows Massacre did happen "IRL" (in real life), as one columnist reported when the series aired.[43] Frank incorporated elements of the popular massacre narrative that had been presented as factual into his account.[44] He unwittingly replicated a litany of massacre tropes, so that *Godless* ended up steeped in American stereotypes about Mormons. "Frank [Griffin] is the dark core of the story."[45] This implicitly communicates the singularity of Mormon violence and the need for its eradication. Though Griffin's evil is not innate, he is too steeped in the religion of violence to escape. For Frank there is no redemption.

In contrast to implicit critique of the Mormons in *Godless*, the 2022 limited series adaptation of Jon Krakauer's *Under the Banner of Heaven* created by Dustin Lance Black returns to a heavy-handed dark and foreboding narrative befitting its chosen true-crime genre. A tale of Mormon sin, the narrative is a curious mix of a nineteenth-century sensational novel and a twenty-first-century faith crisis circling two horrific 1984 murders: that of a modern Mormon woman and her baby girl. The woman unknowingly married into an increasingly more extreme and dangerous family of Mormon patriarchs. The patriarchs' growing beards demonstrate their exit from the mainstream Latter-day Saint church and their extreme devotion. Though the series reworked some of Krakauer's deficiencies, as it moved back and forth between the Mormon past and 1984's present it leaned into many nineteenth-century tropes of Mormon violence while expanding some for the twenty-first century. Everyone speaks in a constant wave of scripture and communicates directly with God. Violence begets violence. Historical rumors evolve into established fact. Following Krakauer's book and revealing Mormonism's dangerous roots, Brigham Young claimed to receive a revelation and God commanded that the Mormons kill "140 people." Moreover, this version extends Young's violence and accountability by insinuating that Young was previously involved in Joseph Smith's death. In this retelling, there were no Paiutes at the massacre; the Mormons were the only ones on the field. Though John D. Lee recruited the Paiutes to initially attack the emigrants, here the Paiutes rejected Lee and chose peace. Rather than the nineteenth-century narratives that saw the Mormons *as savage* as the Indians, or *hypersavage*—more savage than the Indians after the massacre—here the Mormons are the *only* savages. In *Banner's* present, a Mormon bishop longingly looks back to the 1857 massacre. As the series ends, Mountain Meadows once again becomes the ultimate marker of Mormon deficiencies, securely developing the series thesis that Mormonism "breeds dangerous men."[46] Whatever the year—1844, 1857, or 1984—Mormon men will act as they've been conditioned to act, with violence. For *Banner* these are not exceptions, aberrations, or extremists. Mountain Meadows is still shorthand for the whole of the Mormon Problem.

The Mormons are no longer litigated against as a whole. For the Latter-day Saints, there was some redemption in the eyes of other Americans, though never as much as the Saints expect. At present, the situation is a curious sort of détente, with Mormons being regarded as a "model minority" on the one hand and viewed as hiding the potential to commit horrific atrocity on the other. The violence Latter-day Saints perpetrated at the Mountain Meadows is a point in common with a long history of American violence, part and parcel of a bloody nineteenth century, a point that deserves continued interrogation and requires accountability. Latter-day Saints and Americans were more alike than either group wanted to recognize. Yet it is always easier to blame an Other than to recognize its familiarity. For some, this singular tragic event remains a tool—*ex uno disce omnes*—shaped to American anxieties and fears to punish Mormon transgressions.

Acknowledgments

As my path in academia has been rather circuitous, the number of people who have encouraged, sustained, and aided me has multiplied with each bend in my path traveled over years. I don't think it possible to thank everyone adequately. I am grateful for all, named and unnamed.

Several different archival collections have been essential to this work. The remarkable and daunting collection at the National Archives and Records Administration both in Washington, D.C., and College Park, Maryland, was vital—despite the sense at times that I might be circling Dante's inferno. A number of individuals in the Pioche Country Courthouse, the Beaver County Recorder's Office, and the Fifth District Court in Beaver City, Utah, gave me access to their backrooms, basements, and vaults to find documents long thought lost. Archivists, current and now retired, at several depositories went above and beyond their regular scope of duties to help me. I cannot begin to name all of those at the LDS Church History Library in Salt Lake City, Utah, who have provided research assistance, friendship, and feedback. Janet Seegmiller and Paula Mitchell at the Leavitt Special Collections of the Gerald R. Sherratt Library at Southern Utah University; Peter Blodgett at the Huntington Library in San Marino, California; Brandon Metcalf then at the Utah State Archives, Salt Lake City, Utah; and Russ Taylor, John Murphy, Cindy Brightenburg, and so many others at the BYU's L. Tom Perry Special Collections have all kindly and astutely helped augment my research.

I began working on the history of the Mountain Meadows Massacre as a research assistant for the generous Ron Walker in 2001. After several months, I left to continue my graduate education at Vanderbilt University's Divinity School. I didn't feel done with Mountain Meadows but never supposed that after a two-year hiatus I would return to the massacre for more than two decades. I am grateful for Richard E. Turley's role directing that return, offering me my own—ever expanding—project and being a consistent example of faith and dedication. LaJean Purcell Carruth's miraculous work to transcribe nineteenth-century Pitman shorthand provided one of the most fruitful of sources, John D. Lee's trial transcripts. Brian Reeves and Chad Foulger were my men Friday, helping me mine the depths of the Mountain Meadows Massacre Research Files, pointing me to obscure sources I read three years previously but hadn't seen since, and consistently encouraging me in my continued journey. Richard and Claudia Bushman, the late Truman Madsen, the late Stephen Robinson, Carol Madsen, Jessie Embry, Kathleen Flake, and Laurie Maffly-Kipp have all mentored me at critical junctures along my winding path. My colleagues at Brigham Young University's Neal A. Maxwell Institute for Religious Scholarship offered me my first academic home, acted as valuable conversation partners to help me continue to develop as a scholar, and cemented my knowledge that I have a contribution to make.

Amid the more ordinary pandemic experiences of baking sourdough bread and getting a dog, the pandemic allowed me to clear my desk, return to this manuscript, and finally move it toward publication. Elaine Maisner quickly replied to my book proposal with encouragement, and I have not regretted the choice I made to go with the University of North Carolina Press. My UNC editor, Andrew Winters, has been a delight. I appreciate the work of all those at UNC Press who will have contributed to this book, as well as the donor whose contribution will enable this book to reach more people.

George Lewis, James Campbell, Randall Stephens, and my two anonymous UNC readers all read the full manuscript at different stages and aided me as I refined my argument and shaped the manuscript. Various other scholarly friends read and commented on portions of the manuscript. My editor, Jana Riess, has an ability to incisively see a book. She helped me, as I worried about how well my brain functioned after a concussion, to refine my voice, tighten my argument, and make the book accessible to a larger audience.

My friends and family near and far, new and old, have consistently motivated and strengthened me with their late-night surprise visits, packages in the post, cases of Diet Coke, last-minute proofreading, encouraging words over shared meals, illuminating chats, and entertaining breaks. Walks with my sweet dog, Luna, have cleared my head and sharpened my thinking. My parents, Doris and Severin, gave me a foundation of faith as they taught me to think and to work; they continue to sustain me all along the way. Emblematic of my familial support, this last Sunday, my four siblings, Jessica, Jared, Jeremy, and Jackie, and my parents made the trek with me to the hallowed ground that is the Mountain Meadows valley. I will not soon forget the memory of our walking that hallowed ground together.

June 2022

Notes

Source Abbreviations

BYU	L. Tom Perry Special Collections, Harold B. Lee Library, Brigham Young University, Provo, Utah
CCF 31–40	Criminal case files 31–40, Utah State Archives, Salt Lake City, Utah
CHL	Church History Library, The Church of Jesus Christ of Latter-day Saints, Salt Lake City, Utah
Huntington Library	Huntington Library, San Marino, California
JDLT1 (or T2)	Manuscript comparison of four trial transcripts. Comparison of: United States v. John D. Lee. First and Second Trials. Josiah Rogerson Shorthand Notes and Josiah Rogerson Transcript. Josiah Rogerson, Transcripts and notes of John D. Lee trials, 1875–85. CHL, July 1875 and August 1876; United States v. John D. Lee. First and Second Trials. Jacob S. Boreman Transcripts. Jacob S. Boreman Collection, Huntington Library, San Marino, CA, July 1875 and August 1876. mountainmeadowsmassacre.org/legal#supp
LofC	Library of Congress, Washington, D.C.
MMMCLP	Richard E. Turley, Janiece Johnson, and LaJean Purcell Carruth, eds. *The Mountain Meadows Massacre Collected Legal Papers* (Norman: University of Oklahoma Press, 2017).
Mss SDoc 42	Messages of the President, Numbers 10 and 42, 36th Congress, Manuscript, Papers Pertaining to the Territory of Utah, 1849–1870, Records of the U.S. Senate, RG 46, NARA.
NARA	National Archives and Record Association, Washington, D.C., and College Park, Maryland
SDoc 42	Message of the President of the United States, *Communicating, in Compliance with a Resolution of the Senate, Information in Relation to the Massacre at Mountain Meadows, and Other Massacres in Utah Territory,* Senate Executive Document No. 42, 36th Congress, 1st sess., *Message of the President of the United States*, S. Doc. No. 36-42 (1860).
Utah State Archives	Utah State Archives, Salt Lake City, Utah

Prologue

1. C. J. S., 25 March 1877, in "Shooting of Lee!," *Salt Lake Daily Tribune*, 30 March 1877.

2. "The Lee Execution, *New York Herald*, 25 March 1877; Josiah Rogerson to *Deseret News*, 22 March 1877, CHL; "M. M. M. Additional Particulars of the Execution," *Salt Lake Daily Herald*, 25 March 1877.

3. Annie Hoge, "Testimony," JDLT1:13, 18.

4. "The Last of Lee," *Salt Lake Daily Tribune*, 24 March 1877.

5. Rogerson, "Speech of John D. Lee at Mountain Meadows," 23 March 1877.

6. "The Last of Lee," *Salt Lake Daily Tribune*, 24 March 1877.

7. Rogerson, "Speech of John D. Lee at Mountain Meadows," 23 March 1877.

8. Lewis, *Mormon Menace*.

Introduction

1. "Rumored Massacre on the Plains," *Los Angeles Daily Star*, 3 October 1857.

2. "Public Meeting," *Los Angeles Daily Star*, 13 October 1857; "Resoluciones. Adoptadas Por Una Junta Del Pueblo. Sobre El Asesinato de Los Emigrantes Cerca Del Lago Salado," *El Clamor Público*, 17 October 1857.

3. Ekins, *Defending Zion*.

4. "The Mormon Murders," *Daily Alta California*, 28 October 1857.

5. "Mormon Murders."

6. Turley, Johnson, and Carruth, *Mountain Meadows Massacre Collected Legal Papers*.

7. Mason, *Mormon Menace*, 6.

8. Douglas, *Remarks of the Hon. Stephen A. Douglas*.

9. For additional background, see Hafen and Hafen, *Utah Expedition, 1857-58*; MacKinnon, *At Sword's Point*; Moorman and Sessions, *Camp Floyd and the Mormons*; Walker, "Buchanan, Popular Sovereignty."

10. Walker, Turley, and Leonard, *Massacre at Mountain Meadows*, 101-15.

11. Ulrich, "Runaway Wives, 1830-1860."

12. Walker, Turley, and Leonard, *Massacre at Mountain Meadows*, 109-28; Brooks, *Mountain Meadows Massacre*, 46-47.

13. Walker, Turley, and Leonard, *Massacre at Mountain Meadows* 136; Brooks, *Mountain Meadows Massacre*, 31-32.

14. Walker, Turley, and Leonard, *Massacre at Mountain Meadows*, 129-49.

15. Walker, Turley, and Leonard, 141-48.

16. Walker, Turley, and Leonard, 59-61.

17. Walker, Turley, and Leonard, 149-65.

18. Walker, Turley, and Leonard, 145-48.

19. Walker, Turley, and Leonard, *Massacre at Mountain Meadows*, 149-52; Brooks, *Mountain Meadows Massacre*, 69-70.

20. Walker, Turley, and Leonard, *Massacre at Mountain Meadows*, 154-57; Brooks, *Mountain Meadows Massacre*, 53-54.

21. Walker, Turley, and Leonard, *Massacre at Mountain Meadows*, 157-59.

22. Walker, Turley, and Leonard, 159-61.

23. Walker, Turley, and Leonard, 161-65.

24. Walker, Turley, and Leonard, 166-79.

25. Walker, Turley, and Leonard, 151-54.

26. Bradshaw, "Testimony," JDLT1:1162–63.
27. Walker, Turley, and Leonard, *Massacre at Mountain Meadows*, 179–90.
28. Walker, Turley, and Leonard, 180.
29. Walker, Turley, and Leonard, *Massacre at Mountain Meadows*, 199–211; Brooks, *Mountain Meadows Massacre*, 73–83.
30. Scholars of violence consistently debate the precise definition of massacre. Most scholars conform to the *Oxford English Dictionary* definition, which dictates that a massacre comprises "the indiscriminate and brutal slaughter of people or (less commonly) animals; carnage, butchery, slaughter in numbers; an instance of this." Within the current academic discourse, Benjamin Madley defines massacres as "largely one-sided intentional killings of five or more non-combatants or relatively poorly armed or disarmed combatants, often in surprise." Madley's definition is both operable and useful and will be used throughout this project while still acknowledging the complexity of the term. Scholars now agree that 120 persons were murdered, and therefore this work uses the term "massacre" freely. Dwyer and Ryan, "Introduction," xii: Madley, "Tactics of Nineteenth-Century Colonial Massacres," 138.
31. "The Massacre at Mountain Meadows, Utah Territory," *Harper's Weekly* 3:137 (13 August 1859): 1–2; Horace Greeley, "Brigham Young's Religion, Wealth, Wives, Etc.," *Harper's Weekly*, 3:140 (3 September 1859), 561–62.
32. "Mormonism (Jack-in-the-Box)," Charles W. Carter Collection, CHL.
33. Wilson, "Alexander Wilson to Jacob Thompson," 4 March 1859; Cradlebaugh, "Charge to the Grand Jury," 8 March 1859; Cradlebaugh, "Cradlebaugh Dismissal of Grand Jury," 21 March 1859; Cradlebaugh, "Explanation of Grand Jury Dismissal," 4 April 1859; Wilson, "Jacob Thompson to Alexander Wilson," 25 April 1859; Black, "Jeremiah S. Black to Alfred Cumming," 17 May 1859; Cradlebaugh and Sinclair, "John Cradlebaugh and Charles Sinclair to James Buchanan," 16 July 1859; Black, "Alexander Wilson to Jeremiah S. Black," 30 June 1859; Cradlebaugh, "John Cradlebaugh to James Buchanan," 3 June 1859; Eckels, "Delana R. Eckels to Lewis Cass," 27 September 1859; Wilson, "Alexander Wilson to Jeremiah S. Black," 15 November 1859; Cumming, "Alfred Cumming to Lewis Cass," 2 February 1860.
34. As the general editor of the *Mountain Meadows Massacre Complete Legal Papers*, I worked with my team to gather and prepare a complete history of the official investigation and prosecution for the massacre from 1857 to 1890 by searching archives across the United States. Sources were found in a wide swath of repositories, but a considerable segment of the records were found in Utah State Archives in Salt Lake City, Utah; the local state repository at the Southern Utah University, Cedar City, Utah; the United States National Archives and Records Administration in Washington, D.C., and College Park, Maryland; and the Huntington Library in San Marino, California. The effort worked to be comprehensive while acknowledging the limitations in definitive claims. MMMCLP.
35. Pearce, *Savagism and Civilization*; Axeen, "'Heroes of the Engine Room'"; Stocking, *Race, Culture, and Evolution*; Stocking, *Victorian Anthropology*; Cott, "Two Beards"; Bederman, *Manliness & Civilization*.
36. For a comprehensive analysis of Indian captivity narratives, see Slotkin, *Regeneration through Violence*.

37. Ida B. Wells feverishly worked to dispel the myth of the "Negro rapist." See Bederman, *Manliness & Civilization*, 45–76.

38. For salacious convent tales, see Reed, *Veil of Fear*; Franchot, *Roads to Rome*.

39. London, *Star Rover*. While Alexander Fancher was one of the emigrant train leaders, there was not a Jesse among the Fanchers in the emigrant train.

40. London, *Star Rover*, 129–30.

41. London, 135.

42. London, 152.

43. Bederman, *Manliness & Civilization*, 2, 23, 41–43.

44. Auerbach, *Male Call*.

45. London, *Star Rover*, 112, 113, 144.

46. Kershaw, *Jack London*, 257–58.

47. Mill, *On Liberty*, 166.

Chapter One

1. "The Mormons in the Capacity of Savages," *San Joaquin Republican*, 29 October 1857.

2. "Mormon and Indian Depredations," *Daily Evening Bulletin*, November 1859.

3. Tracy, "Journal of Captain Albert Tracy, 1858–1860," 19 March 1859 entry.

4. Kendall, *Forgotten Founding Father*, 73.

5. Haude, *In the Shadow of "Savage Wolves."*

6. Roediger, *Working toward Whiteness*, 63.

7. Jacobson, *Whiteness of a Different Color*, 41.

8. Pearce, *Savagism and Civilization*, 6.

9. Berkhofer, *White Man's Indian*, 90; Clark and Nagel, "White Men, Red Masks," 114; Huhndorf, *Going Native*, 20; Deloria, *Playing Indian*.

10. Deloria, *Playing Indian*.

11. Bashore, "'Bloodiest Drama Ever Perpetrated.'"

12. Clark and Nagel, "White Men, Red Masks," 4–8; Bederman, *Manliness & Civilization*, 207–13; Deloria, *Playing Indian*, 107–10.

13. R. W. Mac, "Mormonism in Illinois," *American Whig Review* 15, no. 82 (March 1852): 221.

14. Givens, *Viper on the Hearth*, 56; Reeve, *Religion of a Different Color*, 64–69.

15. Mac, "Mormonism in Illinois," 221.

16. Reeve, *Religion of a Different Color*, 64.

17. Habitator Montium [perhaps Mountain Inhabitant], "More of Imposture," *New-York Spectator*, 28 July 1836.

18. Givens, *Viper on the Hearth*, 56.

19. Warren Foote, "Autobiography and Journal, May 1837–December 1879," CHL.

20. Mac, "Mormonism in Illinois," 511–36. Interestingly, both Mormons and anti-Mormons were called savage.

21. Mac, "Mormonism in Illinois," 523.

22. Mac, "Mormonism in Illinois," 221. In a distinct series, Joseph Smith: The Yankee Mahomet, Mac demonstrated other deficiencies of the Mormon prophet and Mormonism in general.

23. Walker, Turley, and Leonard, *Massacre at Mountain Meadows*, 146–47.

24. See Farmer, *On Zion's Mount*, 54–104; Jones, "Saints or Sinners?"; Reeve, *Religion of a Different Color*, 75–106; Smith, "Mormon Conquest."

25. *Daily Inter-Ocean*, 20 June 1874, 8.

26. Beadle, "Mormon Theocracy," 394.

27. Fife Mormon Collection I: 814 as cited in Fife and Redden, "Pseudo-Indian Folksongs," 244.

28. Wilford Woodruff, "Journal," 29 September 1857, CHL. Lee also sent an official report in November. John D. Lee, "John D. Lee to Brigham Young," 20 November 1857, CHL. For W. W. Bishop's alternate version, see Lee [with Bishop], *Mormonism Unveiled*, 252–53.

29. Walker, Turley, and Leonard, *Massacre at Mountain Meadows*, 88–100; Brigham Young, "Brigham Young to James W. Denver," 6 January 1858, CHL.

30. Brigham Young, "George W. Armstrong to Brigham Young," 30 September 1857, NARA.

31. Hurt to Forney, 4 December 1857, *SDoc. No. 35-71*, 199–203 and SDoc 42, 92–98. The year is incorrectly given as 1859 in SDoc 42.

32. For a few examples, see "Horrible Massacre of Emigrants by Indians," *Chicago Daily Tribune*, 12 November 1857; "Horrible Massacre of Emigrants—Over 100 Persons Killed," *Daily Cleveland Herald*, 9 November 1857; "Horrible Massacre of Arkansas and Missouri Emigrants," *New York Times*, 17 November 1857; "Horrible Massacre of Emigrants—Over One Hundred Persons Killed," *Weekly Raleigh Register*, 18 November 1857.

33. "The Mormon Outrages," *Chicago Daily Tribune*, 21 November 1857; "The Mormon Outrages," *Omaha Nebraskan*, 2 December 1857; "Mormons and Indians Butchering Emigrants," *Cleveland Herald*, 2 December 1857; "Complicity of the Mormons in the Late Emigrant Massacre—The Indians Were Tools in the Hands of the Saints," *New York Herald*, 4 December 1857.

34. For an evaluation of Indian participation, see Walker, Turley, and Leonard, *Massacre at Mountain Meadows*, 265–70. Beyond written sources, two competing strains of Paiute oral history exist. One claims no participation in the massacre (perhaps in response to unjustly shouldering the burden of the massacre in many sources for more than a century); the other strain recognizes Paiute participation.

35. Ekins, *Defending Zion*, 309–31.

36. "The Immigrant Massacre," *Daily Alta California*, 14 October 1857.

37. [No title], *San Francisco Herald* (Calif.), 17 October 1857.

38. Mitchell, "William C. Mitchell to William K. Sebastian," 31 December 1857, SDoc 42, 42–43.

39. "Extract from a Letter to the Editor," *Little Rock State Gazette and Democrat*, 13 February 1858. Some federal officials gave lip service to prosecuting the Native Americans involved in the massacre, but no substantive action would be taken

against any individual Paiute men. The focus was consistently on Latter-day Saint participants and leaders, and on the Latter-day Saint people as a whole.

40. "Public Meeting of the People of Carroll County," *Arkansas State Gazette*, 27 May 1858. Interestingly, during the Civil War Arkansans were also constructed as savages, or at least semi-savages. See Shea, "Semi-Savage State," 309–28.

41. Mitchell to Sebastian, 31 December 1857, SDoc 42, 42–43; Mitchell to Greenwood, 5 July 1859, Sdoc 42, 42–43.

42. Mitchell to Greenwood; "Extract from a Letter to This Office," *Arkansas Daily Gazette*, 24 September 1859; "Return of the Survivors of the Mountain Meadows Massacre. Meeting of Citizens of Carroll County: Resolutions, &c. &c.," *Fayetteville Arkansan*, 7 October 1859.

43. "Mormon and Indian-uity," *Daily Citizen & News* (Lowell, Mass.), 4 May 1854.

44. Parry, *Bear River Massacre*; Madsen, *Shoshoni Frontier*.

45. Landers to Greenwood, 18 February 1860, 131.

46. Sdoc 42.

47. Eckels to Cass, 27 September 1859, CHL. Emphasis original.

48. Crofutt, print of John Nash, *American Progress*.

49. Greenberg, *Manifest Manhood*, 1–3.

50. Fitz-Hugh Ludlow, "Among the Mormons," *Atlantic Monthly* 13, no. 78 (April 1864): 479. For another supporting view: Rev. Alfred Taylor, "A Peep at the Mormons," *Sunday Magazine* 9, no. 6 (June 1881).

51. Dorson, *American Folklore*, 119–20.

52. "Reminiscences of an Old Traveler," *Congregationalist* (Boston, Mass.) 156 (28 September 1866):39; "Local Intelligence," *Weekly Arizona Miner*, 25 December 1869; "Savage, the White Indian Chief," *Greenville Mountaineer* (Greenville, S.C.), 19 May 1853; "A White Indian," *Cleveland Herald* (Cleveland, Ohio), 8 February 1853; "The White Indian," *Columbia Telescope* (Columbia, S.C.), 14 May 1833; "Notes and Comments," *Delaware Patriot & American Watchman*, 28 October 1828–14 November 1828.

53. "Over the Plains," *Daily Alta California*, 8 July 1857; *San Andreas Independent*, [n.d.]. as cited in "Further from the Plains," *San Joaquin Republican*, 8 November 1857.

54. "Later from Carson Valley—Arrival of Emigrants at Placerville—Affairs on the Plains," *San Joaquin Republican*, 18 August 1857; Cureton, "Trekking to California," entry 23 August 1857; "Immigrants," *Sacramento Daily Bee*, 6 October 1857.

55. "Emigration," *Deseret News*, 13 July 1854.

56. Maxwell, *Crossing the Plains*, 135–39; Greenwood, "A. B. Greenwood to Jacob Thompson, 26 November 1859," 21–22.

57. "The Mountain Meadows Massacre," *Chicago Daily Tribune*, 11 July 1859.

58. Lynch, "Affidavit."

59. *MMMCLP* 1:331–40.

60. *MMMCLP* 1:341–55.

61. *MMMCLP* 1:357–65, 407–11.

62. *MMMCLP* 1:525–40.

63. "Saved from the Mormons," *Galaxy* 24, no. 5 (1872): 677–83; Lynn, "Sensational Virtue," 101–11.

64. Walker, "Stenhouses," 62; Stenhouse, *"Tell It All"* (1874).

65. Stenhouse, *"Tell It All"* (1877), 626.

66. Stenhouse, *Exposé of Polygamy*, 172–78.

67. Her account of Mountain Meadows liberally reproduced material from her husband Thomas B. Stenhouse's own effort—*Rocky Mountain Saints*. Mr. Stenhouse did not see polygamy as the central heresy of Mormonism; he tried to use the Mountain Meadows narrative as one of many evidences of the failure of Brigham Young to entice his followers to join with the Godbeites—an 1870s Latter-day Saint schismatic group.

68. Stenhouse, *"Tell It All"* (1874), 331–32.

69. "A Great Crime Unpunished," *New York Times*, 23 July 1875; "Mountain Meadows," *New York Times*, 24 July 1875; "A Tale of Horror," *Steubenville Daily Herald*, 24 July 1875; "Pacific Coast," *Pioche Daily Journal*, 24 July 1875.

70. "The Lee Trial," *Salt Lake Daily Tribune*, 11 July 1875; "Progress of the Trial of the Mormon Murders," *Los Angeles Daily Star*, 21 July 1875.

71. "Editorial," *Deseret Evening News*, 16 July 1875.

72. "City Jottings," *Salt Lake Daily Tribune*, 25 July 1875; "Tale of Horror"; "Mountain Meadows Massacre," *State Rights Democrat*, 6 August 1875; "The Massacre. The Horrible Details—Brigham Young Will Probably Be Inculpated," *Arkansas Daily Gazette*, 25 July 1875.

73. "Mrs. Lee No. Eleven," *Salt Lake Daily Tribune*, 1 August 1875.

74. "The Beaver Trial," *Ogden Junction*, 28 July 1875; Baskin introduced Phelps to *Tribune* reporter Frederic Lockley, disappointed that he could not use her "interesting story" as testimony. Lockley proceeded to publish her sensational account of the "honors" poured on Lee after the massacre including "being sealed to another wife"—"a dark eyed English hussey." "Mrs. Lee No. Eleven"; "City Jottings," *Salt Lake Daily Tribune*, 3 August 1875; Associated Press interview with "Indian Chief Beaverite," in "Mountain Meadow [sic]," *Elmira Daily Advertiser*, 4 August 1875; "The Lee Trial," *Los Angeles Daily Star*, 4 August 1875; "Pacific Coast," *Pioche Daily Journal*, 4 August 1875.

75. For example, see "City Jottings," *Salt Lake Daily Tribune*, 5 August 1875. This particular report refers to an individual who was "cautioned about expressing himself too freely, or they would *serve him as they did those at Mountain Meadows*"; it also claims a gold watch was stolen from the slaughtered emigrants only to be paid as tithing and then "taken by Brigham and appropriated for his own use."

76. "W. W. Bishop to Editor," *Pioche Daily Record*, 21 July 1875. Bishop would later capitalize on that hunger when he edited and published John D. Lee's confessions. See chapter 5.

77. Tucher, "Newspapers and Periodicals," 404–8.

78. "Brigham's Great Crime," *Salt Lake Daily Tribune*, 7 August 1875.

79. *MMMCLP* 2:607–8.

80. Carey, "Opening Argument," 22 July 1875, JDLT1:1279, 1260.

81. Baskin, "Closing Argument," 5 August 1875, JDLT1:2789. Emphasis added. In contrast, early newspaper accounts cited the seventeen children saved as evidence of Mormon involvement.

82. Baskin, "Closing Argument," 5 August 1875, JDLT1:3011.
83. Baskin, "Closing Argument," 5 August 1875, JDLT1:3153–58.
84. Fluhman, *Peculiar People*, 39–48.
85. Huhndorf, *Going Native*, 31.
86. Carey, "Opening Argument," 22 July 1875, JDLT1:307.
87. Boreman, "Charge to the Jury," 3 August1875, JDLT1:1999.
88. Baskin, "Closing Argument," 5 August 1875, JDLT1: 2694, 2672; Carey, "Closing Argument," 30 August 1875, JDLT1:2047.
89. Baskin, "Closing Argument," 5 August 1875, JDLT1:2673.
90. Baskin, "Closing Argument," 5 August 1875, JDLT1:3430, 3533, 2858.
91. Baskin, "Closing Argument," 5 August 1875, JDLT1:3122.
92. Carey, "Closing Argument," 3 August 1875, JDLT1:2974.
93. Carey, "Opening Argument," 22 July 1875, JDLT1:318.
94. Baskin, "Closing Argument," 5 August 1875, JDLT1:2830.
95. Spicer, "Opening Argument," 29 August 1875, JDLT1:1278.
96. Spicer, "Opening Argument," 29 August 1875, JDLT1:1420.
97. Spicer, "Opening Argument," 29 August 1875, JDLT1:1304.
98. Spicer, "Opening Argument," 29 August 1875, JDLT1:1302.
99. F[rederick] L[ockley], "Judge Spicer's Address," *Salt Lake Daily Tribune*, 30 July 1875.
100. Spicer, "Opening Argument," 29 August 1875, JDLT1:1318.
101. Spicer, "Opening Argument," 29 August 1875, JDLT1:1238; Baskin, "Closing Argument," 5 August 1875, JDLT1:2858.
102. Turley and Walker, *Mountain Meadows Massacre*, 150–51, 160, 202, 209; Walker, Turley, and Leonard, *Massacre at Mountain Meadows*, 141–42, 159–60, 200, 163–64.
103. "Mountain Meadow [sic] Massacre," *Salt Lake Daily Herald*, 5 August 1875; "Pacific Coast," *Pioche Daily Record*, August 5, 1875; "Arguments for the Defence," *Deseret Evening News*, 4 August 1875; "The Great Massacre in Utah," *Daily Alta California*, 5 August 1875; Hoge, "Closing Argument," 3 August 1875, JDLT1:2422–28.
104. Carey, "Closing Argument," 3 August 1875, JDLT1:2093.
105. "A Mormon Plot to Clean Out the Town of Corrine, Utah a la Mountain Meadows," *Daily Inter-Ocean* (Chicago), 19 August 1875.
106. "Press Opinions," *Salt Lake Daily Tribune*, 28 September 1876. Emphasis original.
107. See *The Mormon Monster* for one of the many examples of an anti-Mormon work contributing to the expanding narrative of Mountain Meadows. The copy of *The Mormon Monster* in the British Library includes an approbation and recommendation by six of Dunn's fellow Protestant ministers in Salt Lake City. Folk, *Mormon Monster*.
108. Dunn wanted a constitutional amendment to the free exercise clause of the First Amendment, specifically adding "but Congress shall have power by appropriate legislation to prohibit in any community, the practice of polygamy, polyandry, promiscuity, and every form of crime attempted in the name of religion." Dunn, *How to Solve the Mormon Problem*.
109. Thomas, "Violence across the Land."

110. Triplett, *History, Romance and Philosophy*. Triplett also focused his literary skill on Jesse James, Grover Cleveland, and great American crimes. Settle, *Jesse James Was His Name*, 192–93.

111. Triplett, *History, Romance and Philosophy*, 196–207.

112. Marberry, *Splendid Poseur*, 124.

113. Bashore, "'Bloodiest Drama.'" Bill Cody also included a chapter on Mountain Meadows when he co-wrote *The Great Salt Lake Trail* with U.S. Army colonel Henry Inman. Inman, *Great Salt Lake Trail*.

114. Jones, *Performing American Identity*, 19–21.

115. "The Big Pawnee Bill Wild West and Far East Show," *New York Tribune*, 17 June 1906; "Pawnee Bill's Wild West and Great Far East Show," *Evening Star*, 19 August 1906; "Pawnee Bill's Show," *Socorro Chieftain*, 28 September 1907.

116. De Wolff, *Pawnee Bill (Major Gordon W. Lillie), His Experience and Adventures on the Western Plains; Or, From the Saddle of a "Cowboy and Ranger" to the Chair of a "Bank President,"* 76–81.

117. See Mason, "Disciplinary Democracy," 88–110.

118. Victoria Reed, "The Mormon Church," *Bay State Monthly* 3, no. 5 (October 1885): 350.

119. Carey, "Closing Argument," 3 August 1875, JDLT1:2072.

120. Baskin, "Closing Argument," 5 August 1875, JDLT1:2842, 2848.

121. Baskin, "Closing Argument," 5 August 1875, JDLT1:2858.

122. As quoted in "Crime of the Priesthood," *Salt Lake Daily Tribune*, 31 July 1875.

123. Simms, *Speech of Hon. W. E. Simms*.

124. *Dred Scott v. John F. A. Sandford* (U.S. Supreme Court 1857).

Chapter Two

1. Forney to Johnston, 1 May 1859, MMMCLP 1:56.

2. Forney, "Extract from Superintendent Forney's Annual Report, of September 29, 1859," SDoc 42, 87–89 and MMMCLP 1:93.

3. Forney to Johnston, 1 May 1859 and Forney to Greenwood, August 1859, MMMCLP 1:56, 86.

4. Forney to Greenwood, August 1859, MMMCLP 1:86.

5. Forney to Johnston, 1 May 1859, MMMCLP 1:56.

6. Forney to Johnston, 1 May 1859; MSS SDoc 42, 18–20; SDoc 42, 8–9.

7. Waite, "Charles B. Waite to Edward Bates"; Carleton, "James H. Carleton to William W. Mackall," 24 June 1859; Young, *Wife No. 19*, 230; Forney, "Extract from Superintendent Forney's Annual Report, of September 29, 1859"; Forney, "Jacob Forney to Alfred B. Greenwood"; Jeremiah S. Black, "Jeremiah S. Black to Alexander Wilson," 17 May 1859, NARA; Robert Newton, "Horrible Massacre of Emigrants!! Over 100 Persons Murdered!!," *Los Angeles Daily Star*, 10 October 1857; Baskin, *Reminiscences of Early Utah*, 88; Cragin, *Amendment. Strike out All After . . .* , 15; William Spicer, "Opening Argument," 29 July 1875, 36, MSS JDL T1; spelling and punctuation have been standardized.

8. Carleton, "James H. Carleton to William W. Mackall," 1 July 1859.

9. Jacob S. Boreman, "Charge to the Grand Jury," *Beaver Enterprise*, 9 September 1874. *MMMCLP* 1:381–89.

10. Utah's first federally appointed territorial governor, Alfred Cumming, was one of Forney's few allies in his temperate opinions of the Mormons as a whole. Cumming to Cass, 2 February 1860.

11. Some examples include Cradlebaugh to Buchanan, 3 June 1859, NARA; Cradlebaugh, *Utah and the Mormons*; Eckels to Cass, 27 September 1859, CHL.

12. Forney to Greenwood, August 1859, *MMMCLP* 1:86.

13. Reeve, *Religion of a Different Color*, 22.

14. Johnson, *Dictionary of the English Language*.

15. Fluhman, *Peculiar People*; Reeve, *Religion of a Different Color*.

16. Cragin, *Execution of Laws in Utah*, 15; Forney, "Extract from Superintendent Forney's Annual Report, of Sept. 29, 1859," NARA; SDoc 42, 87–89; Triplett, *Conquering the Wilderness*, 196; Young, *Wife No. 19*, 1875, 230.

17. Madley, "Tactics," 117–39; Madley, *American Genocide*, 45–48.

18. Michno, *Encyclopedia of Indian Wars*; Madsen, *Shoshoni Frontier*, 92; Haymond, *Infamous Dakota War Trial of 1862*, 7–10.

19. McMurtry, *Oh What a Slaughter*, 64–65, 89; Reilly, *Frontier Newspapers*, 1–16.

20. W. R. Hamilton, "History of the Mormon Rebellion of 1856–57," *The United Service. A Monthly Review of Military and Naval Affairs* 4 (November 1890): 446–59.

21. John Turner notes in his recent biography of Mormon leader Brigham Young that the Hawn's Mill Massacre, when a Missouri state militia killed seventeen Mormon men and boys in 1838, stands as perhaps one of the only other examples of a White militia killing other White people. Seventeen and 120 are clearly not numerically comparable, and the Pottawatomie Massacre importantly complicates the claim. This example further highlights the problematic nature of the category of the word "massacre"—six people to seventeen to 120 all are put in the same category. Turner, *Brigham Young*, 279.

22. The classic estimate of people dead over a turbulent seven-year period in Kansas was fifty-four. A modern historian would double that through further documentation. Etcheson, *Bleeding Kansas*; Earle and Burke, *Bleeding Kansas, Bleeding Missouri*; Watts, "How Bloody," 116–29; Potter, *Impending Crisis*, 199–224.

23. While both massacres included religious elements, John Brown believed that he was enacting a kind of Old Testament retribution: an eye for an eye. These proslavery individuals were ready to use violence to enslave other human beings, exterminating free slave advocates by violence if necessary to ensure that Kansas became a slave state, and Brown believed he returned the same. Reynolds, *John Brown*, 40–42.

24. See Reynolds, *John Brown*, 8, 102, 271, 357–59, 424, 456.

25. "Massacre of the Cheyenne Indians"; McMurty, *O What a Slaughter*, 122.

26. Reilly, *Frontier Newspapers*, 11–16; Haymond, *Infamous Dakota War Trial*, 3–4, 47–51.

27. Tucker, *Encyclopedia*, 171.

28. Tucker, 116.

29. In one example from the summer of 1822, Denmark Vesey and those rumored to have planned a slave insurrection in Charleston, South Carolina, were executed in

waves. Vesey and four others were killed within weeks of the accusation, while in the next two months more than 150 were executed and another forty exiled from the limits of Charleston. Pearson, *Designs against Charleston*, 1–17.

30. Wise, *Massacre at Mountain Meadows*, 243, 263; Bagley, *Blood of the Prophets*, 287–306; Denton, *American Massacre*, 149, 215, 222, 245; Krakauer, *Under the Banner of Heaven*, 247–48.

31. Lynch's interaction with Federal Judge John Cradlebaugh possibly led to the initial changes in his account, but the changes continued to grow over time. See *MMMCLP* 1:243–54.

32. In 1893, at age seventy-two, Lynch married Sarah Dunlap, one of the surviving children. Lynch would continue to make published statements regarding the massacre for years; his statements expanded with gripping embellishment over time. Lynch would later augment and expand his involvement with the returned survivor children, claiming that he had dramatically returned them from the hands of the "damned" Mormons. Despite his assertions, the children were already gathered, and Lynch did not return to Arkansas with them. Tales of Lynch's exploits later made their way into the accounts of others. Survivor Sallie Baker Mitchell remembered, "The way Captain Lynch and his soldiers found us was by going around among the Mormons in disguise. I got to know him riht [sic] well later on, and he used to slap his leg and laugh like anything, as he told how he said to those Mormons: 'You let those children go, or I'll blow you to purgatory." Mitchell, "Mountain Meadows Massacre," 15.

33. Margaret Ross, "Arkansas Journeys West to Bring Back 17 Survivors of 1857 Morman Massacre," *Arkansas Daily Gazette*, 1 January 1967; "Blames Mormons for the Massacre: Affidavit of James Lynch of Utah Tells of Slaughter of Arkansas Emigrants," *Arkansas Daily Gazette*, December 1912; William Humphreys Newton, "Death at Mountain Meadows," *Arkansas Daily Gazette*, 6 September 1959; "Late News from Utah," *San Francisco Evening Bulletin*, 24 August 1859; "Mountain Meadows: An Official Narrative of the Atrocity," *California Daily Alta*, 23 August 1875; Parker, *Recollections*; SDoc 42; "Mountain Meadows Massacre: The Butchery of a Train of Arkansans by Mormons and Indians While on Their Way to California," *Fort Smith Elevator*, 20 August 1897; "Mountain Meadows," *St. Louis Globe-Democrat*, 26 July 1875; Ralph R. Rea, "The Mountain Meadows Massacre and Its Completion as a Historic Episode," http://tfancher.tripod.com/rea.htm.

34. Montgomery, "Samuel H. Montgomery to Alfred B. Greenwood," NARA.

35. Montgomery, "Samuel H. Montgomery to Alfred B. Greenwood."

36. The discourse surrounding the massacre does not begin to acknowledge the existence of African American Mormons and the additional racial complexity that could produce. For an overview, see Coleman, "Utah's Black Pioneers," 95–110; Newell, *Your Sister in the Gospel: The Life of Jane Manning James, a Nineteenth-century Black Mormon*; Reeve, *Religion of a Different Color*; and the database *Century of Black Mormons*, https://exhibits.lib.utah.edu/s/century-of-black-mormons.

37. Bartholow, quoted in Coolidge, *Statistical Report*, 300–302. See Givens, *Viper on the Hearth*, 147–49; Fluhman, *Peculiar People*, 113; Reeve, *Religion of a Different Color*, 14–20.

38. Smith, *How Race Is Made*; Kidd, *Forging of Races*, 41–43, 148–50, 215–16, 270–76.

39. Bartholow quoted in Coolidge, *Statistical Report*, 300–302.

40. Walker, *Railroading Religion*, 7–8, 11–12.

41. "Hereditary Descent; Or, Depravity of the Offspring of Polygamy among the Mormons," *Debow's Review, Agricultural, Commercial, Industrial Progress and Resources* 30, no. 2 (February 1861): 206–16.

42. In a similar vein, Marta Erthman argues that the Mormons were guilty of race treason. For Erthman, this includes the social treason of polygamy and the political treason of theocracy. Mountain Meadows expanded the narrative beyond polygamy and theocracy. Erthman, "Race Treason."

43. Kidd, *Forging of Races*; Jacobson, *Whiteness of a Different Color*; Roediger, *Working toward Whiteness*; Smith, *How Race Is Made*; Bederman, *Manliness & Civilization*, 28–41; Gross, *What Blood Won't Tell*.

44. Kidd, *Forging of Races*, 7.

45. Hale, *Making Whiteness*; Roediger, *Wages of Whiteness*; Jacobson, *Whiteness of a Different Color*; Smith, *How Race Is Made*.

46. Deloria, *Playing Indian*, 5; Hale, *Making Whiteness*, 6.

47. Richardson, *West from Appomattox*, 8–38; Goldstein, *Price of Whiteness*, 1–7; Jacobson, *Whiteness of a Different Color*, 22–40.

48. Williamson, *New People*, 1–2, 62, 73–75; Kidd, *Forging of Races*, 11, 126, 235, 259, 261; Davis, *Who Is Black*.

49. Gross, *What Blood Won't Tell*, 1–8. After a hung jury in the first trial, she won the second trial, which was only to be overturned on appeal. The third likewise ended in a hung jury.

50. Kidd, *Forging of Races*, 11. Emphasis added.

51. Kidd, 11–13.

52. Fluhman, *Peculiar People*; Reeve, *Religion of a Different Color*.

53. Fluhman, *Peculiar People*, 103–26.

54. In the 1850 census, almost half of New York City's residents (45.7 percent) were foreign-born and more than half of Chicago's residents (52 percent). In the same year there were 18 percent foreign-born residents in Utah, comparable to Middlesex County, Massachusetts, and Rensselaer County, New York. Gibson and Jung, "Historical Census Statistics," 1 February 2006. See Carleton, "James H. Carleton to William W. Mackall," 1 July 1859.

55. Carleton, "James H. Carleton to William W. Mackall," 1 July 1859.

56. In 1850 the majority of immigrants were English, Canadian, Scottish, Welsh, and Irish. Interestingly Carleton did not note the dubious whiteness of the Irish immigrants. Poll, *Utah Historical Encyclopedia*, 272–73.

57. Carleton, "James H. Carleton to William W. Mackall," 1 July 1859. Paul Reeve likewise considers the racialization of Asian peoples in relation to the racialization of the Mormons, *Religion of a Different Color*, 215–46.

58. Eckels, "Delana R. Eckels to Lewis Cass."

59. Kerstetter, *God's Country, Uncle Sam's Land*, 37. There is not yet an effectual example of class analysis of the Mormon Problem.

60. Eckels, "Delana R. Eckels to Lewis Cass"; Forney, "Jacob Forney to James W. Denver," 18 March 1859, 157–59; SDoc 42, 52–53; Campbell, "Reuben P. Campbell to Fitz-John Porter," 6 July 1859; MSS SDoc 40–44; SDoc 42, 14–16; William H. Rog-

ers, "Details of the Mountain Meadows Massacre in Utah," *Painesville Telegraph*, 21 July 1859; Cragin, *Execution of Laws in Utah*; Hamilton, "History of the Mormon Rebellion of 1856–57," 446; Freece, *Letters of an Apostate Mormon*, 25; Morrill, *On the Warpath*, 226.

61. Carey, "Opening Argument," 22 July 1875, JDLT1:289.
62. Carleton, *Mountain Meadow [sic] Massacre . . . Special Report*.
63. Turley, "Problems with Mountain Meadows Massacre Sources."
64. Cradlebaugh, "Charge to the Grand Jury." Emphasis added.
65. Boreman, "Charge to the Grand Jury," *Beaver Enterprise*, 9 September 1874; MMMCLP 381–89.
66. Jury Interviews, 19 July 1875, JDLT1:32–287, particularly 146–93.
67. Carey, "Opening Argument," 22 July 1875, JDLT1:288.
68. Carey, "Opening Argument," 22 July 1875, JDLT1:292.
69. Carey, "Opening Argument," 22 July 1875, JDLT1:287–88.
70. Carey, "Opening Argument," 22 July 1875, JDLT1:298–308.
71. Carey, "Opening Argument," 22 July 1875, JDLT1:319–23.
72. Carey, "Opening Argument," 22 July 1875, JDLT1:325–26.
73. Carey, "Opening Argument," 22 July 1875, JDLT1:271.
74. Carey, "Opening Argument," 22 July 1875, JDL1:272–74, 283–84.
75. Carey, "Closing Argument," 3 August 1875, JDL T1:2073. All of the numerically comparable nineteenth-century massacres had occurred by this point, save Wounded Knee.
76. Carey, "Opening Argument," 22 July 1875, JDLT1:319.
77. For examples of similar anti-Catholicism, see Franchot, *Roads to Rome*, 102–6; Reed, *Veil of Fear*, vii–xxix.
78. Davis, "Some Themes of Counter-Subversion," September 1960; Givens, *Viper on the Hearth*, 146.
79. Carey, "Opening Argument," 22 July 1875, JDLT1:319–22.
80. Baskin, "Closing Argument," 5 August 1875, JDLT1:2858.
81. Baskin, *Reminiscences of Early Utah*, 88.
82. Prebble, *Glencoe*.
83. Beadle, *Polygamy*, 180.
84. Carleton, "James H. Carleton to William W. Mackall," 24 June 1859.
85. Scotland, Privy Council, *His Majesties Proclamation*.
86. Sir Walter Scott's 1819 novel *The Legend of Montrose* references the children of the mist. Furthermore, the children of the mist were the subject of other sources: an epic poem by Turner, *The Children of the Mist, The Conqueror, and Other Poems* and the play "Montrose; or The Children of the Mist."
87. Carey, "Opening Argument," 22 July 1875, JDLT1:326.
88. Holwell, *India Tracts*, 221.
89. Chatterjee, *Black Hole of Empire*.
90. Fluhman, *Peculiar People*, 28–34; Heise, "Marking Mormon Difference," 82; Reeve, *Religion of a Different Color*, 215–46.
91. Greenberg, *Manifest Manhood*, 184; Hyde, *Empires, Nations and Families*; Horsman, *Race and Manifest Destiny*.

92. Oman, "Natural Law," 661–706; Wagner, *Great Fear of 1857*; Llewellyn-Jones, *Great Uprising in India, 1857–58*; Holwell, *India Tracts*; Chatterjee, *Black Hole of Empire*, 25. Curiously, Holwell originally wrote his account of the Black Hole of Calcutta to demonstrate how civilized decisions could save an individual in even the direst of situations. He described how, despite their apparent civility, both Portuguese and British soldiers died in the Black Hole after focusing more on immediate relief rather than deleterious long-term effects of those choices. Holwell intended his narrative to inspire civilized men to turn from their basest attributes and reach their civilized potential. Only later would the British engage the narrative to warrant imperial expansion.

93. Bederman, *Manliness & Civilization*, 25; Stocking, *Race, Culture, and Evolution*, 112–32.

94. Triplett, *History, Romance and Philosophy*, 196–97; Triplett, *Conquering the Wilderness*.

95. Holwell, *India Tracts*.

96. Chatterjee, *Black Hole of Empire*; Willey, *Eagle's Nest*.

97. Little, *Black Hole*, 1915.

98. Baskin, "Closing Argument," 5 August 1875, JDLT1:3073.

99. Baskin, "Closing Argument." 5 August 1875, JDLT1:3073.

100. Kidd, *Forging of Races*, 1–18.

101. The killing of women and children would become a predictable point of contention in a variety of paradoxical ways by different individuals.

102. Baskin, "Closing Argument," 5 August 1875, JDLT1:2844.

103. Cradlebaugh, "Charge to the Grand Jury," 8 March 1859; Jacob S. Boreman, "Charge to the Grand Jury," *Beaver Enterprise*, 9 September 1874; MMMCLP 1:381–89.

Chapter Three

1. Boreman, "Charge to the Grand Jury," *Beaver Enterprise*, 9 September 1874; repr. in "Charge to the Grand Jury of the Second District Court," *Deseret News*, 16 September 1874, MMMCLP 1:381–89.

2. "Manhood" is the precise term. The term "masculinity" was not appropriated until the very end of the nineteenth century with distinct connotations of physicality.

3. Bederman, *Manliness & Civilization*, 1–44; Horsman, *Race and Manifest Destiny*.

4. Greenberg, *Manifest Manhood*, 135–69.

5. Greenberg, *Manifest Manhood*; Ownby, *Subduing Satan*; Carnes, *Secret Ritual*; Basso, McCall, and Garceau, *Across the Great Divide*; Rotundo, *American Manhood*; Hoganson, *Fighting for American Manhood*; Wyatt-Brown, *Southern Honor*.

6. Though much research remains to be done on Latter-day Saints ideals of manhood, particularly in the nineteenth century, Taylor Petrey and Amy Hoyt's handbook offers a beginning foundation, *The Routledge Handbook of Mormonism and Gender*, 60–99. Essays by Sarah Patterson, Laurel Thatcher Ulrich, and Ben Park offer a glimpse of the foundation.

7. For one example, see Harriet Beecher Stowe's introduction in Fanny Stenhouse, *"Tell It All"*, 1874, x.

8. Though some historians have repeated the nineteenth-century newspaper claims to a connection, Richard E. Turley convincingly argues against any claim of the massacre as vengeance for Pratt's death in "The Murder of Parley P. Pratt and the Mountain Meadows Massacre" in *Parley P. Pratt and the Making of Mormonism*, 297–311. Carleton and Cradlebaugh stand as the only exceptions—both mention the possibility absent any mileage in official channels. Carleton, "James H. Carleton to William W. Mackall," 24 June 1859; Carleton, *Utah and the Mormons*, 21; MMMCLP 1:201–36.

9. "Horrible Massacre of Arkansas and Missouri Emigrants," *New York Times*, 17 November 1857; "Horrible Massacre of Emigrants!! Over 100 Persons Murdered!!," *Los Angeles Daily Star*, 10 October 1857; "Joe Smith, The False Prophet of the Nineteenth Century," n.d., CHL; "Killing of Immigrants–Mormons Falsely Accused–Further Endurance No Longer a Virtue," *Western Standard*, 6 November 1857; "Latest Intelligence," *New York Times*, 20 November 1857; "Topics of the Day," *San Francisco Herald*, 12 October 1857; Carleton, *Utah and the Mormons*, 122; Burton, *City of the Saints*, 340–41. A general assessment of the narrative surrounding Pratt's murder can be found in Matthew Grow, "Martyred Apostle or Un-Saintly Seducer? Narratives on the Death of Parley P. Pratt," in Givens and Grow, *Parley P. Pratt and the Making of Mormonism*, 275–95.

10. J. Spencer Fluhman, *"A Peculiar People": Anti-Mormonism and the Making of Religion in Nineteenth-Century America*, 49–52.

11. Pratt, "Loved Ones in Utah," ca. 1857; Pratt, "Brother Snow," circa 1857.

12. Givens and Grow, *Parley P. Pratt: The Apostle Paul of Mormonism*, 366–92; Mason, "Honor, the Unwritten Law," 245–73.

13. Stenhouse, *"Tell It All"* (1874), 325.

14. "The Sad Story of Mormonism: The Mother and Children," *New Orleans Bulletin*, 14 March 1857.

15. "Tragic End of a Mormon Patriarch," *Farmer's Cabinet*, 4 June 1857.

16. "The Killing of Pratt—Letter from Mr. McLean," *California Daily Alta*, 9 July 1857.

17. McLaren, *Trials of Masculinity*, 8.

18. "Horrible Massacre of Emigrants!! Over 100 Persons Murdered!!," *Los Angeles Star*, 10 October 1857; "News from the South," *Sacramento Daily Bee*, 12 October 1857.

19. "Topics of the Day," *San Francisco Herald*, 12 October 1857.

20. Ekins, *Defending Zion*, 309–31.

21. "Latest Intelligence," *New York Times*, 20 November 1857.

22. "Latest Intelligence," *New York Times*, 20 November 1857; "Horrible Massacre of Arkansas and Missouri Emigrants," *New York Times*, 17 November 1857; Dunn, *Massacres of the Mountains*, 290; "Killing of Immigrants–Mormons Falsely Accused–Further Endurance No Longer a Virtue," *Western Standard*, 6 November 1857; Carleton, *Utah and the Mormons*, 122; Stenhouse, *"Tell It All"* (1874), 325.

23. In his book *Blood of the Prophets*, Will Bagley leaned into narrative of Pratt's murder as the rationale for the massacre most completely, and journalists Sally Denton and Jon Krakauer followed his lead. Richard Turley convincingly dismantles Bagley's analysis in Turley, "Murder of Parley P. Pratt," 297–311; Bagley, *Blood of the Prophets*; Denton, *American Massacre*; and Krakauer, *Under the Banner of Heaven*.

24. "Horrible Massacre of Arkansas and Missouri Emigrants," *New York Times*, 17 November 1857.

25. Stenhouse, *"Tell It All"* (1874), 325.

26. Bundy, *Mormonism Exposed*; Stenhouse, *Rocky Mountain Saints*, 429–30; Stenhouse, *"Tell It All"*, 1874, 325–26; "Mountain Meadows Secrets," *Pioche Daily Record*, 20 August 1875; Pacific Art Company, San Francisco, *History*, 2; McGlashan, *From the Desk of Truckee's*, 132–34; Dunn, *Massacres of the Mountains*, 290; Hamilton, "History of the Mormon Rebellion of 1856–57," *The United Service: A Monthly Review of Military and Naval Affairs* 4 (November 1890): 446–48; "Cause of Mountain Meadow Massacre," *Monroe City Democrat*, 7 May 1903, 325–26; Morrill, *On the Warpath*, 225.

27. Mason, *Mormon Menace*, 3–6; Wyatt-Brown, *Southern Honor*, 306.

28. Stenhouse, *"Tell It All"* (1874), 325.

29. Carleton, *Utah and the Mormons*, 122.

30. Stenhouse, *"Tell It All"* (1874), 326.

31. "Mountain Meadows Secrets," *Pioche Daily Record*, 20 August 1875.

32. Lyford, *Mormon Problem*, 275.

33. Greenberg, *Manifest Manhood*.

34. Leong, "'A Distinct and Antagonistic Race': Constructions of Chinese Manhood in the Exclusionist Debates, 1869–1878," in Basso, McCall, and Garceau, *Across the Great Divide*, 131–48.

35. Bederman, *Manliness & Civilization*, 1–5.

36. Ditz, "New Men's History," 1–35. Ditz's argument comes in response to the work of Kimmel, *Manhood in America*.

37. Stenhouse, *"Tell It All"* (1874), 325.

38. Hamilton, "History of the Mormon Rebellion," 450.

39. The implication was that the child had been murdered—but more likely she was simply moved to another home. Turley and Walker, *Mountain Meadows Massacre*, 45, 49.

40. Langdon, *Authentic History*, 17.

41. Oswalt, *Pen Pictures of Mormonism*, 18.

42. Carleton, *Report on the Subject of the Massacre at the Mountain Meadows*, 8.

43. Carleton, "James H. Carleton to William W. Mackall," 24 June 1859, 16.

44. Morrill, *On the Warpath*, 226.

45. Stenhouse, *"Tell It All"* (1878), 331; Freece, *Letters*, 26.

46. Triplett, *Conquering the Wilderness*, 533.

47. London, *Star Rover*, 144; Wilson, *Lions of the Lord*, 210.

48. William Young, "Testimony," 27 July 1875, 73–77, MSS JDL T1.

49. Hamblin, "Testimony," 16 July 1876, 3428–51, MSS JDL T1.

50. Jones, *Performing American Identity*, 48.

51. Burton, *City of the Saints*, 427–41.
52. Pacific Art Company, San Francisco, *History*, 6.
53. *Crimes of the Latter Day Saints in Utah, By a Mormon of 1831* . . . , 52.
54. Pacific Art Company, San Francisco, *History*, 6.
55. Beadle, *Polygamy; Or, the Mysteries and Crimes of Mormonism*, 1882, 183.
56. Bederman, *Manliness & Civilization*, 46–53.
57. For other examples of this motif, see Burnham, *Captivity and Sentiment*, 50; Dorson, *America Begins*, 180–84; Jason and Graves, *Encyclopedia of American War Literature*, 180; Mather, *Magnalia Christi Americana*, 2:635. For a comprehensive analysis of Indian captivity narratives, see Slotkin, *Regeneration through Violence*.
58. Pacific Art Company, San Francisco, *History*, 6; Beadle, *Polygamy; Or, the Mysteries and Crimes of Mormonism*, 1882, 183; McGlashan, *From the Desk of Truckee's*.
59. Arrington, "Crusade against Theocracy," 7–8.
60. Boreman, "Charge to the Grand Jury."
61. Boreman, "Charge to the Grand Jury."
62. Mason, "Disciplinary Democracy," 88–96.
63. Boreman, "Charge to the Grand Jury."
64. Greenberg, *Manifest Manhood*.
65. Smith, *Virgin Land*, 59–70.
66. Ball, "Cool to the End," 97–108; McLaren, *Trials of Masculinity: Policing Sexual Boundaries, 1870–1930*, 111–31.
67. Utah waited forty-seven years and eleven months for statehood. Only New Mexico's wait was longer, at sixty-one years and seven months. Both included considerable debate over the potential for citizenship of the territory's inhabitants.
68. Walker and Grow, "Affairs of the 'Runaways,'" 1–43; Walker and Grow, "People Are 'Hogaffed or Humbugged,'" 1–52.
69. See Richardson, *West from Appomattox*; Gordon, *Mormon Question*; Milner and Cannon, *Reconstruction and Mormon America*.
70. Dred Scott v. John F. A. Sanford (U.S. Supreme Court 1857).
71. Jacob S. Boreman, "Charge to the Grand Jury."
72. Jacob S. Boreman, "Charge to the Grand Jury," *Beaver Enterprise*, 2 December 1874; repr. in "Second District Court," *Salt Lake Daily Tribune*, 6 December 1874; MMMCLP 1:389–390; Arrington, "Crusade against Theocracy," 7–8.
73. All original versions of Carey's opening argument only mention the women and children. "Men" was later added to one of the transcripts. Carey, "Opening Argument," 22 July 1875, JDLT1:302.
74. Keyes, "Testimony," 23 July 1875, JDLT1:360.
75. Bennett, "Testimony," 23 July 1875, JDLT1:371.
76. Walker, Turley, and Leonard, *Massacre at Mountain Meadows*, 206–8.
77. Keyes, "Testimony," 23 July 1875, JDLT1:368.
78. "The Lee Trial," *Salt Lake Daily Tribune*, 20 July 1875.
79. Carey, "Opening Argument," 23 July 1875, JDLT1:304.
80. Carey, "Opening Argument," 23 July 1875, JDLT1:305.
81. Baskin, "Closing Argument," 5 August 1875, JDLT1:3079.

82. Baskin, "Closing Argument," 5 August 1875, JDLT1:2830.

83. Spierenburg, *Men and Violence*, 197–254; McLaren, *Trials of Masculinity*, 111–32; Wyatt-Brown, *Southern Honor*, 327–496.

84. Baskin, "Closing Argument," 5 August 1875, JDLT1:2830. One of the Mormon temple rituals is called the endowment; Mormons performed this rite in a building specifically for this ritual—the Endowment House—before the completion of the temple in Salt Lake City. The St. George temple had been dedicated a few months earlier 100 miles south of Beaver, Utah.

85. Davis, "Some Themes of Counter-Subversion," 212.

86. Greenberg, *Manifest Manhood*; Welke, *Recasting American Liberty*, 3–42.

87. Baskin, "Closing Argument," 5 August 1875, JDLT1:2844.

88. Baskin, "Closing Argument," 5 August 1875, JDLT1:2998.

89. Baskin, "Closing Argument," 5 August 1875, JDLT1:2989–90. The term "grease vat" is only found in the Rogerson transcript, not in the Rogerson shorthand. Court reporter Rogerson either added it from his memory or added it to further augment Baskin's animosity.

90. Lockley, "Frederic Lockley to Elizabeth Lockley."

91. Lockley, "Frederic Lockley to Elizabeth Lockley."

92. Jones, *Performing American Identity*, 83–116.

93. "Mountain Meadows Secrets" *Pioche Daily Record*, 20 August 1875.

94. *New York Sun* correspondent as reprinted in *Pioche Daily Record*, 20 August 1875.

95. Givens and Grow, *Parley P. Pratt*, 382–84.

96. Lyford, *Mormon Problem*, 275; McGlashan, *From the Desk of Truckee's*, 133.

97. McGlashan, *From the Desk of Truckee's*, 133–34.

98. Hamilton, "History," 447. More recently, Will Bagley similarly placed Eleanor Pratt at the flashpoint of the massacre. She arrived in Salt Lake in the first wagons that arrived after sighting the U.S. Army marching to Utah on the plains. For Bagley, the news of the army and Parley's widow led directly to the massacre. Bagley, *Blood of the Prophets*, 7–9.

99. "Mountain Meadows Secrets," *Pioche Daily Record*, 20 August 1875.

100. Langdon, *Authentic History*, 17.

101. Forney, "Jacob Forney to James W. Denver," 18 March 1859; SDoc 42, 52–53.

102. Carleton, *Utah and the Mormons*, 122.

103. Cragin, *Execution of Laws in Utah*, 17.

104. Young, *Wife No. 19*, 247.

105. Langdon, *Authentic History*, 17.

106. Lyford, *Mormon Problem*, 322, 295.

107. Triplett, *History, Romance and Philosophy*, 200.

108. Lyford, *Mormon Problem*, 304.

109. Lyford, *Mormon Problem*, 306.

110. Walker, *Railroading Religion*, 7–8. Walker specifically addresses the coming of the railroad with the end of Mormonism. However, in the popular narrative, significant change was often thought to be the "death knell" of Mormonism. The death of

Joseph Smith as well as the death of Brigham Young during this period were such moments.

111. Lyford, *Mormon Problem*, 308.

112. Young, *Wife No. 19*, 248.

113. "Biographical.: BRIGHAM YOUNG," *Massachusetts Ploughman and New England Journal of Agriculture*, 8 September 1877; "Brigham Young and His Work," *Chicago Daily Tribune*, 31 August 1877; "Death of Brigham Young," *Maine Farmer*, 8 September 1877.

114. Pacific Art Company, San Francisco, *History*, 6; "Execution of John D. Lee Today," *New York Tribune*, 23 March 1877.

115. James Pearce, "Testimony," 27 July 1875, JDLT1:1284.

116. Lyford, *Mormon Problem*, 307–8.

117. Beadle, *Undeveloped West*, 665.

Chapter Four

1. William W. Bishop, "The Lee Trial," *Pioche Daily Record*, 25 July 1875.

2. "Mountain Meadows Massacre," *Salt Lake Daily Herald*, 15 July 1875.

3. Bishop, "Lee Trial."

4. "The Lee Trial," *Salt Lake Daily Tribune*, 20 July 1875.

5. "The Massacre at Mountain Meadows, Utah Territory," *Harper's Weekly* 3:137 (13 August 1859); Horace Greeley, "Brigham Young's Religion, Wealth, Wives, Etc.," *Harper's Weekly*, 3:140 (3 September 1859).

6. Rogers, "The Mountain Medows [sic] Massacre," *Valley Tan*, 29 February 1860. Emphasis added.

7. Cradlebaugh and Sinclair, "John Cradlebaugh and Charles Sinclair to James Buchanan."

8. Anderson, "Mormon King"; Rice, *Mormon Way*, 8.

9. "The Dead Prophet," *Salt Lake Daily Tribune*, 7 September 1877; Oswalt, *Pen Pictures of Mormonism*, 17.

10. Oswalt, *Pen Pictures of Mormonism*, 17.

11. Anderson, "Mormon King."

12. Wilson, "Alexander Wilson to Jacob Thompson," 4 March 1859; Cradlebaugh, "Charge to the Grand Jury," 8 March 1859; Cradlebaugh, "Cradlebaugh Dismissal of Grand Jury," 21 March 1859; Thompson, "Jacob Thompson to Alexander Wilson," 25 April 1859; Black, "Jeremiah S. Black to Alexander Wilson," 17 May 1859; Cradlebaugh, "John Cradlebaugh to James Buchanan," 3 June 1859; Wilson, "Alexander Wilson to Jeremiah S. Black"; Cradlebaugh and Sinclair, "John Cradlebaugh and Charles Sinclair to James Buchanan," 16 July 1859; Cumming, "Alfred Cumming to Lewis Cass," 2 February 1860; Wilson, "Alexander Wilson to Jeremiah S. Black," 15 November 1859.

13. Eckels, "Delana R. Eckels to Lewis Cass," 27 September 1859.

14. Wilson, "Alexander Wilson to Jacob Thompson," 4 March 1859; Black, "Jeremiah S. Black to Alexander Wilson," 17 May 1859. U.S. Attorney Alexander Wilson fell ill, and his replacement did not move forward with any action.

15. Waite, *Mormon Prophet and His Harem*, 60–77.

16. Waite, 60–77.

17. Waite, 60.

18. Waite, 60–77.

19. Clemens, *Roughing It*, 117.

20. Clemens, 343–51. The first appendix chapter was likewise devoted to the Mormons.

21. Beadle, *Life in Utah*, 181; Beadle, *Polygamy; Or, the Mysteries and Crimes of Mormonism*, 1882, 181.

22. Beadle, *Life in Utah*, 6. In 1882, he essentially republished the same volume under the title more focused on polygamy: *Polygamy; Or, the Mysteries and Crimes of Mormonism*, 1882. Reflecting the mobilization of women in the East against polygamy, the second version included a new dedication "to the Ladies of America, whose sympathies are ever active in behalf of the suffering and oppressed." In both versions, the massacre played a significant role.

23. Beadle, *Life in Utah*, 183.

24. [Wandell], "An Open Letter to Brigham Young," *Daily Utah Reporter*, 12 September 1870.

25. Reeve, *Making Space*, 200n29.

26. This point is absent from Klingensmith's trial testimony. Klingensmith, "Testimony," 23 July 1875, JDLT1:376–769.

27. "A MORMON MONSTROSITY," *New York Herald*, 10 April 1871.

28. Bates, "George C. Bates to Benjamin H. Bristow, Solicitor General," 21 December 1871.

29. By the time of Lee's first trial, Bates was employed as a member of Lee's defense team.

30. Arrest warrant for John D. Lee, 13 October 1874, 289–90; Young, "Brigham Young to Daniel H. Wells," 12 November 1874. Young's important evidence was his letter to Isaac Haight telling him to let the emigrants pass in safety. A portion of the telegram was written using Larrabee's cipher with the code word "Wednesday."

31. Indianapolis Herald (Ind.) as quoted in "Brigham's Great Crime," *Salt Lake Daily Tribune*, 7 August 1875.

32. "A Great Crime Unpunished," *New York Times*, 23 July 1875.

33. Reprinting excerpt from the *Virginia Enterprise*, "That Bloody Deed: The Press of the Country Put It Where It Belongs," *Salt Lake Daily Tribune*, 28 July 1875.

34. Carey, "Opening Argument," 22 July 1875, JDLT1:311.

35. Carey, "Opening Argument," 22 July 1875, JDLT1:314.

36. Wilford Woodruff, present when Lee reported to Young, wrote in his journal the day that Lee reported to Young. John D. Lee also told the story of an Indian massacre as he traveled north. Those who argue that Lee told Young the truth based their claims in *Mormonism Unveiled* as we will discuss in chapter 5. Woodruff, "Journal," 29 September 1857. For an alternate version, see Lee, *Mormonism Unveiled*, 1877, 252–53.

37. Klingensmith, "Testimony," 23 July 1875, JDLT1:647.

38. Klingensmith, "Testimony," 23 July 1875, JDLT1:458–59.

39. Bishop, "Closing Argument," 4 August 1875, JDLT1:2533–34.

40. Bishop, "Closing Argument," 4 August 1875, JDLT1:2533.

41. Klingensmith, "Testimony," 23 July 1875, JDLT1:445.

42. "The Massacre. The Horrible Details—Brigham Young Will Probably Be Inculpated," *Arkansas Daily Gazette* (Little Rock), 25 July 1875.

43. *Indianapolis Herald* (Ind.) as reprinted in "Brigham's Great Crime," *Salt Lake Daily Tribune*, 7 August 1875.

44. Smith was head of the militia in southern Utah, an apostle, and later a member of Young's First Presidency. Young, "Deposition," 30 July 1875, CCF 31; "Brigham's Deposition: His Account of the Mountain Meadows Massacre. He Displays Astonishing Ignorance and Makes a General Denial George A. Smith Also Tells How Little He Knows. Smith's Story," *New York Times*, 3 August 1875.

45. Young, "Deposition," 30 July 1875, CCF 31; Smith, "Deposition," 30 July 1875, CCF 31.

46. Jabez G. Sutherland and Jacob S. Boreman, "Argument," JDLT1:1014–18, 1218–25; Resolutions and Memorials, Ch. 30, § 22.

47. "Brigham's Deposition," *New York Times*, 3 August 1875; "WRONG'S RECORD: The Twenty-Seventh of the Series of Williamson County Assassinations. Brigham Young's Deposition in the Mountain Meadow Case. He Denies All Knowledge of or Responsibility for the Massacre," *Chicago Daily Tribune*, 3 August 1875; "Mountain Meadow Massacre. Deposition of Brigham Young—The Defense Closed," *Daily Alta California*, 3 August 1875; "Depositions of Presidents Brigham Young and Geo. A. Smith Concerning the Mountain Meadow Massacre," *Deseret Evening News*, 2 August 1875.

48. *Leavenworth Commercial* as reproduced in Baskin, *Reminiscences of Early Utah*, 127.

49. "Brigham's Testimony," *Salt Lake Daily Tribune*, 1 August 1875.

50. "Pacific Coast," *Pioche Daily Record*, 5 August 1875; "The Emigrant Butchery," *Los Angeles Daily Star*, 3 August 1875.

51. Citing the Virginia Enterprise (Virginia City, Nev.), "City Jottings," *Salt Lake Daily Tribune*, 6 August 1875.

52. "The Mountain Meadows Massacre," *Chicago Inter-Ocean*, as reprinted in "Mormon Butchery!," *Salt Lake Daily Tribune*, 1 August 1875.

53. Bishop, "Closing Argument," 4 August 1875, JDLT1:2530–32.

54. Bishop, "Closing Argument," 4 August 1875, JDLT1:2530–32.

55. "The Lee Statement," *Deseret Evening News*, 19 July 1875; "Progress of the Trial of the Mormon Murders," *Los Angeles Daily Star*, 21 July 1875.

56. Bishop, "Closing Argument," 4 August 1875, JDLT1:2528–31.

57. Bishop, "Closing Argument," 4 August 1875, JDLT1:2351.

58. "Mountain Meadow Massacre," *Salt Lake Daily Herald*, 6 August 1875.

59. Spicer, "Opening Argument," 29 July 1875, JDLT1:1248.

60. Baskin, "Closing Argument," 5 August 1875, JDLT1:2998.

61. Joshua 7–8.

62. Miller, "Garden of Eden."

63. Shalev, *American Zion*; Miller, "Garden of Eden"; Clemens, *Roughing It*, 576; "Among the Exchanges," *Messenger*, 12 September 1877; "A Mariner on Mormonism: The Dead Prophet Defended. What Capt. John Codman Thinks of Brigham Young and His People Some Alarming Predictions Ridiculed a Bright View of Utah a Land

Flowing with Railroads and Silver Mines the Observations of a Practiced Observer," *New York Times*, 1 October 1877.

64. Baskin, "Closing Argument," 5 August 1875, JDLT1:2937.

65. Baskin, "Closing Argument," 5 August 1875, JDLT1:2988–89.

66. Young's secretary Wilford Woodruff took notes of the meeting, recording that Lee told Young of an Indian massacre at Mountain Meadows. Woodruff, "Journal," 29 September 1857, CHL.

67. Baskin, "Closing Argument," 5 August 1875, JDLT1:2953.

68. Baskin, "Closing Argument," 5 August 1875, JDLT1:2953.

69. Baskin, "Closing Argument," 5 August 1875, JDLT1:2964.

70. Baskin, "Closing Argument," 5 August 1875, JDLT1:2947.

71. Baskin, "Closing Argument," 5 August 1875, JDLT1:2970.

72. Baskin, "Closing Argument," 5 August 1875, JDLT1:3208.

73. Baskin, "Closing Argument," 5 August 1875, JDLT1:2955–56.

74. Baskin, "Closing Argument," 5 August 1875, JDLT1:2966.

75. Baskin, "Closing Argument," 5 August 1875, JDLT1:2975.

76. Baskin, "Closing Argument," 5 August 1875, JDLT1:2998–3000.

77. Baskin, "Closing Argument," 5 August 1875, JDLT1:3008.

78. Baskin, "Closing Argument," 5 August 1875, JDLT1:3019–20.

79. Baskin, "Closing Argument," 5 August 1875, JDLT1:3133–34.

80. The composition of the jury was consistently debated. Some argued that it was split among Mormons and non-Mormons, another that two Mormons voted to convict. The *Salt Lake Daily Tribune* originally reported that one non-Mormon voted for Lee's acquittal. In the following days, the *Tribune* corrected its report, saying that the gentile had been either paid or baptized by the Mormons. The *Deseret News* chided other papers for assuming that the Mormons all voted to acquit. There was no published consensus. "The Verdict," *Salt Lake Daily Tribune*, 8 August 1875; "The Lee Jury Classified," *Eureka Daily Sentinel*, 11 August 1875; "John T. Caine to Joseph F. Smith," *Latter-Day Saints' Millennial Star*, 30 August 1875; "The Lee Trial," *Deseret Evening News*, 9 August 1875; "City Jottings," *Salt Lake Daily Tribune*, 10 August 1875; "City Jottings," *Salt Lake Daily Tribune*, 11 August 1875.

81. Baskin, *Reminiscences of Early Utah*, 147.

82. Carleton, *Utah and the Mormons*, 122.

83. Young, *Wife No. 19*, 233.

84. "The Mountain Meadows Massacre," *Tri-Weekly New Era*, 18 August 1875. Emphasis original.

85. "The Mormons: Special Order," *Hartford Daily Courant* (Conn.), 29 March 1877.

Chapter Five

1. As cited in "Demanding Justice," *Salt Lake Daily Tribune*, 8 August 1875.

2. MMMCLP, 2:667–70.

3. "The Lee Trial," *Salt Lake Daily Tribune*, 15 September 1876.

4. "The Lee Trial," *Salt Lake Daily Tribune*, 16 September 1876; JDLT2:3741–42; MMMCLP 2:670–75.

5. "The Lee Trial," *New York Times*, 30 September 1876.
6. *MMMCLP* 2:672-76.
7. *MMMCLP* 2:676; Sumner Howard, Closing Argument, JDL-T2 3914-68.
8. *MMMCLP* 2:676-77.
9. Ball, "Cool to the End," 97-108.
10. Cohen, *Pillars of Salt*, 29.
11. Ball, "Cool to the End," 100; Banner, *Death Penalty*, 5-52.
12. "Mountain Meadows. An Interview with John D. Lee, the Condemned Murderer," *Daily Morning Call*, 10 March 1877.
13. "Mountain Meadows. An Interview with John D. Lee, the Condemned Murderer," *Daily Morning Call*, 10 March 1877.
14. Beaver, "Further Evidence of the Conspiracy of the Mormon Priesthood," *Salt Lake Daily Tribune*, 24 September 1876.
15. "Beaver. John D. Lee Will Not Be Sentenced for Ten Days," *Salt Lake Daily Herald*, 21 September 1876.
16. "John D. Lee," *Salt Lake Daily Herald*, 11 October 1876.
17. *MMMCLP* 2:677-78, 692-94.
18. *MMMCLP* 2:749-50.
19. *MMMCLP* 2:749-79.
20. William Bishop to John D. Lee, 23 February 1877, John D. Lee Collection, Huntington Library, San Marino, California.
21. Sumner Howard, "Howard's Defence," *New York Herald*, 9 May 1877.
22. *Sacramento Daily Record-Union*, 22 February 1875.
23. *Virginia City Enterprise*, 24 February 1875. For another example: "John D. Lee's Confession of the Mountain Meadows Massacre," *San Francisco Daily Call*, 23 March 1877.
24. Howard, "Howard's Defence," *New York Herald*, 9 May 1877.
25. Howard, "Howard's Defence," *New York Herald*, 9 May 1877.
26. Douglass, "Henry Douglass to Edward D. Townsend," 28 March 1877.
27. Banner, *Death Penalty*, 146-64.
28. Wood, *Lynching and Spectacle*, 8, 12, 77-81.
29. Lee, Cleland, and Brooks, *Mormon Chronicle*, 2:206-7; "New Advertisements," *Beaver Enterprise*, 2 December 1874; "Those That Want a Good Picture," *Beaver Enterprise*, 19 December 1874; "A Splendid Photograph," *Beaver Enterprise*, 13 April 1875; "The Mountain Meadows Massacre," *Daily Graphic*, 18 May 1875; "John D. Lee of Mountain Meadows," *Salt Lake Daily Tribune*, 17 November 1874; "The Old Butcher," *Salt Lake Daily Tribune*, 20 November 1874; "The Mountain Meadows Massacre of 1857," *Frank Leslie's Illustrated*, 9 January 1875; "The Mountain Meadows Massacre," *Harper's Weekly*, 14 August 1875.
30. Rogerson, "Speech of John D. Lee."
31. Rogerson, "Speech of John D. Lee."
32. "City Jottings," *Salt Lake Daily Tribune*, 3 August 1875, 5 August 1875, 25 March 1877, 27 March 1877, 29 March 1877.
33. "Through the Heart," *Salt Lake Daily Herald*, 24 March 1877.
34. C. J. S., 25 March 1877, in "Shooting of Lee!," *Salt Lake Daily Tribune*, 30 March 1877.

35. Rogerson, "Speech of John D. Lee."
36. Rogerson, "Speech of John D. Lee."
37. "A Mormon Scapegoat," *New York Times*, 23 March 1877; "Criminal News," *Chicago Daily Tribune*, 21 March 1877.
38. Langdon, *Authentic History of the Mormons*, 18.
39. MMMCLP 1:493–503, 511–18.
40. Lee, "John D. Lee to Joseph Hyrum Lee," 24 February 1877; Lee, Cleland, and Brooks, *Mormon Chronicle*, 2:449; McGlashan, *From the Desk of Truckee's*; Lee, "John D. Lee to O. A. Patton," 1 November 1876.
41. Bishop, "William W. Bishop to John D. Lee," 23 February 1877.
42. Bishop, "William W. Bishop to John D. Lee," 9 March 1877.
43. "Lee's Confession," *New York Herald*, 22 March 1877; "John D. Lee Makes a Confession of His Crimes," *San Francisco Chronicle*, 22 March 1877; "Mountain Meadows," *San Francisco Daily Evening Post*, 22 March 1877; Turley, "Problems," 142–57.
44. Lee, *Mountain Meadows Massacre with the Life Confession and Execution* (1877, 1882); Lee, *Das Leben Und Bekenntniss von John D. Lee, Dem Mormonen. Nebst Einen Vollen Bericht Über Das Mountain Meadows Massacre Und Die Hinrichtung von Lee*; Lee, *The Life and Confession of John D. lee, the Mormon. With a full account of the Mountains Meadows Massacre and the Execution of Lee: Helpless Women and Children Butchered in Cold Blood*.
45. Lee, *Life, Confession and Execution of Bishop John D. Lee, the Mormon Fiend*; Lee, *La Vie, La Confesion et L'execution de L'eveque John D. Lee, Le Monstre Mormon*.
46. "Lee's Last Confession," *San Francisco Daily Bulletin Supplement*, 24 March 1877; "Lee's Confession," *Sacramento Daily Record-Union*, 24 September 1877.
47. "Lee's Last Confession," *San Francisco Daily Bulletin Supplement*, 24 March 1877; "Lee's Confession," *New York Herald*, 22 March 1877; "The Confession!," *Salt Lake Daily Tribune*, 28 March 1877; "John D. Lee's Confession of the Mountain Meadows Massacre," *San Francisco Daily Call*, 23 March 1877; "Mountain Meadows. An Interview with John D. Lee, the Condemned Murderer," *Daily Morning Call* (San Francisco), 10 March 1877; "THE GREAT MORMON CRIME: JOHN D. LEE'S DYING TESTIMONY," *New York Times*, 24 March 1877; "Confession of John D. Lee," *Anaheim Gazette*, 24 March 1877; "Lee's Confession," *Stark County Democrat*, 29 March 1877.
48. "Lee's Confession," *New York Herald*, 22 March 1877.
49. Chad Orton has most thoroughly analyzed *Mormonism Unveiled* and the different versions of Lee's confessions. Orton, "Confessions of John D. Lee." His work is also the basis of Turley, "Problems," 142–57.
50. "Reported Confessions of John D. Lee," *Ogden Junction*, 26 March 1877.
51. "The Life of John D. Lee," *Eureka Republican*, 5 May 1877.
52. Howe, *Mormonism Unvailed*.
53. Lee, *Mormonism Unveiled* (1877), iv.
54. Fabricant, "Thomas R. Gray," 332–61.
55. Orton, "Confessions of John D. Lee."
56. Hoffman, *Zealots of Zion*, 159.
57. It remains a source for a number of histories, avowedly anti-Mormon works proliferating with the rise of digital publishing, and an ever-growing number of anti-Mormon websites. Abanes, *One Nation under Gods*; Bagley, *Blood of the Prophets*; Bro-

die, *No Man Knows My History*; Denton, *American Massacre*; Harrod, *Deception by Design*; Hyde, *Empires, Nations and Families*, 484–88; Kreig, *Presidential Puppetry*; Newell and Avery, *Mormon Enigma*; "Mountain Meadows Massacre" in *Violent Encounters*; Wise, *Massacre at Mountain Meadows*; Wishnatsky, *Mormonism*.

58. Though the text of Lee's first pretrial confession is not extant, Bishop publicly claimed that the prosecution had not accepted Lee's confession because "John D. Lee shows, beyond the possibility of a doubt, that Brigham Young is innocent and knew nothing of the massacre until many days after the massacre occurred." "The Lee Trial," *Pioche Daily Record*, 25 July 1875.

59. "The Mormons Arming to Resist the Arrest of Brigham Young," *Dallas Weekly Herald* (Tex.), 12 May 1877.

60. Reprinted from the *Chicago Standard*, "Brigham Young," *Cherokee Advocate*, 19 September 1877.

61. "BRIGHAM YOUNG. Death of the Great Mormon Saint at Salt Lake City," *Chicago Daily Tribune*, 30 August 1877.

62. "The Mormons: Special Order," *Hartford Daily Courant* (Conn.), 29 March 1877.

63. "Mountain Meadows: A Review of the Numerous and Conflicting Statements Concerning the Mountain Meadows Massacre," *California Daily Alta*, 26 March 1877.

64. Oswalt, *Pen Pictures of Mormonism*, 20.

65. "Among the Exchanges," *American Messenger* (New York: American Tract Society), 12 September 1877.

66. For a sampling, see "Brigham Young," *Colorado Banner*, 27 September 1877; "Brigham Young and Mormonism," *Independent*, 6 September 1877; "DEATH OF BRIGHAM YOUNG," *New York Times*, 30 August 1877; "BRIGHAM YOUNG. Death of the Great Mormon Saint at Salt Lake City," *Chicago Daily Tribune*, 30 August 1877.

67. For more recent accounts fixing massacre responsibility on Young, see Wise, *Massacre at Mountain Meadows*, 175–87; Denton, *American Massacre*, 119–21, 157–58; Bagley, *Blood of the Prophets*, 88, 112–13; Krakauer, *Under the Banner of Heaven*, 219; Hyde, *Empires, Nations and Families*, 483.

68. Turner's biography did not specifically address the public impression of Young, yet the perception of Young made the stain indelible. Earlier biographer Leonard Arrington reviewed specific journalist interviews with Young, but not the larger image of Young developed in the press. The absence of specific engagement with the popular narrative by either author suggests their dismissal of the caricature of Young in the American mind. Turner, *Brigham Young*, 397; 275–82, 308–10, 389–97; Arrington, *Brigham Young*, 257–60, 78–80, 300, 322–28, 385–86, 479–80, 493.

69. "The Dead Prophet," *Salt Lake Daily Tribune*, 7 September 1877.

70. "Brigham Young and Mormonism," *Youth's Companion*, 20 September 1877.

71. "Brigham Young and Mormonism," *Youth's Companion*, 20 September 1877 and "Brigham Young," *Colorado Banner* (Boulder), 27 September 1877.

72. "Brigham Young and Mormonism," *Youth's Companion*, 20 September 1877; "Brigham Young," *Colorado Banner* (Boulder), 27 September 1877.

73. "Death of Brigham Young," *Christian Secretary*, 5 September 1877.

74. "Death of Brigham Young," *Maine Farmer*, 8 September 1877.

75. "Brigham Young and Mormonism," *Youth's Companion*, 20 September 1877; H, "BRIGHAM YOUNG," *Chicago Daily Tribune*, 9 September 1877; "Death of Brigham Young," *Christian Secretary*, 5 September 1877.

76. "Brigham Young and His Work," *Chicago Daily Tribune*, 31 August 1877.

77. "BRIGHAM YOUNG," *Elyria Constitution* (Ohio), 6 September 1877.

78. "Brigham Young and His Work," *Chicago Daily Tribune*, 31 August 1877; "Death of Brigham Young," *Maine Farmer*, 8 September 1877.

79. "Biographical: BRIGHAM YOUNG," *Massachusetts Ploughman and New England Journal of Agriculture*, 8 September 1877; David Walker, *Railroading Religion*, 11–12.

80. "More Mormon Troubles," *New York Tribune*, 10 May 1877.

81. "Biographical: BRIGHAM YOUNG," *Massachusetts Ploughman and New England Journal of Agriculture*, 8 September 1877; "The Dead Prophet," *Salt Lake Daily Tribune*, 7 September 1877; "Tuesday Afternoon," *Cincinnati Times*, 31 August 1877; "Brigham Young Preparations for the Obsequies of the Prophet," *Sacramento Daily Record-Union*, 1 September 1877.

82. "The Fruits of Mormonism," *New York Times*, 25 March 1877.

83. Rice, *Mormon Way*, 8–9.

84. For a small smattering of examples, see Morrill, *On the Warpath*, 225; Stenhouse, *"Tell It All"*; Taylor, "A Peep at the Mormons," *Sunday Magazine*, June 1881, 9:6; E. C. B., "Brigham Young and Mormonism," *Lippincott's Magazine of Popular Literature and Science*, October 1877; "Brigham Young and Mormonism," *The Independent . . . Devoted to the Consideration of Politics, Social and Economic Tendencies, History, Literature, and the Arts*, 6 September 1877; "Death of Brigham Young," *Maine Farmer*, 8 September 1877; Beadle, *Life in Utah*, 181.

85. Following a conflict between Lee and members of the Harmony congregation, Lee was removed from his office of branch president during the summer of 1856. Lee, "John D. Lee to Brigham Young," 22 August 1856; Haight, "Isaac C. Haight to Heber C. Kimball," 20 August 1856. The offices of bishop and branch president in 1857 Mormonism were two distinct positions. At the same time Lee was branch president, the office of bishop in Harmony was held by William R. Davies. The branch president presided over the local congregations' spiritual affairs, while the bishop handled temporal matters such as the collection and allocation of tithing.

86. *Sacramento Record* as quoted in "Brigham's Great Crime," *Salt Lake Daily Tribune*, 7 August 1875.

87. Oswalt, *Pen Pictures of Mormonism*, 28.

88. Beadle, *Life in Utah*, 182.

89. Young, *Wife No. 19*, 248.

90. Triplett, *Conquering the Wilderness*, 553.

91. Gash, *False Star*, 396; Klingensmith, "Testimony," 23 July 1875, JDLT1:654.

92. Gash, *False Star*, 397; Stenhouse, *"Tell It All"* (1874), 651; Taylor, "Peep at the Mormons," 642.

93. "The Mountain-Meadow Massacre Revenged," *Chicago Daily Tribune*, 25 March 1877.

94. [No Title], *Zion's Herald*, 29 March 1877.
95. Young, *Wife No. 19*, 233.
96. "The Fruits of Mormonism," *New York Times*, 25 March 1877.
97. *Crimes of the Latter Day Saints in Utah*.
98. *Crimes of the Latter Day Saints in Utah*, 48–52.
99. "Death of Brigham Young," *New York Times*, 30 August 1877; "Brigham Young," *Sacramento Daily Record-Union*, 30 August 1877; "Brigham Young Preparations for the Obsequies of the Prophet," *Sacramento Daily Record-Union*, 1 September 1877; "A Damaging Story.: And the Cattle. Brigham's Opinion of the Massacre. 'the Deed's Done.' Concealing a Wholesale Murder. Lee Tells the Crime. How the Truth Was Told. Confessions Became Frequent. Resting at Last. Ghastly Relics," *Chicago Daily Tribune*, 6 January 1875; "Brigham Young and the Mountain Meadows Massacre," *Tiffin Tribune*, 14 June 1877; "Death of Brigham Young," *Christian Secretary*, 5 September 1877; "Death of Brigham Young," *Maine Farmer*, 8 September 1877; "Among the Exchanges," *Messenger*, 12 September 1877.

Epilogue

1. Waite, *Mormon Prophet and His Harem*, 71.
2. *Reconstruction and Mormon America* offers a comprehensive look at the attempt to remake Mormonism beyond the Mountain Meadows efforts. Milner and Cannon, *Reconstruction and Mormon America*, including Mason, "Disciplinary Democracy," 88–110.
3. Hudson, "There Is No Mormon Trail of Tears," 19–51.
4. Blum, *Reforging the White Republic*, 3.
5. Mason, *Mormon Menace*, 2011.
6. Bancroft, *History of Utah, 1540-1886*, 543–70; Walker, Whittaker, and Allen, *Mormon History*, 20–21.
7. Gash, *False Star*, 341.
8. Wilson, *Lions of the Lord*, (1911).
9. *Buffalo Bill's Double or The False Guide*, Buffalo Bill Stories is one example. These novels would be repeatedly published into the 1960s. *Buffalo Bill's Double or The False Guide*, Buffalo Bill Stories in 1964.
10. Kathleen Flake asserts that "the ultimate purpose of the Senate hearing was to determine whether or not Mormonism was to be 'integrated' or 'dismissed.'" Flake contends that once the Senate decided to integrate Mormonism, the Mormon Problem quickly waned and the evils of Mormonism remained only for those who sought to argue for the Mormon heresy. Flake, *Politics of American Religious Identity*, 157, 195.
11. Flake argues they used Mountain Meadows because they didn't have any more recent tales of Mormon atrocity. Flake, *Politics of American Religious Identity*, 195.
12. "Other Editor's Opinions," *Mower County Transcript*, 27 May 1903; "Mormonism in Utah," *Hawaiian Gazette*, 26 September 1905; [No Title], *Los Angeles Daily Herald*, 11 February 1905; [No Title], *Daily Capital Journal*, 17 May 1906; T. S. Childs, "THE MORMON ISSUE. If the Wind Is Sown Now the Whirlwind Will Soon Follow," *New

York Observer and Chronicle, 8 March 1906; "Senate Has Full Power to Exclude Apostolic Senator," *Salt Lake Daily Tribune*, 12 February 1907; "Mountain Meadow Massacre as Text," *Salt Lake Daily Tribune*, 8 February 1907; T. S. Childs, "MORMONISM AND SENATOR SMOOT. What the Recent Action of the Senate Means to the Nation," *New York Observer and Chronicle*, 4 April 1907. When Smoot supported a fellow Utahn for a seat in the House of Representatives, newspapers called the candidate John D. Lee's favorite son-in-law because he had married a Lee (not a daughter of John D. Lee nor either of them Latter-day Saints). "Son-In-Law of Danite Chief Selected by Smoot for Kearn's Seat in the Senate," *Williston Graphic*, 12 January 1905; "Danite Chief's Son for Senator," *Minneapolis Journal*, 9 January 1905; [No Title], 11 February 1905.

13. "How 1,500,000 American Women Are Fighting Mormonism," *Washington Times*, 22 January 1905.

14. The original appendix included a biographical sketch of Brigham Young. After his death, later editions included sketches of contemporary Mormon prophets. Lewis used the first edition's sketch of Young. Lewis, *Mormon Menace*, vii.

15. For other examples, see Lewis, *Mormon Menace*, 5–6.

16. Berry, *Speech of Hon. James H. Berry*; "Berry Would Exclude Smoot," *Deseret Evening News*, 12 February 1907; "Mountain Meadow Massacre as Text," *Salt Lake Daily Tribune*, 8 February 1907.

17. Alfred Henry Lewis, "Viper on the Hearth," *Cosmopolitan Magazine* 50, no. 4 (March 1911): 439–50; Alfred Henry Lewis, "The Trail of the Viper," *Cosmopolitan Magazine* 50, no. 5 (April 1911): 693–703; Alfred Henry Lewis, "The Viper's Trail of Gold," *Cosmopolitan Magazine* 50, no. 6 (May 1911): 823–33.

18. Lewis, "Viper on the Hearth," 444.

19. Lewis, 450.

20. Hutchison-Jones, "Reviling the Revering the Mormons," 121–60.

21. Allen, *Out of a Clear Sky*; Birney, *Zealots of Zion*.

22. Brooks, *Mountain Meadows Massacre*.

23. Mayo, *Cowboys, Mountain Men, and Grizzly Bears*; Newton, *Fire in the Desert*; Moore, *Mormon Reflections*; Merz, *Red Emerald*; Freeman, *Red Water*; Ebershoff, *19th Wife*; *Last Way Station*.

24. Emily Eakin, "Reopening a Mormon Murder Mystery: New Accusations That Brigham Young Himself Ordered an 1857 Massacre of Pioneers," *New York Times*, 12 October 2002.

25. Bagley, *Blood of the Prophets*; Denton, *American Massacre*. Denton's would not be completed for another two years. In her acknowledgments, she cites Bagley and thanks him for the influence of his work on hers. Paul Reeve and Ardis Parshall provide a thorough critique of *Blood of the Prophets* in *Mormon Historical Studies*.

26. Black, Krakauer, and Boyce, *Under the Banner of Heaven*.

27. Krakauer, *Under the Banner of Heaven*.

28. John G. Turner, "The Mountain Meadows Massacre Revisited," *Huffington Post*, 18 October 2012; Sandhya Somashekhar, "Mitt Romney's Mormon Faith Tangles with a Quirk of Arkansas History," *Washington Post*, 20 May 2012.

29. Hulse and Musegades, *When Salt Lake City Calls*; Capurro, *White Flag, America's First 9/11*, 11; Scott, *Mormon Mirage*; Wishnatsky, *Mormonism*; Levenda, *Angel &*

the Sorcerer. The rise of digital printing has opened up the possibilities for self-publishing and caused another rise in Mountain Meadows narratives.

30. Krakauer, *Under the Banner of Heaven*; Capurro, *White Flag, America's First 9/11*.

31. Damon Linker, "The Big Test: Taking Mormonism Seriously," *New Republic*, 14 January 2006; Linker, *Religious Test*.

32. Biggers, *State out of the Union*.

33. Turley, "What's New," 1–13.

34. Penrose, *Mountain Meadows Massacre*; Wilford Woodruff, "President Woodruff Replies," *Illustrated American*, 7 February 1891, 529–33.

35. Reeve, *Religion of a Different Color*, 263–72.

36. Cain, *September Dawn*, 2007. The screen writer published a parallel narrative several years later to continue her work "to inform the general public of an important event that has been kept relatively quiet" and "the extraordinary lessons" to be learned about the Mormons. Schutter, *September Dawn*; Wilson, *Lions of the Lord*.

37. Ebert, "You can't get 'em up in the mornin'."

38. In the pilot's original screenplay, the girl sang "Amazing Grace," furthering the juxtaposition of Christianity and Griffin's counterfeit religion of violence.

39. Frank, *Godless*.

40. Griffin interrogates the townspeople: "Y'all been baptized? Y'all wash your bodies once a week? Have you committed adultery, ma'am? Have you betrayed your brother, sir? Do you preside in your family as servant of God?" mimicking the questions of the 1850s Mormon Reformation.

41. Gross, interview, "'*Godless*' Creator Was Determined."

42. *Godless*, episode 2, "The Ladies of La Belle."

43. Nicolaou, "This Brutal Scene."

44. Sally Denton's *American Massacre* was one of the books that Frank read before writing his screenplay. Denton's account of the massacre is just one of many which replicate nineteenth-century expansions on the massacre and present them as fact. Denton, *American Massacre*.

45. Sophie Gilbert, "What *Godless* Says about America," *Atlantic*, 27 November 2017.

46. *Under the Banner of Heaven*, episode 1, "One Mighty and Strong."

Bibliography

Primary Sources

Unpublished Manuscript Collections

GOVERNMENT RECORDS

Armstrong, George W. "George W. Armstrong to Brigham Young," 30 September 1857. Records of the Utah Superintendency, 1855-1870, Records of the Bureau of Indian Affairs. NARA.

Bates, George C. "George C. Bates to Benjamin H. Bristow, Solicitor General," 21 December 1871, Source Chronological Files, Letters Received from District of Utah, General Records of the Department of Justice, RG 60. NARA.

Black, Jeremiah S. "Alexander Wilson to Jeremiah S. Black," 30 June 1859. Letters Received, Jeremiah S. Black Collection. LofC.

———. "Jeremiah S. Black to Alexander Wilson," 17 May 1859. General Letterbooks, 5:149, U.S. Department of Justice Records, RG 60, entry 10. NARA.

———. "Jeremiah S. Black to Alfred Cumming," 17 May 1859. General Letterbooks, 5:149, U.S. Department of Justice Records, RG 60, entry 10. NARA.

Campbell, Reuben P. "Reuben P. Campbell to Fitz-John Porter," 6 July 1859. File 61.U, 1859, Utah Correspondence, Adjutant General's Office, U.S. Department of War, RG 393, microfilm. NARA. See also MSS SDoc 40-44; SDoc 42, 14-16.

Carleton, James Henry. "James H. Carleton to William W. Mackall," 24 June 1859. Letters and Telegrams Received, Department of the Pacific, Army, U.S. Department of War Records, RG 393, microfilm. NARA.

———. "James H. Carleton to William W. MacKall," 25 May 1859. Microfilm, Records of the Adjutant General's Office, RG 94. NARA.

Clarke, Newman S. "Newman S. Clarke to Lorenzo Thomas," 28 October 1857. Letterbook 10:270-71, Letters Sent, 1857-1859, Department of the Pacific, Army, Department of War. NARA.

Cradlebaugh, John. "Explanation of Grand Jury Dismissal," 4 April 1859. Minute Book C, 4 April 1859, 166-67, Second District Court, Series 5319. Utah State Archives.

———. "John Cradlebaugh to James Buchannan," 3 June 1859. John Cradlebaugh File, James Buchanan Administration, Utah Appointment Papers, U.S. Department of Justice Records, RG 60, entry 350, NARA, enclosing Peter K. Dotson to John Cradlebaugh, 3 June 1859.

Cradlebaugh, John, and Charles E. Sinclair. "John Cradlebaugh and Charles Sinclair to James Buchanan," 16 July 1859. Microfilm, John Cradlebaugh File, James Buchanan Administration, Utah Appointment Papers, General Records of the Department of Justice. NARA.

Criminal Case File 31, Joint Indictment for Conspiracy, Utah State Archives.
Criminal Case File 32, John M. Higbee, Utah State Archives.
Criminal Case File 33, Samuel Jewkes, Utah State Archives.
Criminal Case File 34, William H. Dame, Utah State Archives.
Criminal Case File 35, William C. Stewart, Utah State Archives.
Criminal Case File 36, Ellott Willden, Utah State Archives.
Criminal Case File 37, Isaac C. Haight, Utah State Archives.
Criminal Case File 38, George W. Adair, Utah State Archives.
Criminal Case File 39, Philip Klingensmith, Utah State Archives.
Criminal Case File 40, John D. Lee, Utah State Archives.
Crofutt, George A. Print of John Nash. *American Progress*, 1873. LofC. www.loc.gov/pictures/item/97507547/.
Douglass, Henry. "Henry Douglass to Edward D. Townsend," 28 March 1877. Correspondence Regarding John D. Lee Trial and Execution, Adjutant General's Office, file 1013, AGO 1877, U.S. Department of War Records, RG 94. NARA.
Forney, Jacob. "Extract from Superintendent Forney's Annual Report, of Sept. 29, 1859," 29 September 1859. Messages of the President, nos. 10 and 42, 241–46, 36th Congress, Papers Pertaining to the Territory of Utah, 1849–1870, Records of the U.S. Senate, RG 46. NARA. See also SDoc 42, 87–89.
———. "Jacob Forney to Albert S. Johnston," 1 May 1859. File 27.U.1859, Utah Correspondence, Adjutant General's Office, U.S. Department of War Records, RG 393, microfilm. NARA. See also MSS SDoc 42, 18–20; SDoc 42, 8–9.
———. "Jacob Forney to Alfred B. Greenwood," August 1859. Messages of the President, nos. 10 and 42, 211–21, 36th Congress, Papers Pertaining to the Territory of Utah, 1849–1870, Records of the U.S. Senate, RG 46. NARA. See also SDoc 42, 75–80.
———. "Jacob Forney to James W. Denver," 18 March 1859. Messages of the President, nos. 10 and 42, 157–59, 36th Congress, Papers Pertaining to the Territory of Utah, 1849–1870, Records of the U.S. Senate, RG 46. NARA. See also SDoc 42, 52–53.
Hawley, Cyrus M. "Cyrus M. Hawley to George H. Williams," 9 November 1872. Letters from the District of Utah, U.S. Department of Justice Files, RG 60, entry 556. NARA.
———. "Cyrus M. Hawley to Ulysses M. Grant," 24 February 1872. Selected Documents Relating to the Mountain Meadows Massacre. NARA.
Landers, F. W., to A. B. Greenwood, 18 February 1860, U.S. Congress, Senate, *Message of the President of the United States, Communicating, in Compliance with a Resolution of the Senate, Information in Relation to the Massacre at Mountain Meadows, and Other Massacres in Utah Territory*, 36th Congress, 1st sess., 1860, Executive Document 42, 131.
Lynch, James. "Affidavit," n.d. File 39.U, Letters Received, 1859, Office of the Adjutant General, U.S. Department of War, RG 393, microfilm. NARA.
"Massacre of the Cheyenne Indians" in Report of the Joint Committee on the Conduct of War, at the second session 38th Congress, Part 3, Serial Set vol. 1214, Session vol. 4, 38th Congress, 2nd sess., S. Rpt. 142 pt. 3, 5.

Montgomery, Samuel. "Samuel H. Montgomery to Alfred B. Greenwood," n.d. File M83, Utah Superintendency, 1849-1880, Letters Received by the Office of Indian Affairs, 1824-1881, U.S. Bureau of Indian Affairs, RG 48, microfilm. NARA.

Nast, Thomas. "Religious Liberty Is Guaranteed: But Can We Allow Foreign Reptiles to Crawl All Over Us." LofC, [ca. 1860-1902].

Resolutions and Memorials, Passed at the Several Annual Sessions, of the Legislative Assembly of the Territory of Utah, from 1851 to 1870 Inclusive. Salt Lake City, Utah: Joseph Bull, 1870, ch. 30, § 22.

"Senate Resolution," 16 March 1860. Department of the Interior, Correspondence, 1860. See also Indian Division, Selected Letters, 1858-1877, Office of the Secretary of the Interior, Department of the Interior; Selected Documents Relating to the Mountain Meadows Massacre, 1857-1876. NARA.

Smith, George A. "Deposition," 30 July 1875. CCF 31. Utah State Archives.

Thompson, Jacob. "Jacob Thompson to Alexander Wilson," 25 April 1859. Selected Documents Relating to the Mountain Meadows Massacre, 1857-1876. NARA.

U.S. Bureau of the Census, "Nativity of the Population for the 25 Largest Urban Places and for Selected Counties: 1850," www.census.gov/population/www/documentation/twps0029/tab21.html.

Young, Brigham. "Deposition," 30 July 1875. CCF 31. Utah State Archives.

Waite, Charles B. "Charles B. Waite to Edward Bates," n.d. Utah Appointment Papers, Abraham Lincoln Administration, U.S. Department of Justice, RG 60. NARA.

Wilson, Alexander. "Alexander Wilson to Jacob Thompson," 4 March 1859. Letters Received, Judiciary Accounts, Utah, 1853-1900, U.S. Department of Justice Records. NARA.

———. "Alexander Wilson to Jeremiah S. Black," 15 November 1859. Utah Appointment Papers, James Buchanan Administration, General Records of the Department of Justice. NARA.

PRIVATE COLLECTIONS

Arrest warrant for John D. Lee, 13 October 1874. Minute Book B, Second District Court Records, Leavitt Special Collections, Southern Utah University, Cedar City, Utah, 289-90.

Bishop, William W. "Jacob S. Boreman Collection," n.d. Huntington Library.

———. "W. W. Bishop to William Nelson," 27 April 1877. John D. Lee Collection, Huntington Library.

———. "William W. Bishop to John D. Lee," 23 February 1877. John D. Lee Collection. Huntington Library.

———. "William W. Bishop to John D. Lee," 9 March 1877. John D. Lee Collection. Huntington Library.

Carleton, James Henry. "James H. Carleton to William W. Mackall," 1 July 1859. Cover sheet and addendum to James H. Carleton, Report to Major W. W. Mackall, 1 July 1859. In Collected Material Concerning the Mountain Meadows Massacre, CHL.

Cradlebaugh, John. "Charge to the Grand Jury," 8 March 1859. Proceedings of Judge Cradlebaugh's Court, March–April 1859, Brigham Young Office Files. CHL.

———. "Cradlebaugh Dismissal of Grand Jury," 21 March 1859. Proceedings of Judge Cradlebaugh's Court, March–April 1859, Brigham Young Office Files. CHL.

Cumming, Alfred. "Alfred Cumming to Lewis Cass," 2 February 1860. Letterpress copybook, 476–92, Alfred Cumming Papers, Duke University, Durham, N.C.; microfilm copy at CHL.

Eckels, Delana. "Delana R. Eckels to Lewis Cass," 27 September 1859. Federal and Local Government Files, Brigham Young Office Files. CHL.

Fennemore, James. "Execution of John D. Lee cabinet card." CHL.

Foote, Warren. "Autobiography and Journal, May 1837–December 1879." CHL.

Haight, Isaac C. "Isaac C. Haight to Heber C. Kimball," 20 August 1856, Incoming Correspondence, Brigham Young Office Files. CHL.

Lee, John D. "John D. Lee to Brigham Young," 22 August 1856, Incoming Correspondence, Brigham Young Office Files. CHL.

———. "John D. Lee to Brigham Young," 20 November 1857. General Incoming Correspondence, Brigham Young Office Files. CHL.

———. "John D. Lee to Joseph Hyrum Lee," 24 February 1877. John D. Lee Collection. Huntington Library.

———. "John D. Lee to O. A. Patton," 1 November 1876. John D. Lee Collection. Huntington Library.

Lockley, Frederic. "Frederic Lockley to Elizabeth Lockley," 31 July 1875. Frederic Lockley Collection. Huntington Library.

———. "Romance of a Suspender Buckle," n.d. Frederic Lockley Collection. Huntington Library.

Pratt, Eleanor McLean. "Brother Snow," letter, ca. 1857. CHL.

———. "Loved Ones in Utah," letter, ca. 1857. CHL.

"Provo Utah Central Stake, General Minutes," 27 September 1857. CHL.

Rogerson, Josiah. Josiah Rogerson to *Deseret News*, telegram, 22 March 1877, Office Files, Brigham Young Collection. CHL

———. "Speech of John D. Lee at Mountain Meadows," 23 March 1877. Collected Material concerning the Mountain Meadows Massacre. CHL.

Woodruff, Wilford. "Journal," 29 September 1857, CHL.

Young, Brigham. "Brigham Young to James W. Denver," 6 January 1858, Governor's Letterbook, 1853–1858, 691–94, Governor's Office Files, Brigham Young Office Files. CHL.

———. "Brigham Young to Daniel H. Wells," 12 November 1874. CHL.

John D. Lee Trial Transcripts

Baskin, Robert N. "Closing Argument," 5 August 1875. JDLT1.

Bennett, Ashael. "Testimony," 23 July 1875. JDLT1.

Bishop, William W. "Closing Argument," 4 August 1875. JDLT1.

———. "Closing Argument," 19 September 1876. JDLT2.

Boreman, Jacob S. "Charge to the Grand Jury," 9 September 1874, *MMMCLP*, 381–89.

———. "Charge to the Jury," 3 August 1875. JDLT1.
———. "Charge to the Jury," 20 September 1876. JDLT2.
———. "Death Sentence of John D. Lee," 10 October 1876. JDLT2.
Bradshaw, John. "Testimony," 29 July 1875. JDLT1.
Carey, William. "Closing Argument," 30 August 1875. JDLT1.
———. "Opening Argument," 22 July 1875. JDLT1.
Denny, Pressley. "Closing Argument," 18 September 1876. JDLT2.
Foster, J.C. "Closing Argument," 18 September 1876. JDLT2.
Hamblin, Jacob. "Testimony," 15–16 September 1876. JDLT2.
Haslam, James. "Testimony," 15 September 1876. JDLT2.
Hoge, Annie Elizabeth, "Testimony," 26 July 1876. JDLT1.
Hoge, Enos D. "Closing Argument," 3 August 1875. JDLT1.
Howard, Sumner. "Closing Argument," 19 September 1876. JDLT2.
Johnson, Nephi. "Testimony," 15 September 1876. JDLT2.
Keyes, Robert. "Testimony," 23 July 1875. JDLT1.
Klingensmith, Philip. "Testimony," 23 July 1875. JDLT1.
Knight, Samuel. "Testimony," 15 September 1876. JDLT2.
McMurdy, Samuel. "Testimony," 15 September 1876. JDLT2.
Morrill, Laban. "Testimony," 15 September 1876. JDLT2.
Pearce, James. "Testimony," 27 July 1875. JDLT1.
Spicer, Wells. "Closing Argument," 18 September 1876. JDLT2.
———. "Opening Argument," 29 July 1875. JDLT1.
Wells, Daniel H. "Testimony," 15 September 1876. JDLT2.
White, Joel. "Testimony," 15 September 1876. JDLT2.
Young, William. "Testimony," 27 July 1875. JDLT1.

Contemporary Published Sources

OFFICIAL PUBLICATIONS

"A. B. Greenwood to Jacob Thompson, 26 November 1859." In *U.S. Bureau of Indian Affairs, Report of the Commissioner of Indian Affairs, Accompanying the Annual Report of the Secretary of the Interior for the Year 1859*, 21–22. Washington, D.C.: George W. Bowman, 1860.

Berry, James Henderson. *Speech of Hon. James H. Berry, of Arkansas, in the Senate of the United States, on the Question of Excluding Hon. Reed Smoot, of Utah, from the United States Senate, Monday, Feb. 11, 1907*. Washington, D.C., 1907.

Carleton, James Henry. *Mountain Meadow [sic] Massacre . . . Special Report of the Mountain Meadow [sic] Massacre, by J. H. Carleton, Brevet Major, United States Army, Captain, First Dragoons.* [Washington, D.C.: Government Printing Office], 1902. Also republished: *Report on the Subject of the Massacre at the Mountain Meadows, in Utah Territory, in Sept., 1857, of One Hundred and Twenty Men, Women, and Children, Who Were from Arkansas [. . .].* Little Rock, Ark.: True Democrat Steam Press Print, 1860.

———. *Utah and the Mormons. Speech of Hon. John Cradlebaugh, of Nevada, on the Admission of Utah as a State. Delivered in the House of Representatives, Feb. 7, 1863.*

Appendix to the Congressional Globe. Washington, D.C.: Congressional Globe Office, 1863. Reprinted in pamphlet form: *Mormon Horrors! Judge Cradlebaugh's Speech in Congress in 1863. Terrible Arraignment of the Blood-Stained Mormon Church. Graphic Account of the Mountain Meadows Massacre.* [. . .]. Salt Lake City, Utah: Salt Lake Tribune, 1864.

Committee on Elections, House, U.S. Congress. *McGrorty vs. Hooper . . . Report of the Committee of Elections upon the Contested Election Case of McGrorty vs. Hooper, Sitting Delegate from the Territory of Utah, Referred to the Committee of Elections, First Session, 40th Congress, 1868*. [Washington, D.C.: Government Printing Office], 1868.

Coolidge, Richard H. *Statistical Report on the Sickness and Mortality in the Army of the United States, Compiled from the Records of the Surgeon General's Office; Embracing a Period of Five Years, from Jan., 1855, to Jan., 1860.* Prepared under the Direction of Brevet Brigadier General Thomas Lawson, Surgeon General of the United States Army, by Richard H. Coolidge, M. D., Assistant Surgeon U.S. Army. Washington, D.C.: George W. Bowman, 1860.

Cragin, Aaron H. *Amendment. Strike out All After . . .* [Washington, D.C.: Government Printing Office], 1872.

———. *Execution of Laws in Utah. Speech of Hon. Aaron H. Cragin, of New Hampshire, Delivered in the Senate of the United States, May 18, 1870.* Washington, D.C.: F. & J. Rives & Geo. A. Bailey, Reporters and printers of the debates of Congress, 1870.

Cureton, William H. "Trekking to California." Typescript, Bancroft Library, University of California, Berkeley.

Dred Scott v. John F. A. Sanford (U.S. Supreme Court 1857).

Gibson, Campbell, and Kay Jung. "Historical Census Statistics on the Foreign-Born Population of the United States: 1850 to 2000." U.S. Bureau of the Census, Population Division, Working Paper No. POP-WP081, 1 February 2006. www.census.gov/content/dam/Census/library/working-papers/2006/demo/POP-twps0081.html.

Hawley, Cyrus Madison. "Cyrus Madison Hawley to Edward O. C. Ord," 12 January 1872. U.S. Congress, House of Representatives, Military Post, Beaver City, Utah, 42nd Congress, 2nd sess., Ex. Doc. No. 285, 1–3.

Hurt, Garland. "Garland Hurt to Jacob Forney," 4 December 1857. SDoc 42, 92–98. (The year is incorrectly given as 1859 in SDoc 42.)

Missouri Governor (Boggs). *Governor's Message [To the Senate and House of Representatives]*. [Jefferson: Calvin Gunn], 1838.

Mitchell, William C. "William C. Mitchell to A. B. Greenwood," 5 July 1859. SDoc 42, 42–43.

———. "William C. Mitchell to William K. Sebastian," 31 December 1857. SDoc 42, 42–43.

Phillips, S. F. *George Reynolds, Plaintiff in Error, vs. the United States. In Error to the Supreme Court of the Territory of Utah. Brief for the United States.* [Washington, D.C.], 1878.

Scotland. Privy Council. *His Majesties Proclamation against a Traiterous Band Contrived in the North.* Thomason Tracts. Printed at Edinburgh: by Evan Tyler, Printer to the Kings most Excellent Majestie, 1646.

Simms, William Emmett. *Speech of Hon. W. E. Simms, of Kentucky on Polygamy in Utah. Delivered in the House of Representatives, Apr. 4, 1860.* [Washington, D.C.]: Printed by Lemuel Towers, 1860.

Stewart, Justice Potter, concurring opinion in *Jacobellis v. Ohio* (1964).

U.S. War Department. *The War of the Rebellion. A Compilation of the Official Records of the Union and Confederate Armies. Published under the Direction of The* . . . Washington, D.C.: Government Printing Office, 1880.

NEWSPAPERS AND MAGAZINES

American Messenger
American Weekly
The American Whig Review
Anaheim Gazette
Arkansas Daily Gazette
Arkansas State Gazette
The Atchinson Daily Globe
The Atlantic
The Bay State Monthly
Beaver Enterprise
Birmingham Daily Post
Bisbee Daily Review
Charles W. Carter Collection, CHL
Cherokee Advocate
Chicago Daily Tribune
Christian Advocate
Christian Secretary
Cincinnati Times
El Clamor Público
Cleveland Herald
The Colorado Banner
Columbia Telescope
The Congregationalist
Cosmopolitan Magazine
Daily Alta California
Daily Capital Journal
Daily Citizen & News
The Daily Cleveland Herald
Daily Evening Bulletin
The Daily Graphic
Daily Inter-Ocean
Daily Oklahoman
The Daily Phoenix
Daily Utah Reporter
Dallas (Tex.) Weekly Herald
Debow's Review, Agricultural, Commercial, Industrial Progress and Resources
Decatur (Ill.) Daily Republican
Delaware Patriot and American Watchman (Wilmington, Del.)
Deseret Evening News
Elmira Daily Advertiser
Elyria Constitution (Ohio)
Eureka Daily Sentinel
Evening Star
Farmer's Cabinet
Fayetteville Arkansian
Fort Smith (Ark.) Elevator
Frank Leslie's Illustrated Newspaper
The Galaxy
Greenville Mountaineer
Harper's New Monthly Magazine
Harper's Weekly
Harrison (Ark.) Daily Times
Hartford (Conn.) Daily Courant
The Hawaiian Gazette
The Huddersfield Daily Chronicle
The Hull Packet and East Riding Times
Illustrated American
The Independent (London)
Jackson Amador Weekly Ledger
Latter-Day Saints' Millennial Star
Lippincott's Magazine of Popular Literature and Science
Little Rock State Gazette and Democrat
Liverpool Mercury
Los Angeles Daily Herald
Los Angeles Daily Star
Los Angeles Times
Los Angeles Weekly Herald
Maine Farmer
Massachusetts Ploughman and New England Journal of Agriculture
Messenger
The Minneapolis Journal
Monroe City Democrat
The Morning Post
Mountain Meadows Massacre Newspaper Clippings, CHL
Mower County Transcript (Lansing, Mich.)
Nashville Union and American
New Orleans Bulletin
The New Republic

New York Herald
New York Observer and
  Chronicle
New-York Spectator
New York Times
New York Tribune
North American Review
Ogden (Utah) Junction
Ohio Observer
Omaha Nebraskan
Painesville (Ohio)
  Telegraph
The Pall Mall Gazette
  (London)
The Phrenological
  Journal and Science
  of Health
Pioche Daily Journal
Pioche Daily Record
Puck
Punchinello
Sacramento Daily
  Record-Union
Salt Lake Daily Herald
Salt Lake Daily
  Tribune
San Andreas Independent
San Francisco Chronicle
San Francisco Daily Call
San Francisco Evening
  Bulletin
San Francisco Herald
San Joaquin (Calif.)
  Republican
Scribners Monthly: An
  Illustrated Magazine for
  the People
The Sheffield & Rotterham
  Independent
The Socorro Chieftain
St. Louis Globe-Democrat
The Stark County
  Democrat
State Rights Democrat
Steubenville Daily
  Herald
The Sunday Magazine
The Tiffin Tribune
Tri-Weekly New Era
The United Service. A
  Monthly Review of
  Military and Naval
  Affairs
Valley Tan (Corrine,
  Utah)
Virginia City (Nev.)
  Enterprise
The York Herald
The Youth's Companion
The Washington Post
The Washington Times
The Weekly Arizona
  Miner
The Weekly Raleigh
  Register
Western Mail
Western Standard
Williston Graphic
Zion's Herald

PUBLISHED BOOKS AND PAMPHLETS

Abanes, Richard. *One Nation under Gods: A History of the Mormon Church*. New York: Thunder's Mouth, 2003.

Ahmanson, John. *Secret History: A Translation of Vor Tids Muhamed*. Chicago: Moody, n.d.

Allen, Merritt Parmelee. *Out of a Clear Sky . . . Decorations by James Macdonald*. New York: Longmans, 1938.

Anderson, G. W. "The Mormon King." New York: J. Andrews, n.d.

Anthony, Piers. *Vision of the Tarot*. 230-31. New York: Berkley, 1980.

Bancroft, Hubert Howe. *History of Utah, 1540-1886*. San Francisco: History Company, 1889.

Baskin, Robert Newton. *Reminiscences of Early Utah, by R. N. Baskin, an Ex-Chief Justice of the Supreme Court of Utah*. [Salt Lake City, UT]: [Tribune-Reporter Printer Co.], [ca. 1914].

Beadle, John H. *Life in Utah; Or, The Mysteries and Crimes of Mormonism. Being an Expose of the Secret Rites and Ceremonies of the Latter-Day Saints, with a Full and Authentic History of Polygamy and the Mormon Sect from Its Origin to the Present Time*. Philadelphia, 1870.

———. "The Mormon Theocracy." *Scribners Monthly: An Illustrated Magazine for the People* vol. 14, no. 3 (July 1877): 394.

———. *Polygamy; Or, the Mysteries and Crimes of Mormonism, Being a Full and Authentic History of Polygamy and the Mormon Sect from Its Origin to the Present Time. With a Complete Analysis of Mormon Society and Theocracy, and an Exposé of the Secret Rites and Ceremonies of the Latter-Day Saints, by J. H. Beadle, Later Editor of the Salt Lake Reporter; Utah Correspondent of the Cincinnati Commercial; and Clerk of the Supreme Court for Utah. Assisted by Hon. O. J. Hollister, United States Revenue Collector for Utah*. Philadelphia: National Publishing Co., 1882.

———. *Polygamy; Or, the Mysteries and Crimes of Mormonism. Being an Exposé of Their Secret Rites and Ceremonies; with a Full and Authentic History of Polygamy and the Mormon Sect, from Its Origin to the Present Time. By J. H. Beadle, Late Editor of the "Salt Lake Reporter," and Clerk of the Supreme Court for Utah. Assisted by Hon. O. J. Hollister, United States Revenue Collector for Utah. Illustrated with Nearly 100 Fine Engravings of Scenes in Utah*. Philadelphia: National Publishing Co., 1884.

———. *The Undeveloped West; Or, Five Years in the Territories: Being a Complete History of That Vast Region between the Mississippi and the Pacific, Its Resources, Climate, Inhabitants, Natural Curiosities, Etc., Etc. Life and Adventure on Prairies, Mountains, and the Pacific Coast. With Two Hundred and Forty Illustrations from Original Sketches and Photographic Views of the Scenery, Cities, Lands, Mines, People, and Curiosities of the Great West*. Philadelphia: National Publishing Co., 1873.

———. *Western Wilds, and the Men Who Redeem Them. An Authentic Narrative, Embracing an Account of Seven Years Travel and Adventure in the Far West . . .* Cincinnati: Jones Brothers, 1878.

Beers, Robert W. *The Mormon Puzzle; and How to Solve It*. New York: Funk and Wagnalls, 1887.

Bennett, Fred E. *A Detective's Experience among the Mormons; Or, Polygamist Mormons, How They Live and the Land They Live In, by Fred E. Bennett, Deputy United States Marshall. Mormonism Unmasked. How Slaves Are Made; How Kept in Subjection. Secrets of the Far-Famed and Iniquitous Endowment House. The Veil Drawn aside by One Who Has Been through It*. Chicago: Laird & Lee, 1887.

Bennett, John C. *The History of the Saints; Or, An Expose of Joe Smith and Mormonism*. Boston: Leland and Whiting, 1842.

Biggers, Jeff. *State out of the Union: Arizona and the Final Showdown over the American Dream*. New York: Nation Books, 2012.

Birney, Hoffman. *Zealots of Zion*. Philadelphia: Penn, 1931.

Bostwick, F. E. *As I Found It. Life and Experiences in Utah among the Mormons. Doctrines and Practices of the Mormon Church, Polygamy, Endowment [sic] Secrets, Destroying Angels, Mountain Meadows Massacre, Present Physical and Political Condition*. [St. Louis, Mo.], 1894.

Boyd, James Penny. *Recent Indian Wars, under the Lead of Sitting Bull, and Other Chiefs; with a Full Account of the Messiah Craze, and Ghost Dances*. [Philadelphia]: Publishers Union, 1891.

———. *Red Men on the War Path, a Thrilling Story of Sunset Land and Its Tragedies. The Peculiar Interesting Life, Manners, Customs, Beliefs and Ceremonials of the North American Indians, and a Wholesome, Interesting Narration of the Tragic Events of Their*

Recent History, Delightfully Presented for the Entertainment and Instruction of Youth, with a Wealth of Portraits and Illustrations. Chicago: J. H. Moore, 1895.

Brewer, Charles. *Retribution at Last. A Mormon Tragedy of the Rockies*. Cincinnati, Ohio: The Editor Publishing Company, 1899.

Brown, Marilyn McMeen Miller. *The Wine-Dark Sea of Grass*. Springville, Utah: Salt Press. Distributed by Cedar Fort, 2000.

Buffalo Bill's Double or The False Guide, Buffalo Bill Stories. Vol. 128: 24 October 1903 and repr. Gold Star Books, 1964.

Buffalo Bill's Double or The False Guide, Buffalo Bill Stories. Repr. Derby, Connecticut: Gold Star Books, 1964.

Bundy, L. A. *Mormonism Exposed; a Faithful Expose of the Secrets and Evils of the Mormon Country, by One Who Possessed the Sixteenth Part of a Husband*. New York: Ornum, 1872.

Bunker, Gary L. and Davis Bitton. *The Mormon Graphic Image, 1834–1914: Cartoons, Caricatures, and Illustrations*. Salt Lake City: University of Utah Press, 1983.

Burningham, Kay. *An American Fraud: One Lawyer's Case against Mormonism*. [S.l.]: Amica Veritatis, 2011.

Burton, Richard. *City of the Saints*. New York: Harper and Brothers, 1861.

Call, Cora Pinkley. *Pioneer Tales of Eureka Springs and Carroll County*. Eureka Springs, Ark.: n.p., 930.

Cannon, Frank Jenne, and George L. Knapp. *Brigham Young and His Mormon Empire*. New York: Fleming H. Revell, 1913.

Capurro, Wayne Atilio. *White Flag, America's First 9/11*. Bloomington, Ind.: AuthorHouse, 2009.

Clemens, Samuel L. *Roughing It, by Mark Twain. Fully Illustrated by Eminent Artists*. Hartford, Conn.: American Publishing Co., 1872.

Codman, John. *Through Utah*. New York, 1875.

Cody, William Frederick. *Life and Adventures of "Buffalo Bill" Colonel William F. Cody. This Thrilling Autobiography Tells in Colonel Cody's Own Graphic Language the Wonderful Story of His Long, Eventful and Heoric Career and Is Supplemented with a Chapter by a Loving, Life-Long Friend Covering His Last Days, Death and Burial . . .* Chicago: Charles C. Thompson, 1917.

Coyner, John McCutchen. *Hand-Book on Mormonism*. Salt Lake City, Utah: Hand-book Publishing, 1882.

Crawford, Captain Jack. *Fonda; Or, The Trapper's Dream*, 1888.

The Crimes of the Latter Day Saints in Utah. By a Mormon of 1831. A Demand for a Legislative Commission. A Book of Horrors. San Francisco: A. J. Leary, Printer and Publisher, 1884.

Dawson, Thomas Fulton. *The Ute War: A History of the White River Massacre and the Privations and Hardships of the Captive White Women among the Hostiles of Grand River, Illustrated. Written and Compiled by Thomas F. Dawson and F. J. V. Skiff, of the Denver Tribune*. Denver, Colo.: Printed by the Tribune Publishing House, 1879.

De Barthe, Joseph. *The Life and Adventures of Frank Grouard, Chief of Scouts, U.S.A.* St. Joseph, Mo.: Combe Printing, 1894.

De Wolff, J. H. *Pawnee Bill (Major Gordon W. Lillie), His Experience and Adventures on the Western Plains; Or, From the Saddle of a "Cowboy and Ranger" to the Chair of a "Bank President."* [Pawnee, Okla.]: Pawnee Bill's Historic Wild West Co., 1902.

Dellenbaugh, Frederick Samuel. *Breaking the Wilderness. The Story of the Conquest of the Far West, from the Wanderings of Cabeza de Vaca to the First Descent of the Colorado by Powell, and the Completion of the Union Pacific Railway, with Particular Account of the Exploits of Trappers and Traders . . .* New York: Knickerbocker, 1905.

Denton, Sally. "A Utah Massacre and Mormon Memory." *New York Times*, 24 May 2003.

Desgranges, Daniele. *Autopsie d'un massacre, mountain meadows: une lacune dans la memorie de l'ouest.* Paris: Plebus, 1990.

Dickinson, Ellen E. *New Light on Mormonism by Mrs. Ellen E. Dickinson, with Introduction by Thurlow Weed.* New York: Funk & Wagnalls, 1885.

Didion, Joan. *Slouching towards Bethlehem.* New York: Farrar, Straus and Giroux, 2008.

Douglas, Stephen Arnold. *Remarks of the Hon. Stephen A. Douglas, on Kansas, Utah, and the Dred Scott Decision.* Chicago: Daily Times Book and Job Office, 1857.

Dr. Williams & Company, College of Anatomy. *Descriptive Catalogue of Dr. Williams & Co. College of Anatomy, 298 State Street, Chicago, Ill. Mammoth Gallery of Science, Art, and Curiosities. Mysteries of Man and Woman. Chamber of Horrors.* [Chicago], 1878.

Duke, Thomas S. *Celebrated Criminal Cases of America.* San Francisco: James H. Barry, 1910.

Dunn, Ballard S. *How to Solve the Mormon Problem. Three Letters by Rev. Ballard S. Dunn, Presbyter of the Protestant Episcopal Church.* New York: American News Company, Agents, 1877.

Dunn, Jacob Piatt. *Massacres of the Mountains; a History of the Indian Wars of the Far West, by J. P. Dunn, Jr., M.S. LL.B.E.* New York: Harper & Brothers, 1886.

Ebershoff, David. *The 19th Wife: A Novel.* New York: Random House Trade Paperbacks, 2009.

Fallows, Samuel, and Helen M. Fallows. *The Mormon Menace.* Chicago: Woman's Temperance Publishing Association, 1903.

Faris, John Thomson. *The Romance of the Rivers.* New York: Harper & Brothers, 1927.

Fitzgerald, David. *The Mormons: The Complete Heretic's Guide to Western Religion.* [U.S.]: [CreateSpace], 2013.

Folk, Edgar Estes. *The Mormon Monster or The Story of Mormonism Embracing the History of Mormonism as a Religious System Mormonism as a Social System Mormonism as a Political System with a Full Discussion of the Subject of Polygamy.* Chicago: Fleming H. Revell, 1900.

Franklin, J. B. *The Mysteries and Crimes of Mormonism.* London: E. Eliot, n.d.

Freece, Hans Peter. *The Letters of an Apostate Mormon to His Son. Illustrated by Verona P. Turini.* [New York]: [Arranged and printed by the Wolfer Press], 1908.

Freeman, Judith. *Red Water.* New York: Pantheon Books, 2002.

Gash, Abram Dale. *The False Star: A Tale of the Occident.* Chicago: W. B. Conkey, 1899.

Ghent, William James. *The Road to Oregon, a Chronicle of the Great Emigration Trail. With 32 Illustrations and a Map*. London: Longmans, Green, 1929.

Gibbs, Josiah Francis. *The Essence of Mormonism. Quotations from Mormon Sermons and Writings and a Few Paragraphs of Friendly Criticism, Also a Brief Sketch of the Mountain Meadows Massacre (illustrated)*. [Salt Lake City, Utah]: [J. F. Gibbs], 1909.

———. *The Mountain Meadows Massacre. Illustrated by Nine Full-Page and Five Half-Page Engravings from Photographs Taken on the Ground*. [Salt Lake City, Utah]: Salt Lake Tribune, 1910.

Gilmore, Mikal. *Shot in the Heart*. New York: Anchor Books/Doubleday, 1995.

Greeley, Horace. *An Overland Journey, from New York to San Francisco, in the Summer of 1859*. New York: C. M. Saxton, Barker, 1860.

Grimmett, Gerald. *The Ferry Woman: A Novel of John D. Lee and the Mountain Meadows Massacre*. Boise, Idaho: Limberlost, 2001.

Hafen, LeRoy R., and Ann W. Hafen. *The Utah Expedition, 1857-58*. Glendale, Calif.: A. H. Clark, 1958.

Hardin, J. D. *Bibles, Bullets and Brides*. New York: Berkley Books, 1983.

Harris, Franklin Stewart. *The Fruits of Mormonism*. New York: Macmillan, 1925.

Harrod, Allen F. *Deception by Design: The Mormon Story*. Bloomington, Indiana: WestBow, 2011.

Haslam, James Holt. *Supplement to the Lecture on the Mountain Meadows Massacre. Important Additional Testimony Recently Received*. Salt Lake City, Utah: Printed at Juvenile Instructor Office, 1885.

Hobbs, James. *Wild Life in the Far West; Personal Adventures of a Border Mountain Man. Comprising Hunting and Trapping Adventures with Kit Carson and Others; Captivity and Life among the Comanches; Services under Doniphan in the War with Mexico, and in the Mexican War against the French; Desperate Combats with Apaches, Grizzly Bears, Etc., Etc. By Captain James Hobbs, of California. Illustrated with Numerous Engravings. Published by Subscription Only*. Hartford, Conn.: Wiley, Waterman & Eaton, 1872.

Hollenbeck, Benjamin W. *Zion. A Drama, in a Prologue and Four Acts, by B. W. Hollenbeck, M.D. Author of "After Ten Years,"—to Which Is Added—a Description of the Costumes—cast of the Characters—entrances and Exits—relative Positions of the Performers on the Stage, and the Whole of the Stage Business. Printed from the Author's Original Manuscript*. Clyde, Ohio: A. D. Ames, 1886.

Holwell, John Zephaniah. *India Tracts by Mr. Holwell and Friends*, 1764.

Horton, Emily (McCowen). *Our Family, with a Glimpse of Their Pioneer Life*. [n.p.], 1922.

Howe, Eber D. *Mormonism Unvailed: Or, A Faithful Account of That Singular Imposition and Delusion, from Its Rise to the Present Time [. . .]*. Painesville, Ohio: E. D. Howe, 1834.

Hulse, Rocky, and Michael Musegades. *When Salt Lake City Calls: Is There a Conflict between Mormonism and the Public Trust?* [Longwood, Fla.]: Xulon, 2007.

Hunt, Hiram Morris. *Mormon Tea*. Klamath Falls, Ore., 1966.

Inman, Henry. *The Great Salt Lake Trail, by Colonel Henry Inman, Late Assistant Quatermaster, United States Army . . . and Colonel William F. Cody, "Buffalo Bill" Late Chief of Scouts*. New York: Macmillan, 1898.

James, Jason W. *Memorial Events in the Life of Captain Jason W. James.* [Roswell, N.M.], 1911.

———. *Memories and Viewpoints.* Roswell, N.M.: Privately printed, 1928.

Jarman, William. *Hell upon Earth: Scenes of Mormon Life.* Exeter, England: H. Leducs Steam Printing Works, 1884.

Johnson, Samuel. *Dictionary of the English Language.* London: Reed, Orme, Brown, and Green, 1827.

Kinney, Bruce. *Mormonism: The Islam of America.* New York: Fleming H. Revell, 1913.

Krakauer, Jon. *Under the Banner of Heaven: A Story of Violent Faith.* New York: Anchor, 2004.

Kreig, Andrew. *Presidential Puppetry: Obama, Romney and Their Masters.* Washington, D.C.: Eagle View, 2013.

Langdon, H. Andre. *An Authentic History of the Mormons.* [Chicago]: [M. Stein], 1913.

The Last Way Station. AmazonEncore, 2013.

Lauran Paine. *The Massacre at Mountain Meadows.* London: Transworld, 1958.

Lee, John Doyle. [with William W. Bishop]. *Das Leben und Bekenntniss von John D. Lee, Dem Mormonen. Nebst Einen Vollen Bericht Über Das Mountain Meadows Massacre Und Die Hinrichtung von Lee.* Philadelphia: Barclay, 1877.

———. *La Vie, La Confesion et L'execution de L'eveque John D. Lee, Le Monstre Mormon. Ses Dix—Sept Epouses—Details Terribel Depuiasas Mort—Implication de Brigham Young—Le Massacre Fe Mountain Meadows.* Philadelphia: Old Franklin Publishing House, 1877.

———. *The Life and Confession of John D. Lee, the Mormon. With a full account of the Mountain Meadows Massacre and the Execution of Lee: Helpless Women and Children Butchered in Cold Blood by Merciless Mormon Assassin.* Philadelphia: Barclay, 1877.

———. *Life, Confession and Execution of Bishop John D. Lee, the Mormon Fiend; His Seventeen Wives—startling Details of His Death—implication of Brigham Young—the Massacre at Mountain Meadows. Also the Escape of His Daughter from Salt Lake City—her Pursuit by the Danties for Refusing to Marry Orson Pratt, Her Exposure of the Affairs of the "The Lion House."* Philadelphia: Old Franklin Publishing House, 1877.

———. *Mormonism Unveiled: Confessions of John D. Lee and Brigham Young.* Lewisburg, Pa.: S. T. Buck, Son, and Co., 1882.

———. *Mormonism Unveiled: The Life and Confession of John D. Lee and the Complete Life of Brigham Young.* Albuquerque: University of New Mexico Press, 2001.

———. *Mormonism Unveiled; Or, the Life and Confessions of Late Bishop, John D. Lee; (written by Himself) Embracing a History of Mormonism from Its Origin down to the Present Time, with an Exposition of the Secret History, Signs, Symbols and Crimes of the Mormon Church. Also the True History of the Horrible Butchery Known as the Mountain Meadows Massacre.* St. Louis, Mo.: Bryan, Brand, 1877.

———. *The Mountain Meadows Massacre with the Life Confession and Execution of John D. Lee, the Mormon. Helpless Woman and Children Butchered in Cold Blood by Merciless Mormon Assassins.* Philadelphia: Barclay, 1877, 1882.

Lee, John Doyle, Robert Glass Cleland, and Juanita Brooks. *A Mormon Chronicle: The Diaries of John D. Lee, 1848–1876.* 2 vols. San Marino, Calif.: Huntington Library, 2003.

Levenda, Peter. *The Angel & the Sorcerer: The Remarkable Story of the Occult Origins of Mormonism and the Rise of Mormons in American Politics*. Lake Worth, Fla.: Ibis, 2012.

Lewis, Alfred Henry. *The Mormon Menace; Being the Confession of John Doyle Lee, Danite, an Official Assassin of the Mormon Church under the Late Brigham Young. Introduction by Alfred Henry Lewis with Numerous Illustrations*. New York: Home Protection, 1905.

———. *A Word with You about the Mormon Menace*. [n.p.]: Home Protection, 1905.

Linker, Damon. *The Religious Test: Why We Must Question the Beliefs of Our Leaders*. New York: W. W. Norton, 2010.

Little, J. H. *The Black Hole: The Question of Holwell's Veracity*, 1915.

London, Jack. *The Star Rover*. New York: Macmillan, 1915.

Lyford, C. P. *The Mormon Problem. An Appeal to the American People. With an Appendix, Containing Four Original Stories of Mormon Life, Founded upon Fact, and a Graphic and Thrilling Account of the Mountain Meadows Massacre*. New York: Hunt & Eaton, 1886.

MacKinnon, William. *At Sword's Point*. Norman, Okla.: Arthur H. Clark, 2008.

Manly, William Lewis. *Death Valley in '49. Important Chapter of California Pioneer History. The Autobiography of a Pioneer Detailing His Life from a Humble Home in the Green Mountains to the Gold Mines of California; and Particularly Reciting the Suffering of the Band of Men, Women and Children Who Gave "Death Valley" Its Name*. San Jose, Calif.: Pacific Tree and Vine, 1894.

Martin, Stuart. *The Mystery of Mormonism*. New York: E. P. Dutton, 1920.

Mather, Cotton. *Magnalia Christi Americana; or, The Ecclesiastical History of New-England from Its First Planting, in the Year 1620, unto the Year of Our Lord 1698*. Hartford, Conn.: Silas Andrus & Son, 1853, 2:635.

Maxwell, William Audley. *Crossing the Plains, Days of '57. A Narrative of Early Emigrant Travel to California by the Ox-Team Method*. San Francisco: Sunset Publishing House, 1915.

Mayhew, Henry. *The Mormons or the Latter-day Saints: A Contemporary History*, ed. Charles Mackay. London: National Illustrated Library, 1851.

Mayo, Matthew P. *Cowboys, Mountain Men, and Grizzly Bears: Fifty of the Grittiest Moments in the History of the Wild West*. Guilford, Conn.: TwoDot, 2009.

McAfee, George F. *Map Talk on Missions among the Mormons*. New York: The Presbyterian Church. Woman's Board of Home Missions, 1903.

McGlashan, Charles Fayette. *From the Desk of Truckee's C. F. McGlashan: His Letters to Eliza Donner Houghton, Donner Party Survivor, Investigative Report of a Massacred Wagon Train, Truckee-Tahoe Adventures and More*. Truckee, California: Truckee-Donner Historical Society, 1986.

Merz, Dominique. *Red Emerald: Dirty Secrets behind Precious Stones*. CreateSpace Independent Publishing Platform, 2013.

Mill, John Stuart. *On Liberty*. London: John W. Parker and Son, 1859.

Miller, Joaquin. *'49 The Gold Seeker of the Sierras*. New York: Funk & Wagnalls, 1884.

Moore, Beth Shumway. *Mormon Reflections: The Path to Mountain Meadows*. Cedar City, UT: Jordan, 2007.

Mooso, Josiah. *The Life and Travels of Josiah Mooso. A Life on the Frontier among Indians and Spaniards, Not Seeing the Face of a White Woman for Fifteen Years. . . .* Winfield, Kan.: Telegram Print., 1888.

"Mormonism (Jack-in-the-Box)," Charles W. Carter Collection, CHL.

Morrill, Gulian Lansing. *The Curse of the Caribbean and the Three Guianas (Gehennas).* Minneapolis, MN: Pioneer Printers, 1920.

———. *The Devil in Mexico*. Minneapolis, MN: 1917.

———. *Hawaiian Heathen and Others. By G. L. Morrill*. Minneapolis, MN: 1919.

———. *On the Warpath*. Minneapolis, MN: 1918.

———. *To Hell and Back: My Trip to South America*. Chicago: M. A. Donohue, 1914.

Names, Gerald Wayne. *Home from the Meadows*. Salt Lake City: E.B. Houchin, 1997.

Neal, Rev. Robert B. *The Mountain Meadow [sic] Massacre. Revolting Crime on the Plains of 1857, Now an Historic Incident, Laid at the Door of the Mormon Church*. [Grayson, Ky.?]: The Evangelist and Anti-Mormon Leader, 1910.

Newton, D. B. *Fire in the Desert*. Waterville, Me.: Thorndike, 2005.

Northrop, Henry Davenport. *Wonderful Developments of the Nineteenth Century Containing a Full and Graphic Account of the Marvelous Achievements of One Hundred Years Including Great Battles and Conquests; the Rise and Fall of Nations; Wonderful Growth and Progress of the United States; Famous Explorations, Discoveries, Etc., Etc. . . .* Philadelphia: World Bible House, 1900.

Oswalt, Martin Luther. *Pen Pictures of Mormonism*. Philadelphia: American Baptist Publication Society, 1899.

Oxford English Dictionary. Oxford University Press. http://oed.com.

Pacific Art Company, San Francisco. *History of the Mountain Meadows Massacre, or the Butchery in Cold Blood of 134 Men, Women, and Children by Mormons and Indians, Sept. 1857, Also a Full and Complete Account of the Trial, Confession and Execution of John D. Lee, the Leader of the Murderers*. San Francisco: Spaulding and Barto, Book and Job Printers, 1877.

Paddock, A. G. *In the Toils; Or, Martyrs of the Latter Days*. Chicago: Dixon & Shepard, 1879.

Paddock, Cornelia. *The Fate of Madame La Tour. A Tale of Great Salt Lake, by Mrs. A. G. Paddock*. New York: Fords, Howard, & Hulbert, 1881.

Parker, Basil G. *The Life and Adventures of Basil G. Parker; an Autobiography*. Plano, Calif.: F. W. Reed Printers, 1902.

———. *Recollections of the Mountain Meadows Massacre, Being an Account of the Awful Atrocity and Revealing Some Facts Never Before Made Public*. Plano, Calif.: Fred W. Reed Printers, 1901.

Parry, Darren. *The Bear River Massacre: A Shoshone History*. Salt Lake City, UT: By Common Consent, 2019.

Pearson, Edward. *Designs against Charleston: The Trial Records of the Denmark Vesey Slave Conspiracy of 1822*. Chapel Hill: University of North Carolina Press, 1999.

Penrose, Charles W[illiam]. *The Mountain Meadows Massacre. Who Were Guilty of the Crime?* Salt Lake City, Utah: Printed at Juvenile instructor office, 1884.

Rice, Claton Silas. *The Mormon Way*. [Billings, Mont.?], 1929.

Schutter, Carole Whang. *September Dawn, Based on the Film, September Dawn*. River Ranch Press, 2013.

Scott, Latayne Colvett. *The Mormon Mirage: A Former Mormon Looks at the Mormon Church Today*. Grand Rapids, Mich.: Zondervan, 2009.

Shea, William L. "A Semi-Savage State: The Image of Arkansas in the Civil War," *Arkansas Historical Quarterly* 48, no. 4 (Winter 1989): 309–28.

Stenhouse, Fanny. *Expose of Polygamy: A Lady's Life among the Mormons*. Logan: Utah State University Press, 2008.

———. *Exposé of Polygamy in Utah. A Lady's Life among the Mormons. A Record of Personal Experience as One of the Wives of a Mormon Elder during a Period of More than Twenty Years. By Mrs. T. B. H. Stenhouse, of Salt Lake City. Illustrated by H. L. Stephens*. New York: American News Company, 1872.

———. *A Lady's Life among the Mormons. A Record of Personal Experience as One of the Wives of a Mormon Elder during a Period of More than Twenty Years*. New York: Russell Brothers, 1872.

———. *"Tell It All." The Story of a Life's Experience in Mormonism. An Autobiography: By Mrs. T. B. H. Stenhouse of Salt Lake City, For More than Twenty Years the Wife of a Mormon Missionary and Elder. With Introductory Preface by Mrs. Harriet Beecher Stowe*. Hartford, Conn.: A. D. Worthington, 1874, 1877, 1878.

Stenhouse, T. B. H. *The Rocky Mountain Saints: A Full and Complete History of the Mormons, from the First Vision of Joseph Smith to the Last Courtship of Brigham Young*. New York: D. Appleton, 1873.

Terence Parker. *All Who Can Tell: A Short, Illustrated Account of the Mountain Meadows Massacre / Terence Parker*. Salisbury: Romans, 2008.

Thomas, Rev. J. C. *The Mistakes of Mormon and of Mormons*. Nashville, Tenn.: Publishing House Methodist Episcopal Church, 1899.

Tracy, Albert. "Journal of Captain Albert Tracy, 1858–1860." *Utah Historical Quarterly* 104, no. 58 (1945): 19 March 1859 entry.

Triplett, Frank. *Conquering the Wilderness; Or, New Pictorial History of the Life and Times of the Pioneer Heroes and Heroines of America. A Full Account of the Romantic Deeds, Lofty Achievements, and Marvelous Adventures of Boone, Kenton [and Others] with Picturesque Sketches of Border Life, Past and Present, Backwoods Camp Meetings, Schools and Sunday-Schools; Heroic Fortitude and Noble Deeds of the Pioneer Wives and Mothers . . . the Overland Route and Its Horrors. . . . Brigham Young . . . and Describing Life and Adventure on the Plains and in the Mining Camps of Today . . .* Chicago: National Book and Picture Co., 1883.

———. *History, Romance and Philosophy of Great American Crimes and Criminals; Including the Great Typical Crimes That Have Marked the Various Periods of American History from the Foundation of the Republic to the Present Day, with Personal Portraits, Biographical Sketches . . . by Col. Frank Triplett . . .* New York: N. D. Thompson, 1884.

Trumble, Alfred. *The Mysteries of Mormonism: A Full Exposure of Its Secret Practices and Hidden Crimes. By An Apostle's Wife*. New York: Richard K. Fox, 1881.

Turley, Richard E., Janiece Johnson, and LaJean Purcell Carruth. *The Mountain Meadows Massacre Collected Legal Papers*. Norman: University of Oklahoma Press, 2017.

Vindex. [pseud.] *Mountain Meadows Massacre. Review of Elder Penrose's Exculpatory Address Delivered Oct. 26th, 1884, in Twelfth Ward Meeting House.* [Salt Lake City?], 1884.

Waite, C. V. (Catherine Van Valkenburg). *The Mormon Prophet and His Harem: Or, An Authentic History of Brigham Young, His Numerous Wives and Children*, 1866.

Wilson, Harry Leon. *The Lions of the Lord. A Tale of the Old West.* Boston: Lothrop, 1903.

———. *The Lions of the Lord.* London: Grant Richards, 1911.

Wishnatsky, Martin. *Mormonism: A Latter Day Deception.* Fargo, ND: Xulon, 2012.

Young, Ann Eliza (Webb). *Wife No. 19; Or, the Story of a Life in Bondage, Being a Complete Exposé of Mormonism, and Revealing the Sorrows, Sacrifices and Sufferings of Women in Polygamy, by Ann Eliza Young, Brigham Young's Apostate Wife.* Chicago: Dustin, Gilman, 1875.

Secondary Sources

Books and Articles

Aitken, Robert and Marilyn Aitken. "Legal Lore: Mountain Meadows Massacre." *Litigation* 33, no. 2 (2007), 57–62.

Alexander, Thomas G. *Brigham Young, the Quorum of the Twelve, and the Latter-day Saint Investigation of the Mountain Meadows Massacre.* Leonard J. Arrington Mormon History Lecture Series no. 12. Logan: Special Collections and Archives, Utah State University, 2007.

———. *Mormonism in Transition: A History of the Latter-day Saints, 1890–1930.* Urbana: University of Illinois Press, 1986.

Andrews, Donald Frank. *The American Whig Review, 1845–1852: Its History and Literary Contents.* Knoxville: University of Tennessee, 1977.

Arrington, Leonard J. *Brigham Young: American Moses.* New York: Knopf, 1985.

———. "Crusade against Theocracy: The Reminiscences of Judge Jacob Smith Boreman of Utah, 1872–1877." *Huntington Library Quarterly* 24, no. 1 (November 1960): 1–45.

Auerbach. *Male Call: Becoming Jack London.* Durham, N.C.: Duke University Press, 1996.

Axeen, David. "'Heroes of the Engine Room': American 'Civilization' and the War with Spain." *American Quarterly* 36, no. 4 (1 October 1984): 481–502.

Backus, Anna Jean. *Mountain Meadows Witness: The Life and Times of Bishop Philip Klingensmith.* Spokane, Wash.: Arthur H. Clark, 1995.

———. *Through Bonds of Love: In the Shadow of the Mountain Meadows Massacre.* Orem, Utah: AJB Distributing, 1998.

Bagley, Will. *Blood of the Prophets: Brigham Young and the Massacre at Mountain Meadows.* Norman: University of Oklahoma Press, 2002.

Bain, David Haward. "The Great Utah Mystery: Somebody Massacred 140 People in Southern Utah in 1857, but Not Everyone Agrees Who." *New York Times*, 7 September 2003.

Ball, Durwood. "Cool to the End: Public Hangings and Western Manhood." In *Across the Great Divide: Cultures of Manhood in the American West*, edited by Matthew Basso, Laura McCall, and Dee Garceau, 97–108. New York: Routledge, 2001.

Banner, Stuart. *The Death Penalty: An American History*. Cambridge, Mass.: Harvard University Press, 2002.

Bashore, Melvin. "'The Bloodiest Drama Ever Perpetrated on American Soil': Staging the Mountain Meadows Massacre for Entertainment." *Utah Historical Quarterly* 80, no. 3 (2012): 258–71.

Basso, Matthew, Laura McCall, and Dee Garceau. *Across the Great Divide: Cultures of Manhood in the American West; Cultures of Manhood in the American West*. New York: Routledge, 2001.

Beasley, David. *McKee Rankin and the Heyday of the American Theater*. Waterloo, Ontario, Canada: Wilfrid Laurier University Press, 2002.

Bederman, Gail. *Manliness & Civilization: A Cultural History of Gender and Race in the United States, 1880–1917*. Chicago: University of Chicago Press, 1995.

Bellesiles, Michael. *Documenting American Violence: A Sourcebook*. New York: Oxford University Press, 2005.

Berkhofer, Robert, Jr. *The White Man's Indian: Images of the American Indian from Columbus to the Present*. New York: Vintage, 1979.

Bigler, David L, and Bagley. *Innocent Blood: Essential Narratives of the Mountain Meadows Massacre*. Norman, Okla.: Arthur H. Clark, 2008.

Blackhawk, Ned. *Violence over the Land: Indians and Empires in the Early American West*. Cambridge, Mass.: Harvard University Press, 2009.

Blum, Edward J. *Reforging the White Republic: Race, Religion, and American Nationalism, 1865–1898*. Baton Rouge: Louisiana State University Press, 2005.

Bowman, Matthew Burton. *The Mormon People: The Making of an American Faith*. New York: Random House, 2012.

Briggs, Robert H. "A Seething Cauldron of Controversy: The First Trial of John D. Lee, 1875." *Journal of Mormon History* 39, no. 1 (Winter 2013): 1–35.

Brodie, Fawn M. *No Man Knows My History: The Life of Joseph Smith*. New York: Alfred A. Knopf, 1945.

Brooks, Juanita. *The Mountain Meadows Massacre*. Stanford, Calif.: Stanford University Press, 1950.

Brown, Richard Maxwell. *Strain of Violence: Historical Studies of American Violence and Vigilantism*. Oxford and New York: Oxford University Press, 1977.

Burnham, Michelle. *Captivity and Sentiment: Cultural Exchange in American Literature, 1682–1861*. Hanover, N.H.: University Press of New England, 1997.

Carnes, Mark C. *Secret Ritual and Manhood in Victorian America*. Repr. New Haven, Conn.: Yale University Press, 1991.

Chatterjee, Partha. *The Black Hole of Empire: History of a Global Practice of Power*. Princeton, N.J.: Princeton University Press, 2012.

Clark, David, and Joane Nagel. "'White Men, Red Masks': Appropriation of 'Indian' Manhood in Imagined Wests." In *Across the Great Divide: Cultures of Manhood in the American West*, 114. 1st ed. New York: Routledge, 2001.

Cohen, Daniel A. *Pillars of Salt, Monuments of Grace: New England Crime Literature and the Origins of American Popular Culture, 1674–1860*. Liverpool: Liverpool University Press, 1993.

Coleman, Ronald. "Utah's Black Pioneers: 1847–1869." *Umoja: A Scholarly Journal of Black Studies* 2 (Summer 1978): 95–110.

Cott, Nancy F. "Two Beards: Coauthorship and the Concept of Civilization." *American Quarterly* 42, no. 2 (1 June 1990): 274–300.

Dary, David. *Red Blood & Black Ink: Journalism in the Old West*. New York: Knopf, 1998.

Davis, David Brion. *The Fear of Conspiracy; Images of Un-American Subversion from the Revolution to the Present*. Ithaca, N.Y.: Cornell University Press, 1971.

———. "Some Themes of Counter-Subversion: An Analysis of Anti-Masonic, Anti-Catholic, and Anti-Mormon Literature." *Mississippi Valley Historical Review* 47, no. 2 (1 September 1960): 205–24.

Davis, F. James. *Who Is Black?: One Nation's Definition*. University Park: Pennsylvania State University Press, 2001.

Deloria, Philip Joseph. *Playing Indian*. New Haven, Conn.: Yale University Press, 1998.

Denton, Sally. *American Massacre: The Tragedy at Mountain Meadows, September 1857*. New York: Alfred A. Knopf. Distributed by Random House, 2003.

———. "The Mountain Meadows Massacre Revisited." *Huffington Post*, 18 October 2012. www.huffingtonpost.com/john-g-turner/mountain-meadows-massacre-revisisted_b_1962285.html.

Ditz, Toby L. "The New Men's History and the Peculiar Absence of Gendered Power: Some Remedies from Early American Gender History." *Gender & History* 16, no. 1 (April 2004): 1–35.

Dorson, Richard M. *America Begins: Early American Writing*. New York: Pantheon Books, 1950.

———. *American Folklore*. Chicago: University of Chicago Press, 1977.

Dwyer, Philip G., and Lyndall Ryan. "Introduction: The Massacre and History." In *Theaters of Violence: Massacre, Mass Killing and Atrocity throughout History*, edited by Philip G. Dwyer and Lyndall Ryan. Studies on War and Genocide. New York: Berghahn Books, 2012, xi–xxvi.

Dwyer, Philip G., and Lyndall Ryan, eds. *Theaters of Violence: Massacre, Mass Killing and Atrocity throughout History*. Studies on War and Genocide. New York: Berghahn Books, 2012.

Dykstra, Robert R. *The Cattle Towns*. Lincoln: University of Nebraska Press, 1983.

Earle, Jonathan, and Diane Mutti Burke. *Bleeding Kansas, Bleeding Missouri: The Long Civil War on the Border*. Lawrence: University Press of Kansas, 2013.

Ebert, Roger. "You can't get 'em up in the mornin'." RogerEbert.com, 23 August 2007. www.rogerebert.com/reviews/september-dawn-2007.

Ekins, Roger Robin. *Defending Zion: George Q. Cannon and the California Mormon Newspaper Wars of 1856–1857*. Spokane, Wash.: Arthur H. Clark, 2002.

Erthman, Marta M. "Race Treason: The Untold Story of America's Ban on Polygamy." *Columbia Journal of Gender and Law* 19, no. 2 (2010): 287–366.

Etcheson, Nicole. *Bleeding Kansas: Contested Liberty in the Civil War Era*. Lawrence: University Press of Kansas, 2004.

Evans, Curtis J. *The Burden of Black Religion*. New York: Oxford University Press, 2008.

Fabricant, Daniel S. "Thomas R. Gray and William Styron: Finally, A Critical Look at the 1831 Confessions of Nat Turner." *American Journal of Legal History* 37, no. 3 (1993): 332–61.

Fancher, Burr. *Captain Alexander Fancher: Adventurer, Drover, Wagon Master and Victim of the Mountain Meadows Massacre*. Portland, Ore.: Inkwater, 2006.

Farmer, Jared. *On Zion's Mount: Mormons, Indians, and the American Landscape*. Cambridge, Mass.: Harvard University Press, 2008.

Fife, Austin F., and Francesca Redden. "The Pseudo-Indian Folksongs of the Anglo-American and French-Canadian." *Journal of American Folklore* 67: 265 (July–September 1954): 239–51.

Firmage, Edwin B., and Richard C. Mangrum. *Zion in the Courts: A Legal History of the Church of Jesus Christ of Latter-day Saints, 1830–1900*. Urbana: University of Illinois Press, 1988.

Flake, Kathleen. *The Politics of American Religious Identity: The Seating of Senator Reed Smoot, Mormon Apostle*. Chapel Hill: University of North Carolina Press, 2004.

Fluhman, J. Spencer. *A Peculiar People: Anti-Mormonism and the Making of Religion in Nineteenth-Century America*. 1st ed. Chapel Hill: University of North Carolina Press, 2012.

Foucault, Michel. *Madness and Civilization: A History of Insanity in the Age of Reason*. New York: New American Library, 1965.

Franchot, Jenny. *Roads to Rome: The Antebellum Protestant Encounter with Catholicism*. Berkeley: University of California Press, 1994.

Givens, Terryl L. *The Viper on the Hearth: Mormons, Myths, and the Construction of Heresy*. New York: Oxford University Press, 1997.

Givens, Terryl L., and Matthew J. Grow. *Parley P. Pratt: The Apostle Paul of Mormonism*. New York: Oxford University Press, 2011.

Godless. Rotten Tomatoes aggregate film review. www.rottentomatoes.com/tv/godless/s01.

Goldstein, Eric L. *The Price of Whiteness: Jews, Race, and American Identity*. Princeton, N.J.: Princeton University Press, 2006.

Gonzales-Day, Ken. *Lynching in the West, 1850–1935*. Durham, N.C.: Duke University Press, 2006.

Gordon, Sarah Barringer. *The Mormon Question: Polygamy and Constitutional Conflict in Nineteenth-Century America*. Studies in Legal History. Chapel Hill: University of North Carolina Press, 2002.

Greenberg, Amy S. *Manifest Manhood and the Antebellum American Empire*. Cambridge: Cambridge University Press, 2005.

Gross, Ariela J. *What Blood Won't Tell: A History of Race on Trial in America*. Cambridge, Mass.: Harvard University Press, 2008.

Gross, Terry, interviews Scott Frank. "'*Godless*' Creator Was Determined to Put His Own Spin on the Classic Western." NPR, 29 August 2018. www.npr.org/2018/08

/29/642934417/godless-creator-was-determined-to-put-his-own-spin-on-the-classic-western.

Grow, Matthew J. "The Whore of Babylon and the Abomination of Abominations: Nineteenth-Century Catholic and Mormon Mutual Perceptions and Religious Identity." *Church History* 73, no. 1 (2004): 139–67.

Hafen, LeRoy R., and Ann W. Hafen. *The Utah Expedition, 1857–58: A Documentary Account* . . . Glendale, Calif.: Arthur H. Clark, 1958.

Hale, Grace Elizabeth. *Making Whiteness: The Culture of Segregation in the South, 1890–1940*. New York: Vintage, 2010.

Halttunen, Karen. *Murder Most Foul: The Killer and the American Gothic Imagination*. Cambridge, Mass.: Harvard University Press, 1998.

Haude, Sigrun. *In the Shadow of "Savage Wolves": Anabaptist Munster and the German Reformation During the 1530's*. Boston: Humanities Press International, 2000.

Haymond, John A. *The Infamous Dakota War Trial of 1862*. Jefferson, N.C.: McFarland, 2016.

Heise, Tammy. "Marking Mormon Difference: How Western Perceptions of Islam Defined the 'Mormon Menace.'" *Journal of Religion and Popular Culture* 25, no. 1 (2013): 82.

Hofstadter, Richard. *American Violence*. New York: Knopf, 1970.

———. *The Paranoid Style in American Politics*. New York: Random House, 2012.

Hoganson, Kristin. *Fighting for American Manhood: How Gender Politics Provoked the Spanish-American and Philippine-American Wars*. New Haven, Conn.: Yale University Press, 2000.

Hollon, William Eugene. *Frontier Violence: Another Look*. Oxford: Oxford University Press, 1974.

Horsman, Reginald. *Race and Manifest Destiny: Origins of American Racial Anglo-Saxonism*, Repr. ed. Cambridge, Mass.: Harvard University Press, 1986.

Hudson, Angela Pulley. "There Is No Mormon Trail of Tears." In *Reconstruction and Mormon America*, edited by Clyde Milner and Brain Q. Cannon, 19–51. Norman: University of Oklahoma Press, 2019.

Huhndorf, Shari M. *Going Native: Indians in the American Cultural Imagination*. Ithaca, N.Y.: Cornell University Press, 2001.

Hunt, Aurora. *Major General James Henry Carleton, 1814–1873*. Glendale, Calif.: Arthur H. Clarke, 1958.

Hyde, Anne Farrar. *Empires, Nations and Families: A New History of the North American West, 1800–1860*. New York: Ecco, 2012.

Irwin, Ray W. "The Mountain Meadows Massacre." *Arkansas Historical Quarterly* 9, no. 1 (April 1950): 1–32.

Jacobson, Matthew Frye. *Whiteness of a Different Color: European Immigrants and the Alchemy of Race*. Cambridge, Mass.: Harvard University Press, 1999.

Jason, Philip K. and Mark A. Graves, eds. *Encyclopedia of American War Literature*. Westport, Conn.: Greenwood, 2001.

Jeter, Edje. "The Mormon Cancer." *Juvenile Instructor*, 11 August 2013. www.juvenileinstructor.org/the-mormon-cancer-1-of-2-mountain-meadows-massacre/.

Jones, Megan Sanborn. *Performing American Identity in Anti-Mormon Melodrama*. New York: Routledge, 2009.
Jones, Sondra. "Saints or Sinners? The Evolving Perceptions of Mormon-Indian Relations in Utah Historiography." *Utah Historical Quarterly* 72 (Winter 2004): 19–46.
Kanellos, Nicolás. "'El Clamor Público': Resisting the American Empire." *California History* 84, no. 2 (December 2006): 10–18.
Kendall, Kay. *The Forgotten Founding Father: Noah Webster's Obsession and the Creation of an American Culture*. New York: Berkley Books, 2012.
Kershaw, Alex. *Jack London: A Life*. New York: St. Martin's Griffin, 1999.
Kerstetter, Todd M. *God's Country, Uncle Sam's Land: Faith and Conflict in the American West*. Urbana: University of Illinois Press, 2008.
Kidd, Colin. *The Forging of Races: Race and Scripture in the Protestant Atlantic World, 1600–2000*. New York: Cambridge University Press, 2006.
Kimmel, Michael. *Manhood in America: A Cultural History*, 3rd ed. New York: Oxford University Press, 2011.
Larson, Gustive O. *The "Americanization" of Utah for Statehood*. San Marino, Calif.: Huntington Library, 1971.
"Latter-Day Scholarship." *Huntington Calendar* (August 2003): 5.
Leong, Karen J. "'A Distinct and Antagonistic Race': Constructions of Chinese Manhood in the Exclusionist Debates, 1869–1878." In *Across the Great Divide: Cultures of Manhood in the American West: Cultures of Manhood in the American West*, edited by Matthew Basso, Laura McCall, and Dee Garceau, 131–48. New York: Routledge, 2001.
Lewis, George. "An Un-American Introduction." *Journal of American Studies* 47, no. 4 (2013): 871–79.
Llewellyn-Jones, Rosie. *The Great Uprising in India, 1857-58: Untold Stories, Indian and British*. Woodbridge, U.K.: Boydell & Brewer, 2007.
Lynn, Karen. "Sensational Virtue: Nineteenth-Century Mormon Fiction and American Popular Taste." *Dialogue: A Journal of Mormon Thought* 14, no. 3 (Autumn 1981): 101–11.
MacKinnon, William P. *At Sword's Point*. Norman, OK: Arthur H. Clark, 2008.
Madley, Benjamin. *An American Genocide: The United States and the California Indian catastrophe, 1846–1873*. New Haven, Conn.: Yale University Press, 2016.
———. "Tactics of Nineteenth-Century Colonial Massacre: Tasmani, California and Beyond." In *Theaters of Violence: Massacre, Mass Killing and Atrocity throughout History*, 117–39. Studies on War and Genocide. New York: Berghahn Books, 2012.
Madsen, Brigham. *The Shoshoni Frontier, and the Bear River Massacre*. Salt Lake City: University of Utah Press, 1985.
Marberry, M. M. *Splendid Poseur: Joaquin Miller American Poet*. New York: Thomas Y. Crowell, 1953.
Mason, Patrick. "Disciplinary Democracy: Mormon Violence and the Modern American State." In *Reconstruction and Mormon America*, edited by Clyde A. Milner and Brian Q. Cannon, 88–110. Norman: University of Oklahoma, 2019.
———. "Honor, the Unwritten Law, and Extralegal Violence: Contextualizing Parley Pratt's Murder." In *Parley Pratt and the Making of Mormonism*, edited by

Gregory K. Armstrong, Matthew J. Grow, and Dennis J. Siler, 245–73. Norman, Okla.: Arthur H. Clarke, 2011..
———. *The Mormon Menace: Violence and Anti-Mormonism in the Postbellum South*. New York: Oxford University Press, 2011.
Mauss, Armand L. *The Angel and the Beehive: The Mormon Struggle with Assimilation*. Urbana: University of Illinois Press, 1994.
Mazur, Eric Michael. *The Americanization of Religious Minorities: Confronting the Constitutional Order*. Baltimore: Johns Hopkins University Press, 1999.
McLaren, Angus. *Trials of Masculinity: Policing Sexual Boundaries, 1870–1930*. Chicago: University of Chicago Press, 2008.
McMurtry, Larry. *Oh What a Slaughter: Massacres in the American West, 1846–1890*. New York: Simon & Schuster, 2005.
Michno, Gregory. *Encyclopedia of Indian Wars: Western Battles and Skirmishes*. Missoula, Mont.: Mountain Press, 2003.
Miller, Perry. "The Garden of Eden and the Deacon's Meadow." *American Heritage Magazine* 7, no.1 (1955). https://www.americanheritage.com/garden-eden-and-deacons-meadow.
Milner, Clyde A., II, and Brian Q. Cannon, eds. *Reconstruction and Mormon America*. Norman: University of Oklahoma Press: 2019.
Mitchell, Sallie Baker. "The Mountain Meadows Massacre—An Episode on the Road to Zion." *American Weekly* (1940): 15.
Moorman, Donald R, and Sessions. *Camp Floyd and the Mormons: The Utah War*. Salt Lake City: University of Utah Press, 2005.
"The Mountain Meadows Massacre: An Interview with Will Bagley." In *Violent Encounters: Interviews on Western Massacres*, by Deborah Lawrence and Jon Lawrence. Norman: University of Oklahoma Press, 2006.
The Mountain Meadows Massacre—The Contemporary Documents and a Decent Map. Salt Lake City, Utah: Prairie Dog, 1996.
Mulder, William. *Homeward to Zion: The Mormon Migration from Scandinavia*. Minneapolis: University of Minnesota Press, 2000.
Newell, Linda King, and Valeen Tippetts Avery. *Mormon Enigma: Emma Hale Smith*. Urbana: University of Illinois Press, 1994.
Newell, Quincy. "The Autobiography and Interview of Jane Elizabeth Manning James." *Journal of Africana Religions* 1, no. 2 (April 2013): 251–91.
———. "Playing Jane: Re-Presenting Black Mormon Memory through Reenacting the Black Mormon Past." *Journal of Africana Religions* 1, no. 4 (October 2013): 513–61.
———. *Your Sister in the Gospel: The Life of Jane Manning James, a Nineteenth-Century Black Mormon*. Oxford and New York: Oxford University Press, 2019.
Nichols, Jeffrey. *Prostitution, Polygamy, and Power: Salt Lake City, 1847–1918*. Urbana: University of Illinois Press, 2002.
Nicolaou, Elena "This Brutal Scene from *Godless* Pretty Much Happened IRL." Refinery29, 27 November 2017, www.refinery29.com/en-us/2017/11/182479/godless-frank-griffin-true-story-mountain-meadows-massacre.
Norton, Mary Beth. *A People & a Nation: A History of the United States*. Boston: Wadsworth Cengage, 2012.

Novak, Robert. "Mormon Massacre." *RealClearPolitics*, 3 May 2007, www.realclearpolitics.com/articles/2007/05/mormon_massacre.html.

Novak, Shannon A. *House of Mourning: A Biocultural History of the Mountain Meadows Massacre*. Salt Lake City: University of Utah Press, 2008.

Novak, Shannon A., and Derinna Kopp. "To Feed a Tree in Zion: Osteological Analysis of the 1857 Mountain Meadows Massacre." *Historical Archaeology* 37, no. 2 (1 January 2003): 85–108.

Novak, Shannon A., and Lars Rodseth. "Remembering Mountain Meadows: Collective Violence and the Manipulation of Social Boundaries." *Journal of Anthropological Research* 62, no. 1 (2006): 1–25.

O'Dea, Thomas Francis. *The Mormons*. Chicago: University of Chicago Press, 1954.

Oman, Nathan B. "Natural Law and the Rhetoric of Empire: *Reynolds v. United States*, Polygamy, and Imperialism." *Washington University Law Review* 88 (2011): 661–706.

Ownby, Ted. *Subduing Satan: Religion, Recreation, and Manhood in the Rural South, 1865-1920*. Chapel Hill: University of North Carolina Press, 1993.

Palmer, Louis J. *The Death Penalty: An American Citizen's Guide to Understanding Federal and State Laws*. Jefferson, N.C.: McFarland, 1998.

Panek, LeRoy. *Probable Cause: Crime Fiction in America*. Madison: Popular Press of the University of Wisconsin Press, 1990.

Pearce, Roy Harvey. *Savagism and Civilization: A Study of the Indian and the American Mind*. Berkeley: University of California Press, 1988.

Peterson, Levi S. *Juanita Brooks: Mormon Woman Historian*. Salt Lake City: University of Utah Press, 1988.

Petrey, Taylor, and Amy Hoyt. *The Routledge Handbook of Mormonism and Gender*. New York: Routledge, 2020.

Poll, Richard D. *Utah Historical Encyclopedia*. Salt Lake City: University of Utah Press, 1994.

Potter, David M. *The Impending Crisis, 1848-1861*. New York: Harper Perennial, 2011.

Prebble, John. *Glencoe: The Story of the Massacre*. London: Secker & Warburg, 1966.

Rea, Ralph R. "The Mountain Meadows Massacre and Its Completion as a Historic Episode." Fancher Family website, Accessed 31 August 2013. http://tfancher.tripod.com/rea.htm.

Reed, Rebecca. *Veil of Fear: Nineteenth-Century Convent Tales*. West Lafayette, Ind.: Purdue University Press, 1999.

Reeve, Paul. *Religion of a Different Color: Race and the Mormon Struggle for Whiteness*. New York: Oxford University Press, 2015.

Reeve, W. Paul. *Making Space on the Western Frontier*. Bloomington: University of Illinois Press, 2007.

Reeve, W. Paul, and Ardis Parshall. *Blood of the Prophets*. Review, *Mormon Historical Studies* 4 (Spring 2003):149–57.

Reilly, Hugh J. *The Frontier Newspapers and the Coverage of the Plains Indian Wars (Native America: Yesterday and Today)*. Santa Barbara, Calif.: ABC-CLIO, 2010.

Reynolds, David S. *John Brown: The Man Who Killed Slaver, Sparked the Civil War, and Seeded Civil Rights*. New York, Knopf: 2009.
Richardson, Heather Cox. *West from Appomattox: The Reconstruction of America after the Civil War*. New Haven, Conn.: Yale University Press, 2007.
———. *Wounded Knee: Party Politics and the Road to an American Massacre*. New York: Basic Books, 2010.
Roediger, David R. *The Wages of Whiteness: Race and the Making of the American Working Class*. London: Verso, 1999.
———. *Working toward Whiteness: How America's Immigrants Became White: The Strange Journey from Ellis Island to the Suburbs*. New York: Basic Books, 2006.
Rotundo, Anthony. *American Manhood: Transformations in Masculinity from the Revolution to the Modern Era*. New York: Basic Books, 1994.
September Dawn. Rotten Tomatoes aggregate film review. www.rottentomatoes.com/m/Sept._dawn/
Settle, William A. *Jesse James Was His Name: or, Fact and Fiction Concerning the Careers of the Notorious James Brothers of Missouri*. Lincoln: University of Nebraska Press, 1977.
Shalev, Eran. *American Zion: The Old Testament as a Political Text from the Revolution to the Civil War*. New Haven, Conn.: Yale University Press, 2013.
Slotkin, Richard. *Regeneration through Violence: The Mythology of the American Frontier*. Norman: University of Oklahoma Press, 1973.
Smith, Henry Nash. *Virgin Land: The American West as Symbol and Myth*. Cambridge, Mass.: Harvard University Press, 1950.
Smith, Mark M. *How Race Is Made: Slavery, Segregation, and the Senses*. Chapel Hill: University of North Carolina Press, 2006.
Spierenburg, Petrus Cornelis. *Men and Violence: Gender, Honor, and Rituals in Modern Europe and America*. Columbus: Ohio State University Press, 1998.
Stocking, George W. *Race, Culture, and Evolution: Essays in the History of Anthropology: With a New Preface*. Chicago: University of Chicago Press, 1982.
———. *Victorian Anthropology*. New York: Free Press, 1987.
Trotti, Michael Ayers. *Body in the Reservoir: Murder and Sensationalism in the South: Murder and Sensationalism in the South*. Chapel Hill: University of North Carolina Press, 2010.
Tucher, Andie. "Newspapers and Periodicals." In *History of the Book in America*, edited by Robert A. Gross and Mary Kelley, 404–8. Chapel Hill: University of North Carolina Press, 2010.
Tucker, Spencer C. *The Encyclopedia of North American Indian Wars, 1607–1890: A Political, Social, and Military History: A Political, Social, and Military History*. Santa Barbara, Calif.: ABC-CLIO, 2011.
Turley, Richard E., Jr. "The Murder of Parley P. Pratt and the Mountain Meadows Massacre." In *Parley P. Pratt and the Making of Mormonism*, edited by Gregory K. Armstrong, Matthew J. Grow, and Dennis J. Siler, 297–311. Norman: University of Oklahoma Press, 2011.
———. "Problems with Mountain Meadows Massacre Sources." *BYU Studies* 47, no. 3 (2008): 142–57.

———. "What's New in Latter-day Saint Church History?" *Journal of Mormon History* 28, no. 2 (2002): 1–13.

Turley, Richard E., Jr., and Ronald W. Walker, eds. *Mountain Meadows Massacre: The Andrew Jenson and David H Morris Collections*. Provo, Utah: BYU Studies/Brigham Young University Press, 2009.

Turner, John G. *Brigham Young: Pioneer Prophet*. Cambridge, Mass.: Belknap Press of Harvard University Press, 2012.

———. "The Mountain Meadows Massacre Revisited." *Huffington Post*, 18 October 2012, www.huffingtonpost.com/john-g-turner/mountain-meadows-massacre-revisisted_b_1962285.html.

Ulrich, Laurel Thatcher. "Runaway Wives, 1830–1860" *Journal of Mormon History* 42, no. 2 (April 2016), 1–26.

Wagner, Kim A. *The Great Fear of 1857: Rumours, Conspiracies and the Making of the Indian Uprising*. Bern: Peter Lang, 2010.

Walker, David. *Railroading Religion: Mormons, Tourists, and the Corporate Spirit of the West*. Chapel Hill: University of North Carolina Press, 2019.

Walker, Ronald W. "Buchanan, Popular Sovereignty, and the Mormons: The Election of 1856." *Utah Historical Quarterly* 81, no. 2 (Spring 2013): 108–32.

———. "Mormon Memories and the Tragedy at Mountain Meadows." *BYU Studies* 47, no. 3 (2008): 159–66.

———. "'Save the Emigrants': Joseph Clews on the Mountain Meadows Massacre." *BYU Studies* 42, no. 1 (2003): 139–52.

———. "The Stenhouses and the Making of a Mormon Image." *Journal of Mormon History* 1 (1974): 51–72.

Walker, Ronald W., and Matthew J. Grow. "The Affairs of the 'Runaways': Utah's First Encounter with the Federal Officers, Part 1." *Journal of Mormon History* 39, no. 4 (2013): 1–43.

———. "The People Are 'Hogaffed or Humbugged': The 1851–52 National Reaction to Utah's 'Runaway' Officers, Part Two." *Journal of Mormon History* 41, no.1 (2014): 1–52.

Walker, Ronald W., Richard E. Turley, and Glen M. Leonard. *Massacre at Mountain Meadows*. Oxford: Oxford University Press, 2008.

Walker, Ronald W., David J. Whittaker, and James B. Allen, *Mormon History*. Urbana: University of Illinois Press, 2001, 20–21.

Watts, Dale E. "How Bloody Was Bleeding Kansas? Political Killings in Kansas Territory, 1854–1861." *Kansas History: A Journal of the Central Plains* 18, no. 2 (Summer 1995): 116–29.

Welke, Barbara Young. *Recasting American Liberty: Gender, Race, Law, and the Railroad Revolution, 1865–1920*. Cambridge: Cambridge University Press, 2001.

White, David A. *News of the Plains and Rockies, 1803–1865: Original Narratives of Overland Travel and Adventure Selected from the Wagner-Camp and Becker Bibliography of Western Americana*. Vol. 4. Spokane, Wash.: Arthur H. Clark, 1998.

Willey, Peter. *The Eagle's Nest: Ismaili Castles in Iran and Syria*. London: I. B.Tauris, 2005.

Williamson, Joel. *New People: Miscegenation and Mulattoes in the United States*. Baton Rouge: Louisiana State University Press, 1995.

Wiltenburg, Joy. "True Crime: The Origins of Modern Sensationalism." *American Historical Review* 109, no. 5 (1 December 2004): 1377–404.
Wise, William. *Massacre at Mountain Meadows: An American Legend and a Monumental Crime*. New York: Crowell, 1976.
Wood, Amy Louise. *Lynching and Spectacle: Witnessing Racial Violence in America, 1890–1940*. Chapel Hill: University of North Carolina Press, 2009.
Wyatt-Brown, Bertram. *Southern Honor: Ethics and Behavior in the Old South*. 25th ed. Oxford: Oxford University Press, 2007.

Unpublished Secondary Sources

Foulger, Chad. "The Massacre as Profit." 2013. ms. in possession of author.
Hutchison-Jones, Cristine. "Reviling the Revering the Mormons: Defining American National Values, 1890–2008." Boston University, 2011.
Nicholson, Brid. "Murderous Mormons and Meek Methodists—A Study of Attitudes from the Journals of J.D. Gillilan." Presented at Mormon History Association, Springfield, Ill. May 2008. ms. in possession of author.
Orton, Chad. "Confessions of John D. Lee." n.d., ms. in possession of author.
Smith, Christopher C. "Mormon Conquest: Whites and Natives in the Intermountain West, 1847–1851." Claremont Graduate University, 2016.
Thomas, Scott K. "Violence across the Land: Vigilantism and Extralegal Violence Across Utah." M.A. thesis, History Department, Brigham Young University, 2010.

Film and Television

Godless. Episodes 1–7. Directed by Scott Frank, written by Scott Frank, 2018. Netflix limited series.
September Dawn. Directed by Christopher Cain, 2007. Slowhand Releasing.
Under the Banner of Heaven. Created by Dustin Lance Black, written by Dustin Lance Black, Jon Krakauer, and Brandon Boyce. Based on the book by Jon Krakauer, 2022. FX/Hulu limited series.

Database

Century of Black Mormons, https://exhibits.lib.utah.edu/s/century-of-black-mormons.

Index

Adair, George, Jr., 38, 84, 113, 125
Aden, William, 10–11, 38, 45
Anglo-Saxons, 25, 62, 65, 70–71; Anglo-Norman, 70
anti-Mormonism: literature, 5, 98–101, 127, 134; in massacre narratives, 21; melodrama, 48, 81, 91; and Mountain Meadows Massacre, 2, 30–32, 46, 142–43; profitability, 39; and *September Dawn*, 146; and savagery, 50
Arkansas (Arkansans): migrants from, 6, 13, 39, 41; pleas for indictments, 32–33, 59; and Pratt murder, 75–80, 92–94; and theocracy, 134
Armstrong, George, 31

Baker–Fancher Party, 6, 10–13, 63, 66. *See also* Arkansas
Bancroft, Hubert H., 137–40, 143
Barbarian, 28, 43–45
Bartholow, Roberts, 59–62
Baskin, Robert, 41–45, 50, 68, 71, 89–91, 105–10, 112, 134
Bates, Alfred, 137
Bates, George C., 38, 41, 103
Beadle, John (J.H.), 29, 68, 96, 102, 133
Bear River Massacre, 33, 54
Beaver, UT, 40, 97, 106
Bennett, Ashael, 87
Berry, James H., 142
Bible, 67, 100, 107, 140, 147
Bishop, William W., 41, 97–98, 105–6, 114–17, 125–29, 133
Black Hawk War, 7
Black Hole of Calcutta, 69–70
Blackness, 56, 61–62, 71, 73
Black people (people of African descent), 25, 50, 57, 61, 71, 73, 80, 84, 137

Book of Mormon, 19, 26
Book of Mormon musical, 146
Boreman, Jacob, 43, 52, 63–64, 73, 84–91, 105, 110, 113–16
Bradshaw, John, 12
bravery, 74–75, 86–87, 93–96, 108
Brown, John, 56–57
Buchanan, James, 5, 33
Burton, Richard, 81
butchery, 1, 13, 40, 50, 52, 70, 81

California: Chinese in, 79–80; emigrants to, 1–2, 5–7, 19, 138; federal army and, 11; and alleged Native American savagery, 23, 34, 36, 54; as paradise, 20; in Pratt incident, 74, 77, 92
Camp Grant (Aravaipa) Massacre, 54, 57
Cannon, George Q., 134
captivity narratives, 39, 84
Carey, William, 40–45, 63–70, 87–89, 97, 104–9
Carleton, James Henry (J.H.), 52, 62–63, 68–69, 81
Cass, Lewis, 34
Cedar City, UT, 6–13, 38, 101, 114, 133
children: and Brigham Young narratives, 109; and manhood, 74–81, 84–89, 96; and massacre fiction, 145–48; and Mormon savagery, 38, 41, 43; Mountain Meadows victims, 1, 8, 12–13, 58, 94, 98, 138; in narratives of Mormon-Native alliances, 31, 33, 36; and race, 64–68, 71
China (Chinese), 63, 73–74, 79–80
Chivington, John Milton, 57
Christianity (Christian): burial, 87, 89; and civilization, 107, 115, 117, 119, 124; and Mormonism, 41–46, 145–48; and Native missions, 29, 31, 34; and race, 59–60

211

citizenship: and civilization, 49–50; and manhood, 75, 86–91; and Mormons, 136, 143; and Mountain Meadows Massacre, 1–2; and redemption, 129; and race, 53, 58–61, 64–69, 137; and savagery, 23–27, 41, 44, 135; and theocracy, 109–11
Cody, William, "Buffalo Bill", 26, 48, 140
colonization, 29, 69, 73
confession, 38, 97, 110, 113–18, 124–28, 140–42. *See also* Lee, John D.: Confessions
cowardice, 75, 84–88, 92–95
Cradlebaugh, John, 63–64, 78, 93, 111
Cragin, Aaron, 93–94

Dakota War (Sioux Uprising), 54, 57
Dame, William, 7, 10–12, 38, 41, 97, 113, 133
Dean, William, 61
Deerfield Massacre, 45
Denny, Pressley, 41
despotism, 3, 167, 46, 98, 102, 108, 136
Devens, Charles, 142
De Wolff, J.H., 49
Dred Scott v. Sanford, 50, 86
Dunn, Ballard S., 46–47

Eckels, Delana, 34, 63, 100
Episcopal Church, 46
Eyring, Henry B., 145

fanaticism, 15, 23, 28, 58–59, 70, 78, 94, 96, 109, 127, 132, 134
Fancher, Alexander, 6
Fancher, Jesse, 18
Fennemore, James, 120–23
flag: American, 17, 65–66; white (truce), 12, 19, 43–44, 65–66, 138
Foote, Warren, 28
Forney, Jacob, 31, 51–53, 58–59, 93
Fort Harmony, 9–10
Frank, Scott, 147–48
Fremont, John C., 53

Gash, Abram, 134, 138
gender, 17, 21, 74–75, 79–81, 84–85, 96, 107, 112, 115; feminizing, 34, 79; masculinity, 74–75. *See also* manhood
Gentiles (non-Mormons), 43, 46, 90, 101–2, 148
Glencoe Massacre, 68
Godless, 146–48
Grant, Ulysses, 57
Greeley, Horace, 13, 98–99
Greenwood, Alfred, 51, 59

Haight, Isaac: in anti-Mormon literature, 148; as bishop, 133–34; and Brigham Young, 101; indicted, 38; and manhood, 83–84; and Mountain Meadows Massacre, 7–12, 97; and Native blame, 30; on the run, 125
Hamblin, Rachel, 8–10, 13
Hawley, C. Myron, 41
Hawley, John Pierce, 6
Higbee, John M., 12, 38, 97, 101, 125, 133–34
Hispanics, 73
Hoffman, Birney, 128
Hoge, Enos D., 41
Holy Ghost, 28
honor, 7, 73–80, 91–95, 131, 145
Hooper, William, 134
Howard, Sumner, 113–19, 125–26
Howell, John, 69–71

immigrants (immigration), 23, 25, 61–64, 132, 145
Indians. *See* Native Americans (Indigenous)
Ireland (Irish), 25, 61
Iron County, UT, 7
Islam (Muslim), 70

Jews, 61
Johnson, Nephi, 12–13
Jukes, Samuel, 53

jury/juries: grand juries, 15, 38, 52, 57, 63–64, 73, 85–87, 100, 110, 125; and immigrants, 63–64; Latter-day Saint, 42–46, 49–50, 73, 85–87, 90–91, 109, 113, 125; Nephi trial, 100; in Pratt trial, 76; in second Lee trial, 113–16; in trials for Native massacres, 57

Keyes, Robert, 87
Klingensmith, Philip: as bishop, 133; in Mountain Meadows Massacre, 7; testifies, 10, 38, 41, 45, 47, 102–5, 108
Knight, Samuel, 113
Ku Klux Klan, 101

Lamanite, 26
Lee, Agatha Ann Woolsey, 7
Lee, John D.: adoption to Brigham Young, 7–8; arrest, 38, 94; as bishop, 133–33; born in 1812, 7; as Butcher of Mountain Meadows, 40; *Confessions*, 125–28, 133, 142; coolness (emotion), 94, 115, 124; execution, 4, 57, 95, 112, 115–20, 124–29, 132, 134, 137; faith in Mormonism, 124; lack of penitence, 119; local council consultation request, 8; potential redemption narrative, 96–97, 115, 119–20, 124, 129; as scapegoat, 57, 124. *See also* trial, Lee's first; trial, Lee's second
Lewis, Alfred Henry, 140–42
Lillie, Gordon W. (Pawnee Bill), 48–49
Little, J.H., 70–71
Lockley, Frederic, 91, 110
London, Jack, 17–21, 142
Lucas, Samuel, 27
Ludlow, Fitz-Hugh, 34
Lyford, C.P., 94–95
Lynch, James, 37, 58–59

Mac, R.W., 28
manhood (manliness): and civilization, 4, 17–21, 26, 110, 115, 136; defined, 73–75; dishonorable, 75–79; and execution, 115, 124; hyper-manliness, 75, 84;
individual independence, 75, 87; in the Lee trial, 84–91; martial, 73–74, 79; Mormon failures of, 79–84; relinquished, 3, 73–75; reparation of, 91–93; restrained, 74, 79, 86, 96, 111; and temple rituals, 89–91. *See also* bravery; cowardice
Manifest Destiny, 3, 34–35, 69, 73
Marias River Massacre, 54
marriage: and civilization, 21; interracial, 59; in literature on Mountain Meadows, 138, 148; and manhood, 84; and Mormon-Native alliances, 29–30; and Pratt affair, 74–78. *See also* polygamy
Masons, 101
massacres, narratives of, 4, 8, 21, 47, 75, 84, 136, 143–44, 148
Maxwell, George, 40
McGlashan, C. F., 92
McLean (Pratt), Eleanor, 75–79, 92–93
McLean, Hector, 75–80, 91–93
McMurdie, Samuel, 113
Methodists, 40, 84, 94, 119, 124
Miles, Nelson, 57
militia (military): and Brigham Young, 103–4, 107, 128–29; federal, 33, 40; Iron County, 7–13, 38, 75, 80, 87, 92, 133; and manhood, 95–96; and massacres, 54–57; Mormon militias in fiction, 19; and Mormon-Native alliances, 29, 31, 45
Mill, John Stuart, 21
Mitchell, William C., 32–33
Montgomery, Samuel, 59
Mormon: and dangerous men, 60; death knell thesis, 39, 60, 95, 98, 140; as "fake" religion, 58–59, 148; foreignness, 34, 53, 62–67, 87, 135; as Other, 1, 17, 25, 38, 41, 53, 56, 62–64, 69, 71, 80, 92, 102, 124, 131, 143, 149; potential return to civilization, 42, 53, 72, 115, 137; racialization, 59–60, 71; redemption of, 4, 20, 53, 72, 75, 96–97, 110, 115, 119, 124–25, 129, 147–49; and true Christian beliefs, 42, 147

Mormonism Unveiled, 127–28, 133, 142
Mormon Question *or* Problem: and civilization, 4, 21, 34, 136; and discourses of Mormonism, 13–15; in fiction, 21, 149; and Lee's second trial, 113; and manhood, 94; and polygamy, 5, 21; and race, 62–63, 67–70; and savagery, 40; and theocracy, 99, 102, 140
Morrill, Laban, 10
Morrison, Alexina, 61
Mountain Meadows Massacre, events of, 4–13
Müntzer, Thomas, 25

Nast, John, 34, 138
National League of Women's Organizations, 140
Native Americans (Indigenous): alleged savagery, 23–26, 39–48, 149; and American empire, 65–66; baptisms, 29–30; and the Book of Mormon, 26–27; Buffalo Bill dressed as, 48; captivity narratives, 17–20; and civility, 45, 61; and civilization, 51, 56, 69–70; and dramatic performances of Mountain Meadows, 48–49; interpreter, 12–13; and manhood, 80–84; massacre, 1, 8, 11, 13, 30–34, 44, 58, 84; Mormons feared to be allies of, 1, 21, 26–30, 40, 49–50, 55, 65–66, 134; and Mountain Meadows Massacre, 8–13, 80; "playing" Indian, 23, 26–28, 35, 46–49, 101, 148; and race, 58–61, 71; removal, 25, 29, 33, 137; "white", 35–37. *See also* Paiutes
Nauvoo, IL, 7, 28, 133
Nelson, William, 124, 126

Paiutes, 7–9, 12, 31, 80, 98, 145, 149
Parowan, UT, 7, 11
Pearce, Jim, 95–96
Phelps, Theresa, 41
Philippines, the, 79
photography, 120–21
Poland Act, 38, 64, 91, 110

polygamy: and civilization, 17, 70; fundamentalist, 144; link to Mountain Meadows, 2, 64, 106–7; and manhood, 74–81, 84, 86; and the Mormon Problem, 5–8, 21, 100; opposition to, 46–47; prosecution, 38–39; and race, 59–60, 142; and slavery, 90; and theocracy, 131–34, 136; Woodruff Manifesto, 138
Pottawatomie Massacre, 56
Pratt, Parley, 74–79, 91–93
Protestantism (Protestants), 5, 25, 53, 67, 74, 89, 96, 115, 140

race: and civilization, 17, 21, 112; and manhood, 73, 79, 107; and the Mormon image, 53, 58–62, 65, 68–71; and savagery, 25, 36. *See also* Blackness; whiteness
rape, 81–84
Republican Party, 56, 74
Rogers, William, 98
Rogerson, Josiah, 120
Roman Catholic Church (Catholic), 7, 17, 61, 67, 133
Romney, Mitt, 146
Russia, 107

Sacramento River Massacre, 53–54
Sand Creek Massacre, 54, 57
Savagery: and civilization, 24–26, 34–35, 49–52; and manhood, 83–84, 88; in Massacre drama, 48–49; Mormon, 3, 23–30, 81, 100, 127, 132, 135–36; Native Americans' alleged, 17, 20, 36–40; and race, 58–59, 62, 65–66, 146–49; in trial narratives, 40–48
seduction, 76–79
September Dawn, 146
sex, 17, 81–84, 88
Sinan, Rashid ad-Din (Old Man of the Mountains), 70–71
Sitting Bull, 46
slavery, 50, 56–57, 61, 74, 80, 127, 131; polygamy as, 39, 74, 90

Smith, George A., 105, 111, 129
Smith, Joseph, 7–8, 26, 28, 77, 124, 149
Smith, Joseph F., 142
Smoot, Reed, 140–42
Sorrow, John Calvin, 93
Spicer, Wells, 39, 41, 44–45
St. Bartholomew's Day Massacre, 67–68
Stenhouse, Fanny, 39–40, 78–80
Stenhouse, Thomas H., 38
Stewart, William, 10–11, 38, 45, 83–84, 125, 133
Stowe, Harriet Beecher, 39
Sutherland, Jabez, 41

temples (LDS), 15, 89–91, 134, 146
testimony, witness: and Brigham Young, 103, 105, 109; of enslavers, 61; in Frank Triplett's work, 47; in Lee trial, 88, 93–96, 108–10, 113, 136; of Philip Klingensmith, 41; in Pratt trial, 79; in Smoot hearings, 142
theocracy, 3–5, 17, 21, 46, 86, 97–98, 106–11, 132, 136
trial, Lee's first: Brigham Young a figure in, 97–98, 101–7, 110–11; and civilization, 49–50; court records, 3, 15; jurors for, 64; and manhood, 75, 81, 87–91, 95–96; and Massacre narratives, 47–48, 136–37; and Mormon savagery narratives, 19, 23–24, 40–45; and whiteness, 65–68, 71
trial, Lee's second: and Brigham Young, 130, 135; and confession, 113–119; and conspiracy, 38; and manhood, 81; and Native peoples, 46; and punishment, 112
Triplett, Frank, 47–48, 70, 94, 133
Turley, Richard, 145
Twain, Mark, 101

Under the Banner of Heaven (book), 144; series, 148–49
U.S. Army, 5–6, 35, 40, 53–54, 57–59, 62
U.S. Constitution, 1, 144

U.S. Indian Affairs, 29, 51
U.S. v. Reynolds, 142
Utah Expedition (War), 5, 29, 59
Utah Territory Supreme Court, 100, 117

vengeance, 1, 28, 33, 58, 75–78, 92–93, 112, 127, 146–47
vigilantism, 7, 27, 47, 50, 57, 86, 91–94, 119, 137
violence: and Brigham Young, 99, 101, 107; against Native Americans, 29; and the Irish, 25; and manhood, 74–79, 84, 91–94; and oaths, 47, 134–35; perceptions of Mormonism as, 2–3, 15, 17, 22, 32–36, 46–50, 127–28, 131–34, 137, 144, 147–49; white on Native, 51–58

Waite, Catherine Van Valkenburg (C. V. Waite), 100–2, 105, 107, 132, 136; *ex uno disce omnes*, 136, 149
Waite, Charles, 100
Walker, William, 73–74
Wandell, Charles (Argus), 102–3
Webster, Noah, 24
Wells, Daniel H., 133
Whedon, David P., 106
White, James, 61
White, Joel, 10, 45
whiteness: and American empire, 65–67; and civilization, 24, 112, 136–37, 148; in dramatic performances, 48–49; and the Irish, 25; manhood, 73–74; massacres of Native Americans, 54–57; and Mitt Romney, 146; Mormons as non-whites, 17–21, 59–63, 69–70, 87; Mormon-Native collaborations, 40–45; and Mountain Meadows Massacre involvement, 3, 8, 10; narratives of Natives massacring whites, 28, 31–34, 46; Naturalization Act of 1790, 60–61; one-drop rule, 61, 71; and rape, 17, 84; restoration of, 71–72, 110; vexed, 62, 65, 73; white hell hounds, 51–53;

whiteness (cont.)
  white Indians, 35–37, 44, 51; white on white violence, 54. *See also* Native Americans: "playing" Indian
Wild West Shows, 26, 48, 140
Willden, Ellott, 38, 113, 125
Wilson, Harry Leon, 138
Women: against Mormonism, 140; and civilization, 59, 147–48; comments made in lead up to Massacre, 6–8; and manhood, 22, 74–84, 87–90, 94–96; Mountain Meadows Massacre victims, 1, 12–13, 31, 33, 36, 43, 145, 147; Native American, 29; in political cartoons, 15–16; and whiteness, 17, 65, 71
Woodruff, Wilford, 138
Wounded Knee Massacre, 54, 57
Wyoming Massacre, 45

Young, Ann Eliza, 94–96, 111, 133–34
Young, Brigham: alleged responsibility for Mountain Meadows Massacre, 4, 15, 116–18, 134–35, 143–44; Bureau of Indian Affairs, 29; death and legacy, 129–32, 137; governor, 8; as Great Grand Archee, 101, 132; and Lee's confessions, 124–29, 142; in Mountain Meadows Massacre discourse, 97–103, 112–13; and Native Americans, 29–33; prophetic office called blasphemous, 46; and savagery, 24, 149; tears, 102; and theocracy, 106–11; "unnamed defendant" in Lee trial, 103–10; and Utah's federal courts, 78; and the Utah War's climate, 5–6, 10–11

www.ingramcontent.com/pod-product-compliance
Lightning Source LLC
Chambersburg PA
CBHW031811220426
43662CB00007B/604